The Judas kiss

MANCHESTER
1824

Manchester University Press

The Judas kiss

Treason and betrayal in six modern Irish novels

GERRY SMYTH

Manchester University Press

Published by Manchester University Press
Altrincham Street, Manchester M1 7JA
www.manchesteruniversitypress.co.uk

British Library Cataloguing-in-Publication Data
A catalogue record for this book is available from the British Library

Library of Congress Cataloging-in-Publication Data applied for

ISBN 978 0 7190 8853 7 hardback
ISBN 978 1 5261 2710 5 paperback

First published 2015

The publisher has no responsibility for the persistence or accuracy of URLs for any external or third-party internet websites referred to in this book, and does not guarantee that any content on such websites is, or will remain, accurate or appropriate.

Typeset by Out of House Publishing
Printed in Great Britain by
TJ International Ltd, Padstow

For my friend and colleague Jo Croft

Historical revisionists are now convinced
'Judas is the only Irishman among the Twelve Apostles'.
Certain local historians are incensed
Yet this new theory has a large following.
Some revisionists say Judas was born in Cork
Others say he was a Dublinman
Others still insist he came from Kerry,
A cute hoor who'd steal the salt out of the holy water.
After all that, I ask myself, who am I?
And then I wonder, does it matter a tinker's curse?
Am I you or Uncle Ted or Carney pilgrimming to Knock?
I know this morning I shall never die.
Because like God I'm everywhere although
I think that I may settle in Foxrock.

Brendan Kennelly
The Little Book of Judas, 69

Contents

Acknowledgements

I have discussed various aspects of this book with a wide range of friends, family and colleagues over a long period of time. Of the many who have helped with comments and constructive criticism I would particularly like to thank the following: at Liverpool John Moores University – Timothy Ashplant, Jill Drummond, Kevin Egerton, Elspeth Graham, Sonny Kandola, Lew Llewellyn, Frank McDonough, Tina McGeehan, Joe Moran, Glenda Norquay, Andrew Sherlock, Lucinda Thompson, Joe Yates and Andrew Young; Werner Huber and all the academic and administrative staff of the Department of English and American Studies at the University of Vienna, where I was Visiting Professor of Irish Studies between September 2010 and February 2011; colleagues from the international Irish Studies community – Aidan Arrowsmith, John Brannigan, Scott Brewster, Christine Cusick, Caroline Elbay, Roberta Gefter, Derek Gladwin, Liam Harte, Keith Hopper, John McCourt, Eamon Maher, William Meier, Eugene O'Brien, Noel O'Grady, Michael Parker, Laura Pelaschiar, Lance Pettitt, Shaun Richards, Ian Campbell Ross, Richard Rankin Russell, Hedwig Schwall, Mark Traynor; Matthew Frost at Manchester University Press; David Lloyd and Jack Wilson Foster; facilitators for some of the public engagement work undertaken in relation to this book: Marie Augertin (London Irish Centre), Margot Power (Irish World Heritage Centre, Manchester) and Caroline Foulkes (London Irish Women's Centre); Chris Peters (Liverpool Picturehouse), Jake Roney (Liverpool Irish Festival) and Karen Wall (Irish Film Institute); for their unstinting hospitality and support, Jim and Jane Marshall; and my children, Kevin, Esther, Holly and Duncan.

Finally, and most of all, I thank my wife Stacey for her continuing love and support.

Introduction: betrayal and the Irish novel

Supporting characters are, on the whole, credibly drawn,
The style simple but effective, the plot
Swings through various worlds, heavens and hells.

That grisly scene on the hill verges on
Melodrama but the aftermath has a joyous
Magic. I recommend a large paperback edition.
I'll bet it sells.

Brendan Kennelly, The Little Book of Judas, 213

In a speech in the United States in May 2012, the President of Ireland, Michael D. Higgins, spoke of the 'righteous anger' that Irish people were feeling in light of the revelation 'that various institutions and individuals betrayed the trust placed in them' (Marlowe 2012). What he was referring to on that occasion was the economic recession that had put paid to the Celtic Tiger – more precisely, he was referring to the practices and attitudes that had precipitated Ireland's calamitous fall from economic grace in 2008. Always a figure of suspicion to some, the Tiger had been exposed as a wantonly dangerous beast which thrived only by taking reckless chances with the lives of ordinary people. Hovering in the shadows of the President's speech, meantime, was the spectre of another high-profile modern Irish 'betrayal' – that of its constituents by the Catholic Church. By the second decade of the new century, in fact, the words 'Irish' and 'betrayal' had become closely linked – one never too far from the other when questions of identity, meaning or value were at issue.

What does the emergence of 'betrayal' as a prominent theme within modern Irish life signify?[1] To begin to address that question we must (unsurprisingly) turn to the past, or at least to 'the past' as it's imagined in various narrative discourses – by which I mean those stories, related by itself and by others, through which a society learns about itself.

One such story is the 'Theme of the Traitor and the Hero' (1944), in which the Argentinian writer Jorge Luis Borges imagines the mysterious death of a fictional nineteenth-century Irish revolutionary named Fergus Kilpatrick. A hundred years after his murder in a Dublin theatre, the circumstances surrounding this event begin to intrigue Kilpatrick's great-grandson, a historian named Ryan. As he looks further into the case, certain parallels begin to emerge between Kilpatrick's slaying and the assassination of Julius Caesar, as depicted in Shakespeare's famous play. When Ryan delves deeper still, he also finds connections (some of them linguistic) with *Macbeth*.

Eventually the truth emerges: Kilpatrick was a traitor who, once his treachery had been exposed, agreed to participate in an elaborate theatrical performance designed to cement his own heroic profile and thus to expedite the revolution. Kilpatrick must be assassinated, and his 'martyrdom' must become a rallying point for those whom he had betrayed. This performance was to be set across the whole of Dublin and was to involve large numbers of 'actors', including the central character, Kilpatrick himself, who embraces his role as doomed hero with alacrity. The man who came up with this plan, Kilpatrick's lieutenant James Alexander Nolan, turned to the English dramatist Shakespeare to find effective scenarios and appropriate language with which to mount the show – hence the echoes from two of his most famous tragedies. 'In Nolan's work', the narrator writes,

> the passages imitated from Shakespeare are the *least* dramatic; Ryan suspects that the author interpolated them so that in the future someone might hit upon the truth. He understands that he too forms part of Nolan's plot ... After a series of tenacious hesitations, he resolves to keep his discovery silent. He publishes a book dedicated to the hero's glory; this too, perhaps, was foreseen. (1964: 104, original emphasis)

Borges's text (more 'parable' than 'story') is a useful point of departure for a study of betrayal in modern Irish fiction in at least three important respects. First, it broaches the apparently seminal role of treachery in Irish history – a role with which anyone possessed of even a passing knowledge of that history will be familiar. Modern Irish history might in some respects be said to begin with an act which combines marital infidelity with political treason: Dermot Mac Murrough's abduction of the wife of a rival king in 1152, and his pact with the Norman Richard de Clare (Strongbow) after that liaison was thwarted. Thus the 'English' gained their foothold in Ireland; thus the idea of 800 years of dispossession and oppression took hold.

Interestingly, one of the first reports of the Irish character (by the Anglo-Norman cleric Gerald of Wales, written in 1185) emphasised a national genius for deceit:

> [Above] all other peoples they always practise treachery. When they give their word to anyone, they do not keep it. They do not blush or fear to violate every day the bond of their pledge and oath given to others – although they are very keen that it should be observed with regard to themselves ... You must be more afraid of their wile than their war; their friendship than their fire; their honey than their hemlock; their shrewdness than their soldiery; their betrayals than their battles; their specious friendship than their enmity despised.[2]

Despite Gerald's admonitions, it would be difficult to say if medieval Irish society was more treacherous than any other, or if the Irish people of that period possessed a greater propensity to deceive than their contemporaries in other lands. After all, Gerald was a propagandist, looking for reasons to justify a particular political programme – invasion and domination; and while there may be contextual factors (a caste system, the role of honour in social structure, the development of language and literature, etc.) bearing upon the ways in which the idea of betrayal functions in any society, I want to reject at the outset the idea of some kind of inherent Irish proclivity for or susceptibility to treachery.

It's through textual interventions such as Gerald's, nevertheless, that the idea of treachery as a crucial element of Irish history was established and continued to circulate; and this is an idea that the story by Borges picks up on and contributes to. The fact is that Irish history since Gerald has been in large part one of faction and strife, and that is a context primed for deception. Thus we find the landscape of Irish history littered with acts, exchanges and personalities redolent of betrayal: Hugh O'Neill, Kinsale, the Flight of the Earls, Aughrim, the Penal Laws, the Act of Union, Emmet, the Famine, the loss of Gaelic, Parnell, Casement, Haughey, and so on. Betrayal, from this perspective, is deeply embedded within Irish history – the punctuation and the grammar of the Irish historical narrative. Things, people, situations – these are never what they seem; the representation always masks an underlying reality which is in some senses always 'other' to itself.

Nolan's employment of Shakespeare is another interesting aspect of 'Theme of the Traitor and the Hero'. Of course, it's somewhat ironic that the work of a great English literary icon should be invoked in order to facilitate the Irish revolution; thus the spectres of authenticity and fidelity (and their opposites: inauthenticity and treachery) are raised, not for the first or last time, in Irish cultural history. Leaving that aside for a moment, Borges's story invites us to acknowledge that Shakespeare is in some respects the 'inventor' of the modern human subject, and it's to his work that we turn when we wish to find iconic representations of the traits and emotions that constitute 'the human'. One of those key constituents, as the Shakespearean canon so readily demonstrates, is betrayal.

I shall be expanding in Chapter 1 upon the Shakespearean depiction of treachery and its influence upon the wider cultural imagination. Here it's enough to note that because of its central role in the idea of 'the human', treachery has constituted a recurring theme for the artistic imagination throughout history; and that when artists come to depict the act of treachery, they invariably defer to a recurring repertoire of 'scenes' – incorporating characters, actions, emotions, motives, justifications, etc. – many of which have received their quintessential articulation in Shakespearean drama. Whenever betrayal is the issue (and, given human nature, it's so often the issue), the shadows of Caesar and Macbeth – as well as Othello, Hamlet, Coriolanus, Lear and a host of other Shakespearean characters – lie over the pages of the Western literary imagination.

The metaphor of 'punctuation' introduced above alerts us to a third interesting aspect of Borges's story – Ryan's decision to write a book ignoring his ancestor's treachery, and thus to compound the original treacherous act with a second, textual, one. Borges himself, of course, was no stranger to the duplicities of narrative and language – indeed, his entire *oeuvre* is in some senses an extended exploration of the failure of language as a medium of communication, and of the lengths to which people (including the author named 'Borges') will go to mitigate, or even to deny, its inadequacy. Borges anticipates a perspective that would become theoretical orthodoxy in the late twentieth century: the idea that every textual trace is in some sense an exercise in bad faith, in betrayal – of the thing by the word, the real by the virtual, the event by the representation. Ryan's deceitful history of a deceitful man is thus an allegory of the remorseless drive – constantly thwarted, constantly renewed – to find a means to represent the truth of the human condition.

There's a particular cultural form which is intimately connected with the discourse of betrayal: the novel. This is so for a number of reasons. Firstly (and probably least significantly), there's a sense in which the novel form itself represents a kind of betrayal of the artistic mission itself. Hopelessly mortgaged to the bourgeois world view, hopelessly limited in its focus on individual consciousness and its reliance on crude narrative forms, the novel represents a late, thoroughly compromised contribution to the repertoire of artistic media – one lacking purchase and/or seriousness in comparison with music, poetry or the plastic arts. The charges stack up: all art retains an economic dimension, but only the novel is so fully *determined* by economics; all art (even sculpture) retains a narrative dimension, but only the novel is so fully *determined* by narrative; all art negotiates a relationship between human experience and nature at large, but only the novel locks the former into such a limited model of perception and growth. The novel pretends to be on the side of the angels, but is deeply implicated in the ways of the devil.

Such a pejorative estimation has shadowed the novel throughout its modern evolution, and has prompted generations of practitioners and critics into elaborate defences of the form. The debate has tended to coalesce around a particular issue: the extent to which the novel is concerned with the connection between language, narrative and truth – 'truth', that is, as a function of the relationship between the world represented inside the text (no matter how fantastic or how removed in time or space) and the 'real' world in which the text is consumed. And this is the second sense in which the novel is intimately connected with a discourse of betrayal: while this drive towards truth is always looking to register in some form of social, political or existential context, the former two elements (language and narrative) are constantly undermining that connection – constantly picking away at the knot with which the author or the critic attempts to tether the text to the real world.

This study enters the story of the Irish novel (in 1922, two years before Ryan's fictional biography of his treacherous ancestor) just at the point when the novel has begun to ruminate self-consciously on both its own form and its aesthetic legacy. *Ulysses* (1922) is, as we shall see in the chapter dedicated to it, a treacherous book about treachery – which is to say, it's a novel in which the betrayals perpetrated at the level of plot resonate in relation to the betrayals embedded within the medium of language, *and* within that medium's projection (in the form of narrative) into the 'real' world of space/time. Thus, the modern Irish novel falls into a knowledge of its own treacherous status; and whatever else it may be about in the decades that follow, *after Ulysses* the Irish novel will always in some degree be *about* betrayal.

There's a final sense in which the novel is ineluctably enmeshed with betrayal (illustrated, not coincidentally, in no novel ever written better than in *Ulysses*). In so far as the novel is concerned with the fate of the individual in society, in so far as its formal constitution is based on the author's ability to manipulate a relationship between appearance and underlying reality, the novel has been, is, and will continue to be to a defining degree a prose dramatisation of the politics of betrayal. The reason for this is that behind the Irish experience of treachery (whatever it may be) lies a more fundamental story – of a species with a capacity for duplicity hardwired into its physical and mental composition.

In recent years, a range of 'postal' philosophies (postmodernism, poststructuralism, posthumanism) have speculated on the ordering of discourse (knowledge and ethics, for example) in terms of the evolution of, and relationship between, the various species that share the planet. What are the bases for comparison between species? What's the role and status of justice, of rights, of emotional traffic between different animals, including the human animal? Whatever the answer to those questions might be, there's seems little doubt that only humans possess the levels of high-order intentionality required to betray – to go beyond mere (first-level) intention or (second-level) feigning in order to expedite secret desires or affiliations. The paleoanthropologist Chris Stringer has explored some of the evolutionary reasons for this, claiming that the human brain has 'evolved via selection for life in large groups', and that this has in turn led to the ability to 'mind-read' – that is, to 'observe and interpret the actions of [others] in the group, to learn and pass on "cultural" behaviour within the group, and to cooperate not only for mutual benefit, but for the benefit of others in the group' (2011: 112).

The evolution of the group has been essential to the success of *homo sapiens* in a number of ways. It has brought us co-operation, trust, cumulative knowledge and numerous other evolutionary benefits. When people start to congregate together in groups, however, the ability to 'mind-read' can be put to other, less salubrious uses. Stringer quotes the evolutionary psychologist Robin Dunbar, who has explored the human capacity for 'mind-reading'

> with reference to Shakespeare's play *Othello*, where the playwright had to simultaneously handle four mind-states: Iago intends that Othello should believe that Desdemona loves Cassio and Cassio loves her. But Shakespeare moved beyond that because, to be successful, he also had to be able to visualize the audience's reaction to what he was writing – and so he was working to at least a fifth-order intentionality, right at the limits of human mind-reading abilities. (2011: 112)

In *The Science of Love and Betrayal* Dunbar goes on to make a special study of the kinds of emotional turmoil to be found in *Othello* – of the kind only to be found, that is, in a species capable of high-order linguistic and mental manipulation. 'With the acquisition of theory of mind,' he writes, young children

> can, for the first time, do two key things they had not previously been able to do, and which no other species of animal can do: engage in pretend play and lie convincingly. The second of these is particularly crucial: they can now understand the mind behind your behaviour, and so appreciate much better how they can manipulate your knowledge of the world to mislead you. (2012: 76)

That the complexity of the human mind should be exemplified by a classic narrative of betrayal alerts us to the centrality of a capacity for treachery in the evolution of the species. Few of us, thankfully, ever experience the levels of disorientating, debilitating suspicion that prompt Othello to murder Desdemona. Each society includes enough 'Othellos' to maintain the currency of the stereotype, but a community containing a large number of violent, suspicious husbands simply could not function; and it's generally regarded as a sign of psychosocial dysfunction if a person maintains too high a level of intentionality – something of the kind demonstrated in Dunbar's example: '*I suppose that you think that I wonder whether you want me to believe that* [something is the case]' (76, original emphasis). Each one of us, however, constantly has to manage an innate capacity, bequeathed by millennia of evolution and natural selection, for high-order intentionality – for working out, that is, the relationship between appearance and reality.

The psychoanalyst Jacques Lacan extended this insight to the level of language. In his essay on 'The Subversion of the Subject and the Dialectic of Desire in the Freudian Unconscious' (2006: 671–702), Lacan notes the prevalence of first-level pretence throughout the natural world – as when, for example, a bird feigns injury in order to lure a predator away from its nest, or a predator uses camouflage to expedite a successful hunt. A capacity for play (noted by Dunbar in the quotation above) might also be regarded as a form of feigning, as when wolf cubs play-fight – 'pretending' that they are attacking each other.[3] 'But an animal does not feign feigning', Lacan writes:

> It does not make tracks whose deceptiveness lies in getting them to be taken as false, when in fact they are true – that is, tracks that indicate the right trail. No more than it effaces its tracks, which would already be tantamount to making itself the subject of the signifier … But it is clear that Speech only begins with the passage from the feint to the order of the signifier, and that the signifier requires another locus – the locus of the Other, the Other as witness, the witness who is Other than any of its partners – the Speech borne by the signifier to be able to lie, that is, to posit itself as Truth. (683–4)

For Lacan, it appears, Subjectivity is defined by Speech, and Speech itself is defined by an ability to lie. The consequences for our understanding of language and for human experience are profound – as Jacques Derrida, one of Lacan's illegitimate intellectual heirs, explains:

> There is, according to Lacan, a clear distinction between what the animal is capable of, namely, strategic pretence … and what it is incapable of and incapable of witnessing to, namely, the deception of speech [*la tromperie de la parole*] within the order of the signifier and of Truth. The deception of speech … involves lying to the extent that, in promising what is true, it includes the supplementary possibility of telling the truth in order to lead the other astray, in order to have him believe something other than what is true … According to Lacan, the animal would be incapable of this type of lie, of this deceit, of this pretense in the second degree, whereas the 'subject of the signifier,' within the human order, would possess such a power and, better still, should emerge as subject, instituting itself and coming to itself

as subject by *virtue of this power*, a second-degree reflective power, a power that is *conscious* of being able to deceive by pretending to pretend. (1991b: 26–7, original emphases)

Derrida was sceptical (as was his wont – indeed, his reflex and his credo) as to the 'presence' of deceit within the human order, and its facilitation of the Lacanian 'subject of the signifier'. Nevertheless, I quote these passages at length because the points made here have a seminal bearing on what follows throughout this book – namely, the connection between language, identity and treachery, and the articulation or exploration of this complex connection (or set of connections) within the compromised cultural form known as the novel.

Given the situation – the politico-cultural context of decolonisation, the socio-historical genealogy of the novel form, the focus on an inherently conflicted subject – I think it would be surprising if the modern Irish novel was *not* engaged at some level or to some degree with issues of betrayal. Of course I'm not claiming that every modern Irish novel is self-consciously *about* betrayal: rather, that in so far as the modern novel emerges (during the eighteenth century) as a means to explore and to articulate human experience at a particular phase of its social, cultural, economic and political evolution, and in so far as that form is subsequently co-opted as part of a revolutionary programme in which issues of identity are of paramount importance, then it seems inevitable that treason and betrayal will emerge as recurring themes within the discourse of modern Irish fiction – within the texts themselves as well as within the critical discourses which attend those texts.

Such at least is the assumption which motivates the six analyses comprising Part II of this study: James Joyce's *Ulysses* (1922), Liam O'Flaherty's *The Informer* (1925), Elizabeth Bowen's *The Heat of the Day* (1949), Francis Stuart's *Black List, Section H* (1971), Eugene McCabe's *Death and Nightingales* (1992) and Anne Enright's *The Gathering* (2007). Between them, I believe, these novels engage with some of the most potent instances of betrayal as it impinges upon the modern Irish consciousness, whether it be adultery in Joyce, touting in O'Flaherty, spying in Bowen, writing in Stuart, murder in McCabe or child abuse in Enright. Read together in this way, these books locate betrayal running like an artery through the body of modern Irish history. They also stand as testament, however, to a need – as potent and as persistent as that which it resists – to identify betrayal and to try to counter its effects in the name of something else – betrayal's 'Other': truth.

And herein lies the irony, of course. A drive towards the truth of the Irish historical condition generated the possibility of betrayal which so many of the country's writers have identified and explored in their work. Such is the subject of this book. But truth itself persists beyond that essentially deconstructive gesture: on the other side of betrayal, as it were – betrayal's own secret affiliation. In that place, at that time, these writers are more concerned with reconstruction than deconstruction, ready to contribute to the reconstitution of Ireland as a Utopian rather than an English colony. Betrayal appears to be in essence a doctrine of despair: those whom we trusted proved untrue. But betrayal has more positive connotations also – as a defining moment of change, as that which enables insight, understanding, transformation and growth – and these resonate likewise throughout Irish history and Irish art. Within the treacherous moment lie the seeds of a hope that treachery itself will pass and that some kind of rapprochement between representation and reality – between the way things *seem* and the way things really *are* – will emerge. And just as truth lies on the far side of treachery, so Utopia lies on the far side of the various Irelands we have been made to endure since 1922.

That's the theory, anyhow.

Part I

There must have been a first time.
Something was broken, a grace lost,
A man sidestepped himself, a woman lied.

In that moment, persecution and martyrdom
Happened, two hearts learned not to trust,
A remarkable person was betrayed.

Brendan Kennelly, *The Little
Book of Judas*, 22

1

A short history of betrayal

If we swapped questions, o my brother,
Would we know why we betrayed each other?
Brendan Kennelly, *The*
Little Book of Judas, 90

Introduction

Betrayal is everywhere: in the books we read, the films we watch and
the music to which we listen. There are, moreover, 'infinite types of
betrayal'; as Gabriella Turnaturi puts it in her book *Betrayals: The*
Unpredictability of Human Relations:

> We betray ourselves, our families, our friends, our lovers, our coun-
> try. We betray out of ambition, for vengeance, through inconstancy,
> to assert our autonomy, and for a hundred passions and a hundred
> reasons. (2007: 1–2)

Images of betrayal accost each of us every day – in newspapers,
on television and radio; in advertisements, editorials and news
broadcasts; in soaps and reality shows. The Internet provides us
with a constant stream of visual and textual information in which
ideas and examples of betrayal are readily available. We encounter
betrayal at work amongst our colleagues, in public spaces amongst
our friends, and at home within our family. It is, moreover, something each of us carries around with himself or herself from the
onset of consciousness, something we must learn to live with on a
day-to-day basis: the fear of being betrayed, and the suspicion that
one may be a betrayer. Because it so much a part of life, betrayal
is simply there like life itself. To adapt the old adage: where there's
life, there's betrayal.

Because it's so much a part of life, I think it's probably fair to suggest that as a species we must have been thinking about betrayal since the dawn of civilisation – since, that is, we began to gather together in groupings of various kinds and sizes, and, more importantly, to reflect on the nature of those groupings (Dunbar 2012: 76ff. and *passim*). By the onset of recorded history, certainly, betrayal already figures as a crucial element influencing the ways in which people interacted, the societies they organised, the politics they practised and the wars they fought. In Homer's *Iliad*, we encounter a range of characters – Helen, Paris, Menelaus, Achilles and Hector – caught up in a web of desire and deceit; in the *Odyssey*, the hero returns home from war to find his wife importuned and his position usurped. In each case, betrayal is both interpersonal and political: people betray themselves and one another, and this leads on to – and is inextricably enmeshed with – larger betrayals involving cultures, beliefs and ideas. Thus, the pattern is set.

My suggestion is that betrayal figures prominently within the species in terms of its evolution, its history, its culture and the psychological make-up of its individual units. When we come to contemplate our own existence, in other words, betrayal is an ineluctable part of the story. Betrayal plays a central role in some of the most potent and most enduring discourses treating of the human condition. Before going on to consider one particular sub-narrative (the modern Irish novel) it's necessary to familiarise ourselves with some of the ideas, images and issues emerging from more general engagements with this inheritance. Hopefully, this will sensitise us to the ubiquity of betrayal as an element within human experience, while at the same time introducing us to some of the theories and critical approaches to which we shall have recourse in Part II.

Judas and the politics of friendship

The concept of betrayal is deeply embedded within the Christian world view. It is in fact impossible to contemplate Christianity without reference to the idea of treachery; indeed, some of the most resonant and most potent images of betrayal abroad within Western cultural history derive from Christian discourse.

An omnipotent, omniscient, monotheistic God would appear to obviate the discourse of betrayal: there is no 'Other' upon whom the Singularity must rely for His sense of Self, and therefore no subject who might in time attempt to practise deceit by pretending to be loyal whilst secretly harbouring malevolent intentions. The possibility of betrayal only becomes active once the 'Other' – in the form of the angels – enters the scene.

In *Paradise Lost*, the English republican poet John Milton refers to Satan as 'that traitor angel' (1667: 50, line 689); he is an 'artificer of fraud; and was the first / That practised falsehood under saintly show / Deep malice to conceal, couched with revenge' (88, lines 121–3). Note the spatial conceit invoked here: 'falsehood' operates '*under* saintly show', and the malice is 'deep', presumably beneath a surface show of loyalty. Satan plotted against God, but maintained an outward show of fidelity and friendship. This represents one crucial aspect of betrayal which we shall come to recognise across many different scenarios and contexts: the subsistence of a malevolent reality *beneath* the appearance of fidelity and good will.

A number of issues immediately present themselves in this instance, two of the most obvious being: (1) how could Satan have deceived (or believed that he could deceive) an omniscient God? (2) how could he have operated outwith a divinely sanctioned plan? In other words, if God has ordained the way matters will unfold, has He not also ordained Satan's betrayal, thereby negating the subject-to-subject relationship on which the possibility of betrayal relies?

We're straying here into the minefield of 'free will', something I wish to avoid at this stage. Besides providing a precedent for the manifold betrayals which populate the Christian narrative, however, Satan himself is instrumental in the next one: humanity's betrayal of God. In Genesis, Satan it is who, in the form of a serpent, entices Eve to eat the fruit of the forbidden tree. After Adam joins her and their offence is discovered, they are cast out of the Garden of Eden and condemned to the life of toil and pain that is the result of their Original Sin. According to Christianity, this is an act and a consequence to which all humans are heir. Thus, to be human is to be implicated in an act of betrayal; our progenitors owed fealty to God but chose to forswear that allegiance, and we are all condemned to suffer as a consequence. To be human, according to Christianity, is to be a traitor.

Thereafter the Bible is peppered with instances of disloyalty, duplicity and infidelity. Cain kills Abel; Delilah hands Samson over to the Philistines; David commits adultery with Bathsheba, after which his son Absalom mounts a rebellion against his father's rule; and so on.

As these examples testify, betrayal may take different forms: fratricide, adultery, interpersonal deceit, political sedition, etc. All these examples are echoes to some degree of the original acts of betrayal perpetrated by Satan, Eve and Adam. In both their personal and their public lives, it appears, humans are fated to act out the failure of loyalty – a failure that became possible only after the One (the Subject) imagined an Other. Throughout the Old Testament, the moment of absolute identification between Subject and Other – embodied in the concept of Love – remains an elusive ideal.

Thus, both the Jewish tradition and the Christian one which emerged from it were well primed for the infamous act of betrayal on which the New Testament narrative turns: Judas Iscariot – the twelfth apostle, Christ's friend and confidant – delivers his master up to his enemies. In so doing he becomes both 'a figure of crucial and ... abiding ethical and psychological consequence' (Gubar 2009: 337) as well as a figure to 'think with' (Ehrman 2006: 51). To put it figuratively, the career of Judas provides an arena wherein the most fundamental questions attending the human condition may be performed.

Judas is established as an arch traitor in the accounts which began to emerge in the decades following the death of Jesus: the four gospels and the various writings of Paul. The actions of Judas are motivated either by some unknown grievance – possibly jealousy of Christ's relationship with Mary Magdalene – (Mark), by greed (Matthew) or by Satan (Luke). From this early period also emerges (in John) the idea that Judas's betrayal was part of a preordained plan, long established in Hebrew scripture, to which Jesus was consciously working.

The representation of Judas as an evil traitor is confirmed and consolidated in the following centuries as Christianity begins to mobilise into an international religion. In various commentaries, and for various reasons, Judas is portrayed as the malevolent agent bringing about the capture and subsequent death of the Saviour. This is the figure – 'fratricide, patricide, incestuous thief, and Christ-killer' (Ehrman 2006: 49) – around whom in time the discourse of anti-Semitism will coalesce.

Clearly, Judas is a figure of seminal importance to Christianity, and to the generations of historians, philosophers and artists whose own world view has been so thoroughly informed and shaped by the Christian world view. Judas provided Shakespeare with a readily available, universally recognised example of treachery. He is described (in *Love's Labour's Lost*) as 'a kissing traitor' (Craig 1965: 167); while in *Henry VI Part III* Gloucester self-consciously likens himself to the twelfth apostle as he kisses the infant Prince: 'To say the truth, so Judas kiss'd his master / And cried "all hail!" when as he meant all harm' (595). Although not invoking the name, Richard II clearly alludes to Judas when he describes allies who have switched allegiance as 'villains, vipers, damn'd without redemption' (395), as does Polixenes in *The Winter's Tale* when he fears he may be likened to the hated historical figure who 'did betray the best' (329).

We should not be surprised, perhaps, that a figure so roundly condemned for so long should, after a period of time, begin to be rehabilitated by those bringing new perspectives to bear upon the orthodox line. The discovery and publication in 2006 of the so-called 'lost gospel of Judas Iscariot', for example, has added considerable fuel to the debates surrounding the twelfth apostle. This document, when placed in the context of contemporary history, allows for a very different reading of both the career of Jesus and his 'betrayal' by Judas. The religious historian Bart D. Ehrman argues that the incident needs to be approached with reference to two key religious discourses which were vying with contemporary Jewish orthodoxy: Apocalypticism and Gnosticism.

According to Ehrman, Jesus emerged (as did his predecessor John the Baptist) from a radical strand within contemporary Judaism which believed that the Kingdom of God was imminent. The established world order was patently evil: God was coming to destroy it, and He was coming soon. Jesus and his followers were living at the end of an age. The few who would survive the apocalypse would be those chosen by God to establish his Kingdom on earth – that is, Jesus, the 'Son of Man', and his followers, including the twelve men (representing the twelve tribes of Israel) who made up the inner circle of his retinue.

If Jesus 'is best understood as a first-century Jewish apocalypticist' (Ehrman 2006: 151), *The Gospel of Judas* portrays the twelfth apostle as an adherent of Gnosticism. The latter connotes an arcane religious philosophy which offers to '[reveal] the secrets of how this miserable world of pain and suffering came into existence as a cosmic disaster, and how those of us in the know … can escape the material trappings of this world to return to our heavenly home'

(Ehrman 2006: 10). The seeds of this philosophy were already in place before Jesus commenced his ministry; and the Gnostic interpretation of Jesus' career came to represent a powerful strain within early Christianity, before it was systematically eradicated by a range of first-millennium 'authorities'.

In *The Gospel of Judas*, the relationship between the two principals is revealed as that obtaining between a divinely sponsored agent and the human who most fully understands what is at stake, and who most closely adheres to that agent's wishes. Jesus needs to be freed from the human form he has temporarily adapted in order to impart his secret information, and in order to return to his place in the highest echelon of the gods – a location above and beyond that occupied by the inferior Jewish deity known as Yahweh, he who was responsible for the disaster of human existence. Judas's 'betrayal' expedites this release; in the gospel fragment named for him, he is, as Ehrman puts it, 'the "hero" of the account. He alone is said to understand Jesus and his message ... The betrayal is characterized as a good deed done by Judas for Jesus ... [that which] allows Jesus to escape the trappings of his material body' (2006: 63).

Regarded from the perspective of Apocalypticism and Gnosticism, the 'betrayal' of Jesus by Judas – in some respects *the* key act of the Christian imagination – begins to look quite different from its orthodox representation. That orthodoxy – commencing with the writings of Paul, and established by a variety of Christian writers over the following centuries – portrays Judas as an unequivocally 'bad' man, and it does so with reference to a combination of categorically 'evil' conditions: greed, jealousy, demoniacal possession, lust, etc.

Orthodoxy is never *received*, however, it is always *achieved*. 'Heresy' provides us with the possibility (one in fact broached by 'heretical' artists throughout the ages) that Judas 'betrayed' Jesus because he was frustrated at the non-arrival of the apocalypse, and – as one of the more committed of the apostles – he wished to push matters to a climax. He may have become confused (as so many have done over the centuries) as to whether the Kingdom of God was a figurative or a literal proposition; and he may as a consequence have been shocked at the Romans' frankly political interpretation of Jesus' claim to 'Kingship', and at their brutal response to it.

Alternatively, the marginalised discourse of Gnosticism offers us the possibility that Judas was acting under orders from his master, and that the 'betrayal' expedited Jesus' return to his true form. Handing over a beloved master to his enemies – on that master's own command – represents an extremely difficult and dedicated act: in performing it, Judas renders 'the greatest service imaginable', at the same time becoming 'the greatest of all the apostles' (Ehrman 2006: 180).

The orthodox representation of Judas bears out the truism that it is the winners who get to write history. In this instance, it was the 'winners' – that is, a dominant strain which succeeded in asserting itself over and above a wide variety of Christian communities – who got to differentiate the loyal from the treacherous. Ultimately, however, the historical reclamation offered by *The Gospel of Judas* is not as interesting as the philosophical and theological debates that have emerged around the traditional figure of the arch-betrayer. It is the history of this archetypal figure that Susan Gubar undertook to write in her book *Judas: A Biography* (2009).

This title, of course, is ironic: it is not possible to write the 'biography' of a figure about whom so little is known. Rather, Gubar's book is a study of the representation of Judas (in a variety of media) throughout the centuries since his notorious act of betrayal. In one sense, this is a religious history as, quoting the philosopher Søren Kierkegaard, she acknowledges that '[one] will get a deep insight into the state of Christianity in every age by seeing how it interprets Judas' (42). Beyond this, however, lies the more radical claim that 'the condition of Judas ... profoundly reflects some of the most stubborn psychological and ethical issues human beings face now, as always' (xxi).

Gubar describes at length the 'knot' (93) of inconsistencies formed by traditional representations of Judas – a knot comprising various strands including his uncertain motivation, the existence and/or extent of his free will, the existence and/or extent of Jesus' foreknowledge, the apparent necessity of an act of betrayal, Judas's fidelity to his role as traitor, the unavailability of forgiveness for Judas as opposed to the redemption of Peter the denier, the relationship between power and loyalty, etc. This is the 'knot' that has been teased out by generations of artists and religious commentators as they look to interpret the twelfth apostle's actions in the light of contemporary concerns.

For Gubar, in fact, Judas embodies a fundamental and irresolvable paradox underpinning the Christian world view; and her book is a study of the various ways in which artists – sometimes against their will – have represented that paradox throughout the ages since his notorious act. The relationship between Jesus and Judas, and the act of betrayal with which that relationship comes to be identified, affords a crucial insight into the immemorial human condition. It is an insight, in other words, subsisting above and beyond the merely contextual reinterpretations afforded by temporal and/or spatial perspective.

That insight emerges from a recognition of 'the inscrutability of why betrayal occurs' (192), and what the author describes as 'the disturbing infidelity or treachery always inherent or potential in any and all acts of affection or love' (207). Christianity teaches that Jesus offers us a way of being human, one based on love and empathy; Judas (and the similarity in name is surely not coinciden-tal) is the implicit rejoinder to that assertion – the embodiment of an undeniable impulse within the self, dormant perhaps yet always available for animation. That impulse engenders scepticism with regard to received narratives of redemption and – more frighten-ingly – a suspicion that the concept of love is predicated on the potential for its own annihilation. Gubar writes:

> A seeming exception who proves to be the rule, Judas haunts Western culture because he stands for mendacity or vacillation, confusion or qualms not externalized in others but instead dwelling within each and every human psyche. Judas is our mirror. (352)

What this means is that while Judas may continue to function in some senses as the ultimate incarnation of treachery, he is also and at the same time a constant reminder of the potential for treachery subsisting within the human subject. No matter the strength of the fealty, the intensity of the trust or the purity of the love, Judas waits in the wings, asking: 'Is this the way things *really* are? Is this the way things *have* to be?' To quote Gubar again, the career of Judas

> dramatizes the divisions human beings feel as they are simultaneously pulled toward trust and towards the betrayal of trust or distrust, the reciprocity or interdependency of the graced and the disgraced, illus-trating how each may work for the other, and therefore how depend-ent good is on evil, evil on good. (334)

There's one final, radical, blasphemous possibility raised by the figure of Judas, and it's broached in the story 'Three Versions of Judas' (1964: 125–30) by Jorge Luis Borges, which was originally published in the same volume (*Ficciones*, 1944) as the short story ('Theme of the Traitor and the Hero') with which I commenced this book. Besides the usual points relating to Judas's role in expediting the act of sacrifice upon which the Christian myth is based, Borges proposes that, in so far as he's the one who takes on the burden of irredeemable suffering and unforgivable guilt throughout history, *Judas*, rather than *Jesus*, is God's manifestation on Earth. The traitor as saviour: now, there's a thought to conjure with.

Sigmund Freud and the betraying animal

What was going through Judas's mind when he opted to hand his master over to his enemies? We cannot know, but we can speculate (and many have) as to the psychological processes that enabled that infamous deed to be done. But this in turn begs an important question: how can we ever know what someone – including ourselves – is thinking? How can we ever understand why we act the way we do, or why we desire the things we do?

It's possible to regard psychoanalysis as a modern form of religious discourse – specifically, as a secular rendering of the Judeo-Christian narrative. Suzanne R. Kirschner explains:

> Long-standing cultural themes persist not only in the plot structure of psychoanalytic developmental theories, but also in the ends or goals of development as depicted in those theories. The ideals of self-reliance, self-direction, and even intimacy are articulated in terms that recapitulate several Judaeo-Christian images of salvation. Specifically, these images of the ideal self are secularized versions of Protestant ascetic and mystical visions of the soul's election by God or reunion with him. (1996: 5)

This being so, it should not be surprising to find that betrayal – so prevalent in the one – should feature so significantly in the other; and indeed, when we examine the matter we find that the discourse of psychoanalysis is indeed thoroughly infused with the scandal of betrayal at every level of its deployment – that is, in terms of what it takes to be its field of operations (the human mind), but also in terms of its operational rationale (the discipline of psychoanalysis).

In the Judeo-Christian narrative the human subject is obliged to function with constant reference to the series of betrayals in which it's implicated: Satan's betrayal of God, and the foundation of hell as a consequence; Adam and Eve's betrayal of God, which bequeathed to us the burden of original sin; and Judas's betrayal of Jesus, which, although paradoxically bringing about a desired end – Christ's salvific act – once more places the human in the dock. The Judeo-Christian tradition offers the individual subject a way of negotiating this blighted inheritance; despite the extent of the damage, redemption and reintegration are possible. The prize awaiting is twofold: firstly, we can achieve a state of individual authenticity – a condition in which, by being 'true' to oneself, the dangers of self-betrayal are offset; as a consequence, and secondly, it's possible to attain a state of intimacy *between* subjects – a state which obviates the otherwise constant possibility of interpersonal betrayal.

Kirschner argues that the modern subject is still patently modelled on an established narrative (Judeo-Christian and romantic in provenance) which is itself structured in terms of a drama of integration, alienation and reintegration. She argues further that the discourse of psychoanalysis which emerged to service that subject is similarly structured, and operates with reference to the same endpoint – one orientated towards the goal of two fully self-present subjects (Subject and Other) entering into a relationship of transparency and implicit trust.

The problem with such a model, according to Sigmund Freud, is that there are many obstacles preventing the Subject from attaining such a goal; and that such obstacles, moreover, can never be overcome until both their derivation and their manifest forms are identified and understood. Logically, that process of identification and understanding should in turn lead to the individual authenticity and the interpersonal intimacy that would make the subject happy. For Freud, indeed, psychoanalysis is the royal road to happiness.

As mentioned above, the discourse of Freudian psychoanalysis is informed by the possibility of betrayal at each and every level. In the first instance, the classical structure of the unconscious – comprising the id, the ego and the superego – is characterised by constant internal struggle. The ego 'betrays' the id by repressing instinctive desire; in a classic Freudian effect, however, that process of repression will in turn 'betray' the ego by emerging in certain observable patterns of behaviour and expression. Despite our conscious and unconscious attempts to keep the secret, betrayal, as Freud famously put it in his 'Fragment of an Analysis of a Case of Hysteria', 'oozes out of [us] at every pore' (1905b: 114). Thus it is possible to talk of the Subject 'betraying' itself, as when Milton describes Satan: 'Thus while he spake, each passion dimmed his face / Thrice changed with pale, ire, envy and despair, / Which marred his borrowed visage, and betrayed / Him counterfeit' (1667: 87–8, lines 114–17). Satan pretends to feel a certain way, that is, but is 'betrayed' by the true feelings which are apparent in his face.[1]

In their different ways, the id and the ego represent a betrayal of the ideals animating the superego. On the other hand, the superego constantly betrays – with reference to a putative moral authority exercised in the name of the father – the instinctive drives of the id, as well as the ego's attempts to channel those drives for practical purposes. When the id drives towards death, the superego insists upon life; when the ego organises the drives to ensure life, the superego threatens death with its powerful sanctions against those acts it deems to be transgressive. As in any three-cornered relationship, any combination of two may feel at any time that the excluded one may be working to a secret agenda which it's attempting to hide.

The tripartite structure of the unconscious comes into focus in relation to another classical Freudian trope: the Oedipal and Electra complexes which supposedly organise the child's burgeoning sexual consciousness. Freud proposed that the child moves between aggression towards, and identification with, the parent of the same sex. The infant experiences a feeling of betrayal when it realises that the same-sex parent enjoys a level of physical intimacy with the other parent which is denied to the child. The complex feelings that ensue can in turn lead the child to self-identify as a traitor towards the same-sex parent and towards the family unit itself. Failure to work through this narrative, moreover, will result in pathological behaviour that will continue to have an impact upon the subject's life into adulthood.[2]

What's true for the individual subject might also be true for the community at large. In *Civilization and its Discontents* (1930), Freud speculated on the psychological processes bearing upon social and cultural development. In particular he was concerned with what he identified as the ceaseless, ongoing struggle between our animal inheritance – instinctive fears and desires – and the sanctions placed upon those instincts by the exigencies of communal life. When people begin to form communities the individual is obliged to negotiate a range of emotional relationships with a series of other people (family, friends, fellow citizens or subjects, etc.); these emotions are orientated towards empathy and co-operation, certainly, but also – fired by those instincts that have been repressed in order to enable communal life to occur – by feelings of resentment and aggression.[3]

The Oedipus complex likewise resonates in socio-historical terms. As soon as people start living together, generational relationships come to be characterised by deeply ambivalent feelings moving along a continuum which runs between resentment on the one hand and gratitude on the other – themselves representative 'of the external struggle between Eros and the instinct of destruction or death' (95). 'What began in relation to the father', Freud concludes,

> is completed in relation to the group. If civilization is a necessary course of development from the family to humanity as a whole then – as a result of the inborn conflict arising from ambivalence, of the external struggle between the trends of love and death – there is inextricably bound up with it an increase of the sense of guilt, which will perhaps reach heights that the individual finds hard to tolerate. (96)

Betrayal, in other words, is one of the motors of civilisation – hence the ubiquity of its presence and the multiplicity of its forms. For Freud, the human is the animal that betrays – itself and the others with whom it necessarily enters into relations.

It's in this context, Freud claimed, that the historical figure of Jesus might be regarded as a kind of cultural 'superego' – a man 'of overwhelming force of mind ... [who set] up strict ideal demands, disobedience to which is visited with "fear of conscience"' (1930: 107). The most radical of those demands was to love one's neighbour as oneself – 'radical' because it's so at odds with the irrational demands of the id *and* the rationality of the ego. If Jesus is Western civilisation's 'superego', moreover, then it may be that Judas represents one of the other elements of the cultural consciousness – the id, with its orientation towards the immediate gratification of pleasure; or the ego, with its attempt to mediate a realistic path between the competing sanctions of the id and the superego. In the evolutionary terms described in *Civilization and its Discontents*, Judas represents Thanatos – the death drive, 'the human instinct of aggression and self-destruction' (111) – in relation to Jesus' Eros. It's an immemorial, ongoing struggle, the outcome of which none can tell.

The consequences of such a model are highly suggestive. In the first place, it becomes possible to approach the archetypal traitor as a much more integrated figure – as, in some respects, one aspect, along with Jesus himself, of a single cultural impulse. Gubar acknowledges this when she points out that '[the] resemblance of Jesus and Judas ... can cause innocence and guilt to change places' (2009: 331). Following on from that, an adherent of Freudian discourse would be obliged to acknowledge the extent to which treachery is fundamentally encoded into the development of civilisation itself. Reading from Freud, in other words, would lead us to believe that we are all at heart treacherous subjects living in a treacherous world.

More specifically, it was in relation to the developmental similarities between the individual and society at large that Freud asked whether 'some civilizations, or some epochs of civilization ... have become "neurotic"' (1930: 110). A related issue which will exercise us in the latter stages of this book is whether a society such as Ireland in the years after 1922 experienced a specific form of neurosis related to its decolonising mission; and further, the extent to which a discourse of betrayal is implicated in either the development or the diagnosis of that condition.[4]

Freud's initial impulses, as we have seen, were diagnostic and interventionist: to help people overcome the psychological obstacles put in their way by civilisation and by their own consciousness, and to help them develop an authentic sense of self as a precursor to viable, respectful relations with the Other. This impulse came to inform a multitude of remedial discourses which emerged in the wake of the discovery of the unconscious, including those offering vulgar popularisations of Freudianism itself. It comes as no surprise to find 'betrayal' featuring in many of these systems.

Beth Hedva's *Betrayal, Trust and Forgiveness* (2001) is unusual inasmuch as the author does not regard betrayal as a necessarily negative experience. It is, rather, one element of 'a universal rite of passage' through which all individuals – in so far as they *are* human and part of a community – must pass. Betrayal survival is an ancient instinct which we can use to help us to live in the modern world. Hedva tracks the experience of betrayal across a series of emotional responses, from resentment, through denial, cynicism and self-betrayal, ending with paranoia. These are the experiences undergone by the Subject as the implicit trust of the child is overpowered by the inevitable betrayals of adult life. Betrayal, then, is to be welcomed as it precipitates the emotional states which the individual must experience if they are to be 'reborn into Self-awareness' (18). As with Freud, then, the reward is an integrated sense of the self – one primed and ready to encounter an Other who has been similarly healed of the wounds of betrayal.

As with Freud, moreover, there are larger issues at stake:

> Betrayal is part of the mystery. Betrayal is a natural process that has the potential to open one's heart and awaken expanded states of consciousness: a deeper sense of knowing, a sense of purpose in life, and a sense of wholeness – a oneness with all creation. As we apply the ancient mystery teachings on initiation to our everyday life, we begin to use personal, social, and planetary betrayal wounds as a creative stimulus for personal, social, and planetary spiritual evolution of consciousness. (29)

The postulation of arcane ancient knowledge, as well as the remedial promise held out by the practical application of such knowledge to everyday life, is typical of many 'New Age' self-help discourses, including those indebted in some degree to the developments of psychology and psychoanalysis. While such discourses may appear unconvincing to those with a professional interest in the genealogy of ideas, Hedva's positivity with regard to betrayal is refreshing when set against the overwhelmingly negative portrayal of it (in all periods and in all kinds of contexts) as in some respects an 'unnatural' act – one, moreover, that implicates the entire species in a discourse of sin and failure.[5]

Many people would reject the basic precepts of New Age self-help discourse. Life is never as simple as it's described in such discourses; neither the courses of actions, nor the consequences of such actions, are ever so straightforward as they are portrayed. Just as many people probably cannot accept what they regard as the counterintuitiveness of psychoanalysis itself – its apparent distance from manifest reality – and they refuse the model of personal and cultural development that Freud elaborated so carefully over the course of a long career. Freudianism itself is in fact regarded as treacherous in some accounts: a betrayal of the scientific and humanistic imagination (including the literary and religious imagination) which in some respects it looked to replace. Where it was instituted as a pseudo-medical practice, moreover, psychoanalysis created the potential for a whole series of betrayals: of the 'patient' by the analyst; the layman by the 'professional'; the individual by society. While claiming to diagnose the impact of betrayal in human affairs, psychoanalysis could (and frequently did) in fact function as an agent of treachery in the lives of many individuals.[6]

Such a critique, of course, does not need to be mounted from without: Freudianism itself was riven from the outset. Given its scope and complexity, it would be a surprise were it not so. It's a commonplace to regard Freud himself as a sort of father-figure against whom various key figures from the history of psychoanalysis – Carl Jung, Melanie Klein, Jacques Lacan, perhaps even Anna Freud – rebelled as they would against any authority figure towards whom they experienced feelings of affection and submission on the one hand, hostility and defiance on the other. Indeed, everyone writing in Freud's wake necessarily partakes to a greater or lesser extent in that universal process of betrayal whereby the present constantly redefines itself in relation to a past that it can perforce no longer be.

The capital importance of psychoanalysis in this study is that its founder imagined his work to be nothing less than a key to human behaviour – to *all* human behaviour; and so much of that behaviour concerns people changing their minds, feeling or doing other that they 'should', acting treacherously towards themselves and towards others. Psychoanalysis has plenty to say about the two forms of betrayal which most concern me in this book: political treason and interpersonal infidelity. The scope and force of these analyses will emerge in Part II in the course of close readings of novels in which these forms are engaged. It may be possible, for example, to regard political treason as an act in which the 'fatherland' becomes a symbol of the father, with betrayal representing an act of aggression against his resented authority (in which regard see Chapter 5, on Elizabeth Bowen's *The Heat of the Day*). Interpersonal infidelity may arise (at least in the case of the male) from what Freud described as 'the psychical impotence that results from the failure of affectionate and sensual impulses to coalesce' (1912: 253) – that is, from the difficult and dangerous gap that emerges between instinctive desire and romantic love. At the same time, he recognised that 'the uncertainties and disappointments of genital love … [whether] through unfaithfulness or death' (1930: 56) – are part and parcel of any form of communal life beyond the level of the individual.

Here it's enough to note that both acts (treason and infidelity) may be approached as instances in which manifest actions – selling out your homeland, for example, or cheating on your partner – have their bases in hidden psychic processes; and that these processes function in relation to wider socio-historical formations as well as to the individual subjects who comprise such formations.

Betrayal in Shakespeare: 'I am not what I am'

The Freudian system is based on a particular understanding of the human condition. As mentioned at the outset of the previous section, that understanding was derived in significant part from earlier discourses – religious and cultural in derivation – in which the human subject is presented as functioning in a particular relationship with the external world (nature) and/or with a putative authority figure (God). A typical gesture in the post-Freudian world has been to 'read' cultural phenomena – artistic artefacts, say, or social trends – with reference to that understanding and that relationship.

One particularly happy hunting ground for psychoanalytical criticism has been Shakespearean drama. This celebrated body of work provides such a vast array of characters experiencing such a wide range of apparently fundamental human emotions that it would be strange had they not attracted Freud's attention in some way or to some degree, or had he not been influenced by them in some way or to some degree in his imagination of human consciousness. Matters turn out to be a lot more complicated than such a straightforward narrative of example and influence might initially suggest, however.

Harold Bloom regards Freudianism as both an intellectually degraded and an emotionally impoverished response to Shakespeare's representation of what it is to be a human. Arguing that 'Shakespeare is the inventor of psychoanalysis; Freud its codifier' (1994: 374), Bloom claims that the latter produced 'a reductive parody' (391) of the former's vision; that the latter-day Austrian was 'haunted' (372) by his great English predecessor and that the former's major works represent 'essentially prosified' (371) versions of the great plays. In an ironic reversal of standard psychoanalytical method, Bloom claims that 'Shakespeare, much more than the Bible, became Freud's hidden authority, the father he would not acknowledge' (371). 'Shakespeare', Bloom concludes, 'is everywhere in Freud, far more present when unmentioned than when he is cited' (391).

Bloom asserts further that '[if] there is an essence of Freud, it must be found in his vision of civil war within the psyche' (377).

The contending forces which Freud perceived to be at the core of the individual Subject, and indeed of civilisation as a whole, were anticipated by Shakespeare in his plays. It's in particular relation to perhaps his most complex work – *Hamlet* – that Bloom discerns the keenest influence, and the most industrious disavowal of that influence. He suggests that 'Oedipus … was hauled in by Freud and grafted onto Hamlet largely in order to cover up an obligation to Shakespeare' (377).

The 'Hamlet complex' represents a fascinating counterfactual possibility; one wonders what the landscape of modern critical theory would look like had such a possibility been engaged. Even more interesting from the present perspective is the emphasis that Bloom places upon the role of ambivalence and betrayal in the Shakespearean canon. If Shakespeare is 'our prime authority on love and its vicissitudes' (392), and if deception and betrayal feature so strongly in his vision, then surely this is a crucial consideration for an appraisal of the role of betrayal in human affairs generally, and for the model of humanity which has been so profoundly influenced by that vision.

We should also acknowledge that Shakespeare was writing during a period of extremely heightened sensitivity towards the crime of political treason (Bellamy 1970, 1979). The religious and political tensions of the Tudor era had spilled over into the reign of James I, and provided a legacy of spectacular treason plots involving high-profile figures such as Babington, Essex and Guy Fawkes. This meant that the language of treason was an established element of contemporary political rhetoric, and that Shakespeare – as a cultural commentator whose principal medium was language – would have been particularly sensitised to its deployment. Thus, treason resonates throughout the plays, just as it resonated throughout contemporary Elizabethan and Jacobean society.

Shakespeare's plays provide numerous examples of the two forms of betrayal with which we are most concerned here: political treachery and interpersonal deceit. More or less all the Histories and the Tragedies incorporate the idea of treason as a significant (if not a key) element of their plots. Melun impugns 'discarded faith' in *King John*, for example, and points out how treachery is a crime that begets treachery (Craig 1965: 378). In *Henry V* the traitors are referred to as 'English monsters … Ingrateful, savage and inhuman'; indeed, the King is so particularly affronted by Scroop's treason that he likens it to 'Another fall of man' (477). *Coriolanus* points up the potential contradictions between political allegiance and personal integrity: the tragic hero's resolute desire to remain 'constant' (703) to himself soon implicates him in 'Manifest treason' (718). While in a famous speech from another of the Roman tragedies, *Julius Caesar*, Antony uses rhetoric to unpick the rhetorical distinction between honour and treason (834–6).

In many of the plays, interpersonal deceit and political treason are interconnected – at least in the minds of the characters – so that the suspicion of the one leads inevitably to accusations of the other. The ghost of Hamlet's father (877) and King Leontes in *The Winter's Tale* (330) perceive an implicit link between adultery and treason. Likewise, Cleopatra describes Antony's suspected infidelity as 'treason' (982), while the happy union between the King and Katharine at the conclusion of *Henry V* takes place in the shadow of the 'fell jealousy' (501) that can undermine both the marriage bed and the political settlement. Betrayal is a constant threat in Shakespeare; once conceived, moreover, it becomes a nail upon which the fabric of reality itself can unravel. With the hysterical claim that 'All's true that is mistrusted' (330) Leontes also exemplifies the tendency for suspicion to poison every relationship of trust and to undermine every conviction of faith.

In *Julius Caesar*, Octavius says: 'And some that smile have in their hearts, I fear, / Millions of mischiefs' (837). This adumbrates a trope running throughout the plays: the opposition between surface show and inner reality, as with Hastings' 'show of virtue' in *Richard III* (617), or Cordelia's indictment of 'that glib and oily art / To speak and purpose not' (226–7) in *King Lear*. With his claim that 'we have been / Deceiv'd in thy integrity, deceiv'd / In that which *seems* so' (327, emphasis added), moreover, Leontes uses one of Shakespeare's favourite word to describe this process of dissembling. So, Henry V's anger against Scroop is all the greater because 'so finely bolted didst thou seem' (477), while in *Cymbeline* Imogen indicts men's use of 'seeming' to mask their villainy (1028). Most famously, Hamlet turns his mother's use of the word 'seem' (872–3) back on herself in order to expose what he believes to be her adulterous crimes.

Hamlet is a play in which role-playing plays an important part in the plot: thus, the hero disdains the mere actions of sorrow and distraction 'that a man might play: / But I have that within which passeth show: / These but the trappings and the suits of woe' (873). The difference between surface appearance and underlying reality is central to many of Shakespeare's plays; more fundamentally, it's central to the theatre as an art form. The stage enacts a relationship between different realities: the world of the drama and the 'real' world outside the theatre – each, as it happens, populated by actors who (like Hamlet) assume stock roles with greater or lesser self-consciousness. The playwright uses this similarity to reflect upon the dissembling and internally conflicted individuals who populate his dramas, as well as upon the phenomenon of human subjectivity in general.

The scope for (self-) deception within such a structure is significant. 'Is not the truth the truth?' asks Falstaff (*Henry IV Part I*, 420); and despite its comic resonance in this instance, this is a question which re-echoes throughout the Shakespearean dramatic canon, peopled as it is with characters in search of the truth about themselves and others. Falstaff himself is clearly 'not what [he] seem'st' (437): he is a character who pretends to be brave (that is, *acts* bravely) in order to disguise an underlying cowardice. Beyond that, moreover, there is an actor acting the part of a character who acts bravely in order to disguise an underlying cowardice. Thus the levels of duplicity multiply. The Chorus in *Henry V* points out the discrepancy between 'true things' and their staged 'mockeries' (487) – a point which resonates deeply in relation to contemporary debates regarding the nature of authority. Henry himself wakes from a dream of 'Hal' – his wild younger self – and banishes Falstaff with the words: 'Presume not that I am the thing I was' (*Henry IV Part II*, 468). Coriolanus wishes only to 'play the man I am' (720). The acting metaphor is ironic when used by a character who abhors any form of 'show', while the fantasy of a complete correlation between internal 'reality' and external appearance recalls the remedial programmes of both Christianity and psychoanalysis.

Shakespeare's infatuation with deception both political and interpersonal is exemplified in two of his most powerful tragedies: *Macbeth* and *Othello*. The first is a dramatisation of political treason in action, from the moment of its conceptualisation to the moment of its supposed defeat by the forces of legitimate power. The play is, moreover, replete with the language and the imagery of betrayal mentioned in previous paragraphs. Thus, shortly after Duncan bemoans the absence of an 'art / To find the mind's construction in the face' (849), Lady Macbeth warns her husband that '[his] face ... is as a book where men / May read strange matters'; to counter this she instructs him to 'look like the innocent flower / But be the serpent under't' (850). Macbeth's recognition, that 'False face must hide what the false heart doth know' (851), is a tacit acknowledgement that the internal 'truth' he masks is his own treacherous intentions towards the King.

It's Donalbain who voices the typical Shakespearean insight that 'There's daggers in men's smiles' (854), but it is his brother Malcolm who learns the lessons of deception and treason most fully. Malcolm it is who reports on the death of the first Thane of Cawdor, and who rehearses the traitor's stereotypical speech in which the victim admits his treason and begs forgiveness of his wronged monarch. This is what a Jacobean audience – schooled in a genre of scaffold speeches long in the development – would have expected (Lemon 2006: 79–106). Even as Malcolm pronounces the words, however, Macbeth – the new Thane of Cawdor – is contemplating his own act of betrayal. Thus, the 'lesson' of Cawdor's execution – the unnaturalness of treason, the justice of punishment – is exposed as a rhetorical device which is in service to established power.

Soon after, Malcolm again experiences the uncertain nature of language when, confronted with Macbeth's impassioned (but duplicitous) speech in the aftermath of Duncan's death, he mutters in an aside to his brother: 'Why do we hold our tongues / That most may claim this argument for ours?' (Craig 1965: 854). The materiality of language, it appears – its apparent meaning – may be appropriated by those who lack the matching internal emotion, which is to say, the feelings that language is supposed to express. As Malcolm puts it: 'To show an unfelt sorrow is an office / Which the false man does easy' (854).

According to Rebecca Lemon, this is the lesson that Malcolm learns over the course of the play. In his long exchange with Macduff (Act IV, Scene III), Malcolm pretends – ostensibly in order to test Macduff – that he will be a worse ruler than Macbeth by laying claim to an array of vices and faults. It's not true; he's not the monster he depicts himself to be. But the fact that he's obliged to have recourse to such duplicity shows the extent to which duplicity has entered the language of power in the wake of the first Thane of Cawdor's treason. Especially in the speech (lines 114–37: 864) in which he reveals his 'true' nature, the economy of truth and deception is extremely uncertain. In short, 'Macbeth's and the witches' treasonous language reappears', writes Lemon

> in the mouth of Malcolm. He adopts the hero's traitorous speech and, in doing so, exhibits how the verbal duplicity, typical of traitors, proves necessary in sustaining Scotland's monarchs as well. (2006: 87)

Macbeth is the principal victim of the discrepancy between apparent meaning and actuality. The witches' ambivalent words appear to describe conditions which ensure his victory, only to leave him exposed before the duplicity of their language: Birnam Wood *does* come to Dunsinane, Macduff *is* of no woman born. Having exploited the materiality of language to betray his king, Macbeth is in turn betrayed by language; he will not, however, repeat the rhetoric of his predecessor, the first Thane of Cawdor, and (pretend to) repent before his death. His decision to die a traitor in the eyes of his killers exposes the rhetoric of the scaffold, and leaves the discourse of treason extant and at large even as the play ends.

Othello is another play lacking the normal redemptive impetus of Shakespearean tragedy. On this occasion, the treachery is interpersonal: Othello, a general in the service of Venice, is ensnared within a web of deceit woven by his chief advisor, Iago. Believing himself to be cuckolded by his wife, Desdemona, Othello murders her; on discovering her innocence, he stabs himself, pausing only long enough to kiss the corpse of his wife before he too dies.

Othello is rife with the discourse of betrayal from the outset, and Shakespeare brings to bear much of the imagery and language with which he was wont to treat that theme. 'I am not what I am' (Craig 1965: 944) muses Iago in the opening scene, half in wonder at both the source and the extent of his own perfidious nature. His self-description encapsulates the paradoxical nature of a medium (language) which is inherently treacherous, inasmuch as its grammatical and syntactic formulations ('I am ...') are at odds ('... not what ...') with its meaning ('... I am'). As we observed in the Introduction, language is the medium which enables treachery to thrive, and which indeed alerts us to the elemental presence of treachery within both the evolutionary inheritance and the psychological disposition of the species.

Language is a sign system, and the traitor's art, as Iago describes it, is to 'show out a flag and a sign of love, / Which is indeed but sign'

(944). Brabantio's description of his daughter's relationship with Othello as 'treason of the blood' (945) prefigures the other treacheries upon which the plot will turn: Desdemona's imagined infidelity, and Iago's actual deception of his master. Desdemona plays a dangerous game with this professional traitor when she looks to 'beguile / The thing I am by seeming otherwise' (951). Nothing is as it seems, and it's only fitting that it should be the two-faced Iago who invokes Janus (945) as this world's reigning deity; and he also who provides the supreme irony when he says to his master: 'Men should be what they seem' (958).

It's not difficult to observe how the relations between the three principal characters in *Othello* reproduce the confusions and conflicting alliances of the Oedipal triangle. Perhaps more interestingly, the triangulation of desire between Othello, Iago and Desdemona recalls a similar pattern formed between Jesus, Judas and Mary Magdalene. Such a comparison would seem to demand a straightforward identification of Iago with Judas – both, after all, appear to betray a master to whom they owe implicit allegiance. From the revisionist perspective introduced in the first section of this chapter, however, it might be possible to regard Othello himself as a sympathetic Judas figure: an outsider, a seeker after truth, doomed to kill both the person he loves and – on learning of that person's innocence – himself also. The kiss Othello bestows upon his beloved wife just before his own self-inflicted death likewise draws him towards Judas.[7]

A number of questions emerge from such a reading: Does Othello betray Desdemona through his lack of faith in her fidelity, and through his own fear of being labelled a cuckold? Does the play expose the 'unnaturalness' of adultery, even as it (re)confirms the 'naturalness' of racial difference? To what extent does Shakespeare encode jealousy and infidelity as 'natural', inevitable elements within the discourse of erotic desire? And how, finally, would such a reading modify an understanding of those other discourses which bear so tenaciously upon modern human experience, and in which treachery figures so powerfully: religion and psychoanalysis?

Conclusion

Shakespeare was obsessed with betrayal – its derivation, definition and dynamics. If this obsession had an immediate political provenance – derived from the extremely fraught religious and governmental issues of his time – part of his genius was to track the psychological origins of betrayal, and to anatomise its impact on interpersonal relations in a range of contexts. In doing so, he looked backwards to the origins of Christianity: the betrayal of Jesus by an intimate acquaintance, and his consequent accession thereby to the predestined role of Saviour. Shakespeare also anticipated the 'science of the self', the great twentieth-century movement focused on the psychological structure of the human individual, and indeed of humankind itself. As we have seen, betrayal emerged as a key element of that discourse, underpinning the subject's internal constitution while also determining its socio-sexual orientation.

As with Christianity and the works of Shakespeare, one does not have to subscribe to the discourse of psychoanalysis to find oneself engaging with the Freudian account of subjectivity, nor indeed with the concept of betrayal which plays so central a part in that account. These discourses are abroad in the culture, navigating their way across an ultimately unmappable network of channels, conduits and connections, influencing the ways in which we observe the world and ourselves in relation to the world. Judas, Macbeth, Dora: these figures are both historical *and* fictional – the product of creative imaginations with an investment in how things *are* and how they *should be*. They speak to us as we go about our daily lives – thinking, talking, acting, reacting – implicating us in discourses of existence and in discourses of betrayal.

I have described these networks as 'ultimately unmappable', although in fact people do attempt to make such maps all the time. The discipline of Cultural History represents one such map-making practice. As I understand it, Cultural History is the academic discipline that looks to trace the genealogy of ideas and discourses which underpin beliefs and actions in 'the present' (whenever that present happens to be). The six novels addressed in Part II of this study represent six 'presents' extracted from the experience of modern Ireland, and each will come with its own 'map' – which is to say, an account of the ideas and practices which have contributed to the representation of each particular 'present' in each particular way. Before that, however, we need to familiarise ourselves with the varieties of betrayal that were at large in Irish culture in the period immediately preceding the one that is our main focus. Such is the task of Chapter 2.

2

Déirdre and the sons of Usnach:
a case study in Irish betrayal

If betrayal is a service, learn to betray
With the kind of style that impresses men
Until they dream of being me.
            Brendan Kennelly, *The*
            Little Book of Judas, 18

Introduction

The story of Déirdre and the sons of Usnach[1] is one of the best known from the Ulster Cycle, a body of work offering a miraculous portal onto pre-Christian Ireland and its characteristic La Tène Iron Age culture. Known as *Longes mac nUislenn* in Gaelic (translating as *Exile of the Sons of Uisliu*), a late eighth-/early ninth-century version of the tale appears in the twelfth-century *Book of Leinster* (although this redaction may have been written as early as 1000).[2] Other sources include the *Yellow Book of Lecan*, and a version by Aindrias MacCuirtin from 1740 entitled *Oidhe Chloinne Uisnigh*. Along with *The Death of the Children of Tuireann* and *The Death of the Children of Lir*, the story of the doomed love between Déirdre and Naoise was known to late medieval Irish writers as one of the 'Three Sorrows of Storytelling'. If it's probably, as Sarah del Collo claims, 'the most famous of the Red Branch stories' (1999: 158), it's also, as Douglas Hyde avers, 'perhaps the finest, most pathetic, and best-conceived of any in the whole range of our literature' (1899: 302).

This famous saga rehearses various classic elopement tropes, such as may be found in, for example, the stories of Tristan and Isolde, Paris and Helen and (closer to home) Diarmuid and Grainne.[3] Conor mac Nessa is the King of Ulaid (Ulster), overlord to various heroes (including Cuchulain, Fergus mac Roy and Conall Cearnach), and leader of his people in an ongoing war against Connacht and its queen, Mève. Having manoeuvred his way (past the rightful heir Fergus) to the throne, Conor rules from his hall at Emania where he resides with the Red Branch warrior caste he has established. A baby girl is born to the woman of a house at which the King is lodging for the night. The druid Cathbad names the baby Déirdre (meaning 'alarm' in Gaelic) and prophesises death and destruction on her account. The king refuses to countenance the baby's slaughter, decreeing instead that she be raised in secret in preparation for marriage to himself. Déirdre lives in seclusion with her nurse Lavarcam until she's of marrying age. After hearing of the heroism and beauty of Naoise the eldest son of Usnach, she persuades him (against his will and judgement) to elope with her. Conor is outraged, and he hunts the 'traitors' out of Ulster and eventually out of Ireland. They flee to Scotland, and thereafter (to avoid the attentions of another lustful, jealous king) to a small island in the sea between Ulster and Scotland.

Conor hatches an elaborate plot to expedite his revenge. He sends Fergus – a hero of unimpeachable integrity – as emissary to convince the exiles of the King's forgiveness. Thoroughly homesick for the land of their birth, the sons of Usnach need little convincing to return; Déirdre has forebodings of doom from the outset, however. Her fears appear well founded when Fergus is forced to abandon the party as soon as it lands in Ulster; Conor has arranged with a local chieftain named Barach to invoke Fergus's *geis* (taboo), which stipulates that he must never refuse the offer of a feast. Arriving at Emania with Fergus's two sons as surety, the exiles take refuge in the hall of the Red Branch, where they are soon besieged by Conor's forces. One of Fergus's sons (Iollann) remains true, but the other (Buinne) deserts them. After an energetic defence, the brothers are disarmed by the magic of Cathbad, then captured and executed. Fergus is appalled at this treachery, and switches allegiance to Mève of Connaught; all three characters will feature in the *Táin Bó Cuailnge* (The Cattle Raid of Cooley), which is the central tale of the Ulster Cycle. In the meantime, Déirdre fades in grief, and eventually kills herself when Conor, no longer enamoured, looks to marry her off to one of his supporters.

It's fascinating to consider the historical circumstances wherein the events and actions described in this story might have taken place.

One imagines a highly stratified society, a range of finely calibrated honour protocols, a complex gender politics – the circumstances, in other words, which historians of Celtic Ireland are still in the process of uncovering (James 2005). Compelling as such a history remains, this chapter focuses on an alternative – equally partial, equally fascinating – history: one based on the production and consumption of texts, each of which represents an 'essay' (in the sense of 'attempt') to (re)produce a necessarily absent 'original' in terms of certain concerns and values which resonate in the present.

With that in mind, we note that the 'original' versions mentioned above began to fall within the purview of modern scholarly discourse as it was developing during the eighteenth century. One of the earliest moments in the tale's anglophone career was provided by a typically florid version entitled 'Dar-thula', published by James MacPherson in 1760 as part of his bastardised Ossianic cycle.[4] Outraged by 'the vast liberties taken with the original' (1808: 1) – and also with the claims to Scottish precedence underpinning Macpherson's project – the Irish antiquarian Theophilus O'Flanagan was moved to produce two versions in the proceedings of the Gaelic Society of Dublin in 1808: one his own translation of the version included in *The Book of Leinster*, the other a translation of the account included in Geoffrey Keating's *The History of Ireland* (c. 1634: 191–7). These versions were the inspiration for Thomas Moore's popular ballad 'Avenging and Bright' (1910: 199), as well as the influential treatments penned by Samuel Ferguson (1834, 1864) over the course of his career.[5]

Richard Cave has pointed out that '[one] of the attractions of dramatizing saga, legend, or early history (which almost has the status of myth) is that the sources offer a sequence of events but suspend insight into motivation and generally withhold judgement' (2004: 125). In other words, the reinterpreter in the present has the freedom to imagine a complex emotional and ethical consciousness within the otherwise limited structure of the narrative. An important moment in the history of the Déirdre legend occurs when O'Flanagan commends what he recognises as the 'capital knowledge of human nature' (1808: 75) demonstrated by the medieval composer. This is an acknowledgement that while there remains significant discrepancy with regard to plot detail amongst the different versions of the story that survived into the modern era, the basic outlines (which remain the same) allow for a wide range of complex psychological and political possibilities; and it's precisely this range that recommended the saga to such a great array of scholars and artists during the heightened cultural activity of the nineteenth century.

Editions, translations and treatments of the legend continued to be produced regularly after O'Flanagan's effort: Eugene O'Curry (1862), Robert Dwyer Joyce (1876), Standish James O'Grady (1878), Patrick Weston Joyce (1879), Ernst Windisch (1880), Aubrey de Vere (1884), Whitley Stokes (1887). Interest and activity seemed to intensify around the turn of the century, with versions appearing by Standish Hayes O'Grady (1894), Georges Dottin (1892), Douglas Hyde (1887), John Todhunter (1896), George Sigerson (1897: 107, 109–10, 110–13), Eleanor Hull (1898), William Sharp (Fiona MacLeod) (1900), Herbert Trench (1901), George Russell (AE) (1901), Lady Gregory (1902), Máire Ní Siúdlaig (1904), A.H. Leahy (1905), Charles Squire (1905) and T.W. Rolleston (1911).

The story of Déirdre and the sons of Usnach was an extremely important reference point during the *Kulturkampf* of the 'Celtic Revival'. One contemporary commentator, for example, hinted at the 'symbolism' implicit in the resurrection of interest in Déirdre in the context of a national revival (Bickley 1912: 254); another, during the course of a typically partial apology for Irish cultural history, describes the tragic heroine as 'the highest type of Celtic womanhood' (Macdonell 1913: 347). The 'barrage' (del Collo 1999: 159) of activity that took place around this time is testament to the power of the Déirdre legend, certainly; more than that, however, it speaks to the legend's flexibility of realisation in an increasingly sensitive politico-cultural context. Both that power and that flexibility resonate, I would suggest, with specific reference to the growing importance of 'betrayal' as a key concept within the discourses of cultural and political nationalism. For the story of Déirdre and the sons of Usnach is, in fact, infused with betrayal – in many different forms and degrees – from beginning to end. Here's a list of some of those instances:

1   Conor is King of Ulaid only because he and his ambitious mother Nessa have outmanoeuvred the rightful heir to the throne, Fergus mac Roy. Conor retains the latter's services, but their relationship is uncertain (something borne out by the equally uncertain relationship each shares with Queen Mève).

2 Conor betrays his people by allowing Déirdre to live, against the advice of his counsellors.

3 In pursuit of her own desires, Déirdre betrays the man who saved her from death, the man to whom she is betrothed.

4 Naoise and his brothers betray the King, who is also their uncle.

5 Lavarcam betrays her master by countenancing and indeed expediting the elopement of her charge.

6 In some versions there is an implication that Naoise betrayed Déirdre by consorting with a princess of Scotland.

7 The Scottish king with whom the exiles initially take refuge betrays his guests by coveting Déirdre and plotting the murder of the brothers.

8 Conor betrays the Red Branch knights by implicating them in a plot to exact vengeance on the outcasts; he compounds his initial betrayal of Fergus by devising a plot reliant on the latter's absolute integrity.

9 Barach acts treacherously towards Fergus, inviting him to a feast which he knows will prevent the hero from observing his duty towards Déirdre and the sons of Usnach.

10 Conor acts treacherously towards his returned guests, boarding – and then besieging – them in the hall of the Red Branch.

11 Fergus's son Buinne deserts his charges after accepting a bribe from the King.[6]

12 Lavarcam once again betrays Conor by misreporting Déirdre's beauty when sent by the King to spy on her.

13 Conor lies to the druid Cathbad, promising safety for the sons of Usnach should they be disarmed by enchantment.

14 Conor rescinds his former desire for Déirdre, offering her to one of his retainers.

15 Déirdre 'betrays' herself by refusing to live in such a way, choosing self-inflicted death instead.

16 In protest as Conor's treachery, Fergus turns his back on his fellow Ulstermen and joins with the Connaught enemy.

Back in 1808 O'Flanagan had written that Conor's treachery was popularly regarded as 'the first breach of public faith in Ireland' (3). If so, it was not to be the last. In any event, the emphasis on betrayal continued to be a touchstone for the versions subsequently produced, especially during the fraught decades on either side of

1900. Thus we read of 'Traitors false and tyrants strong' (Ferguson 1864: 80); of how 'Bewney the Ruthless Red ... betrayed the children of Usna' (O'Grady 1878: 119); of 'Concobar's treacherous design' (Joyce 1879: 439); and of Déirdre's insight that 'The pledge of Fergus is no pledge – We are betrayed!' (Todhunter 1896: 118). In his poetic treatment of the story Douglas Hyde made no bones about 'the treachery of Conor' (1887: 29); although in the prose version contained in his *Literary History of Ireland* he introduced a level of irony by having Conor prevent the infant Déirdre's death with the words: 'I do not submit to, nor do I praise, the committing of a base deed, or a deed of treachery, in the hope of quenching the anger of the power of the elements' (1899: 305). AE shifts the emphasis by having Conor swear 'vengeance on the traitors to Ulla' (1901: n.p.); while Lady Gregory also makes provision for Conor's counter-claims when she has the King say to Naoise and his brothers: 'it is not the deed of sister's children you have done me, but you have done harm to me with treachery in the sight of all the men of Ireland' (1902: 189).

In short, a discourse of betrayal features centrally in all of the treatments of the Déirdre saga that were produced in the heightened atmosphere of pre-revolutionary Ireland. A full survey of all this material would constitute a book in itself. As a gesture towards that project, however, the remainder of this chapter looks in detail at four such treatments, and attempts to compare and contrast the different characterisations and emphases of each. This is by way of providing a genealogy for the discourse of betrayal that, as we shall see, comes to feature so prominently in the Irish novel during the post-revolutionary era.

W.B. Yeats, *Deirdre* (1907)

Like every other version, Yeats's drama unfolds across a range of political and interpersonal scenarios: the former encompasses the relations between Conor, Fergus, the sons of Usnach, the Red Branch knights and the general populace; the latter, a triangular relationship between the three principals – as Yeats puts it: 'One woman and two men; that is the quarrel that knows no mending' (1907: 70).[7]

The action is condensed into one act, displaying that 'reticence almost Greek' that Una Ellis-Fermor discerned in Yeats's maturing

work (1939: 113). Bypassing the two traditional starting points –
the birth of Déirdre (from the *Book of Leinster*) and Conor's recall
of the exiles (from the *Yellow Book of Lecan*) – Yeats opts to commence his version after Déirdre and Naoise have returned to Emania,
when they are ensconced in the Red Branch hall waiting, supposedly,
to be called into the King's forgiving presence. The appearance of
a chorus of three female musicians underscores the Greek influence; here also we may discern the influence of Nietzsche – particularly *The Birth of Tragedy* (1872) – with which Yeats began
to engage from late 1902 (Foster 1997: 272). The plot device of
Fergus's detention by the character Yeats elsewhere described as
'Cook Barach, the traitor' (1933: 437) is ignored; instead, the hero
who will feature so centrally in the *Táin Bó Cuailnge* is 'an old man'
(49) who hovers anxiously at the edge of the action, concerned that
his intercession should reconcile the contending parties and thus
restore the *status quo ante*.

   Fergus's hopeful assertion that 'all's forgiven now' is balanced by
the chorus's insistence that 'old men are jealous' (Yeats 1907: 52).
In claiming that the King's forgiveness derived in the main from
'his own natural impulse' (52), Fergus reveals himself as a representative of Apollonian order; with their experience of life on the
margins of society (they are travellers) and their access to music,
however, the chorus is tapped into a Dionysian impulse towards
ritual, violence and the destruction of individualism as a cultural
norm. The irony of Fergus's statement – 'I have known his mind
as if it were my own' (61) – will grow as the play proceeds, as will
the allusions to a different 'tale of treachery' (56) from the Red
Branch cycle, concerning another couple (Lugaidh Redstripe and
his wife) who played chess while awaiting death. Fergus's faith in
the King's word is bolstered by Naoise; indeed, one of the principal
themes of the play is the discrepancy between representation – the
'word' so venerated by Fergus and Naoise in the first half – and
the reality of desire. This division assumes a gendered dimension
when Déirdre reveals that she shares the female chorus's scepticism
towards Conor's aptitude for forgiveness. She pleads with Naoise to
escape with her, even offering to maim herself so as to quench the
King's desire: 'Whatever were to happen to my face / I'd be myself'
(63), she claims, revisiting the discourse on individual integrity initi-
ated by Fergus.

The first half of the play ends with counter-charges of betrayal: the King's servant declares Naoise to be a 'traitor', to which the accused replies: 'So, then, it's treachery' (64). Thereafter the action proceeds rapidly towards its tragic denouement. In a departure from all previous sources, Conor enters and confronts the lovers, claiming to be the wronged party: Déirdre and Naoise betrayed him, he points out – one by denying a betrothal, one by setting aside a political affiliation. Mixing reasonableness with threat he says: 'I but ask / what is already mine' (71). He offers the young lovers a deal: if Déirdre comes to him willingly before the people, he will allow Naoise to depart. Conor has Naoise executed as Déirdre temporises, however: 'The traitor who has carried off my wife / No longer lives' (74), he crows, although this statement does not make it clear whether Naoise is a traitor in a political (acting against the King) or a personal (acting against a betrothed man and a relative) sense. In any event, Déirdre is determined to join her lover in death; she uses 'feminine' guile to convince Conor to allow her to see Naoise's body. The duplicity of language is revealed one last time, as she calls to the chorus to sing,

> Knowing that all is happy, and that you know
> Within which bride-bed I shall lie this night,
> And by what man, and lie close up to him,
> For the bed's narrow, and there outsleep the cockcrow. (77)

By this stage, only Conor believes that she is talking about him (and even he has suspicions). Déirdre kills herself using a dagger she has taken from a member of the chorus, whereupon Fergus enters with an angry mob, demanding retribution. The king refuses to be cowed, however, pouring magisterial scorn on any

> traitor that dare stop my way.
> Howl, if you will; but I, being King, did right
> In choosing her most fitting to be Queen,
> And letting no boy lover take the sway. (78)

Yeats had no doubt read, and been influenced by, the most recent versions of the legend, including those by acquaintances, friends and collaborators such as Todhunter, Rolleston, AE and Lady Gregory herself. Indeed, it may have been when writing the preface to the latter's *Gods and Fighting Men* – in which he contrasted the 'clear outlines' of the Déirdre legend with the 'succession of detached episodes' comprising the story of Diarmuid and Grainne (Gregory 1904: 14) – that Yeats decided 'to put his mark on the story of "Ireland's Helen" (or, as Dublin would have it, "The Second Mrs Conchobar")' (Foster 1997: 321). Del Collo maintains, however, that Yeats's main sources were the ones he had encountered in his youth – specifically, the versions produced by Samuel Ferguson and Standish James O'Grady.[8] This genealogy of influence may indeed be one source for the ambivalence that characterises Yeats's own version: whereas Ferguson depicts Conor as a 'beast' and a 'traitor king' (1897: 43, 86), James O'Grady 'consistently revises and re-interprets events in order to present a more congenial image of … the king' (del Collo 1999: 160–1). The voices of the passionate, doomed heroine and the wilful aristocrat resound throughout Yeats's version.

That version, Christopher Murray claims, remains 'the best of the many adaptations of the Deirdre legend, largely because Yeats stayed true to Conchubar and his fierce, obsessive passion' (1997: 24). This is of a piece, Murray notes, with the combativeness that became such a useful weapon within Yeats's armoury during the early years of the new theatre enterprise. But Murray also notes the Nietzschean influence; and it certainly seems likely that the radical German philosopher (whose work had begun to appear in English translation during the 1890s) was another profound source (besides the Ferguson/James O'Grady opposition) for the moral complexity of *Deirdre*. 'Music and tragic myth', as Nietzsche observed, 'are equally expressive of the Dionysiac talent of a nation and cannot be divorced from one another' (1872: 145). The heroine's passion and the King's aristocratic disdain speak, according to Yeats's aesthetic imagination, of elemental forces underpinning what passes for reality. And so, the relationship between Déirdre and Conor could provide contemporary Irish audiences with an experience of 'imaginative delight in energetic characters and extreme types, [enlarging] the energy of a people by the spectacle of energy' (quoted in Murray 1997: 24).

It will be noted that critical attention here has shifted to the Conor/Déirdre relationship, and that Naoise has been marginalised to a certain extent; this may result from an alternative provenance for the playwright's particular treatment of the legend, and may in turn impact upon his characterisation of the discourses of betrayal which so thoroughly inform it.

In his celebrated biography, Roy Foster writes that Yeats began work on a play about the legend of Déirdre and the sons of Usnach in mid-July of 1904. It was over a year since Yeats had learned of the engagement of his soul mate Maud Gonne to a man of whom he deeply disapproved: Major John MacBride, a veteran of the Boer War and a hardline republican of militarist persuasion. Yeats had received the news by telegram on 7 February 1903, just before delivering a lecture on 'The Future of Irish Drama' to a London audience. In his earliest extant letter after learning of her decision, he had accused Gonne of two forms of betrayal: of the spiritual marriage (to him) to which she had acquiesced a number of years earlier, and of her own pride and dignity. His own position – a cuckold in spirit if not in law – began to weigh on him. To add insult to injury, MacBride was a political enemy inasmuch as he subscribed to a form of bourgeois Catholic nationalism against which Yeats had set out his stall. The marriage broke down almost immediately, and Yeats had much time over the following year to ruminate on events that had been both psychologically and publically traumatic.

My suggestion is that the relations between the three principal characters in *Deirdre* may be read as a symbolic representation of the Yeats/Gonne/MacBride triangle, with Yeats assuming the role of the haughty, revengeful king, and MacBride the role of the younger, vigorous soldier in possession of both an eye for the ladies and the ear of the rabble. Such a model requires a radical reorientation of the saga's moral structure, and in particular of the various forms of betrayal which it had traditionally encompassed.[9]

Yeats was the same age as MacBride when the latter married Maud Gonne in February 1903, yet it's certain that he would have claimed an intellectual and cultural maturity far in excess of his rival. This left him exposed in other areas, however. Yeats was particularly sensitive to the accusation that his chosen profession had to some degree marginalised him from real life – the 'living stream' – leaving him an effete commentator watching the performance from the wings, but with no role in the real drama of life. Much of his work – in all forms: poetry, drama, criticism and autobiography – is by way of an elaborate, multi-faceted apology for the poet's activity, indeed, for the poet's very existence; especially in the context of a politically and socially volatile country such as pre-revolutionary Ireland. There's no doubt also that Yeats was, and continued throughout his life to be, intimidated by men of action

like MacBride. This emerges most clearly in his extended response
to the blood sacrifice made by the men (although not necessarily the
women) of the Citizen Army, the Irish Volunteers and Cumann na
mBan during the Rising of Easter 1916. In some senses, the entire
theatre enterprise may be regarded as an attempt to redress the psychological inadequacy he experienced when confronted by men like
the Major, whose anti-British exploits during the Boer War made
him a hero amongst certain parties back in Ireland.

Conor may be old (or at least 'older', but 'still strong and vigorous' (Yeats 1907: 49) as the author's description tells us), but he
remains a compelling figure, animated throughout by a sense of the
legitimacy of his own desires and of the offence that has been perpetrated against him. He is in many ways an unsympathetic figure;
but then, it's precisely the bourgeois morality that looks to organise the audience's conventional response to characters (as sympathetic or otherwise) that the playwright – infused with the energy
of Nietzschean philosophy – is looking to counter. Conor may be
cruel, cunning and unforgiving; he may have to live with the tacit
acknowledgement of a younger's man's physical (and by implication sexual) prowess: what he absolutely refuses to do, however, is
to be ignored. And this is an image that must have appealed to Yeats
in the period after his 'public humiliation' (Foster 1997: 284) by
Gonne and her soldier boy.

Yeats harboured serious doubts regarding both the strength and
the depth of Gonne's commitment to MacBride – doubts that were
vindicated in a very short time; but he could not 'rewrite' the legend
in line with his preferred image of reality. Déirdre's passion for
Naoise remains true until the end; his death precipitates hers, and
in some ways there's an inevitability about the latter act. She does
what tragic heroines do; the only dramatic interest arises from *how*
she does it – hence the plot with the borrowed knife and Déirdre's
flirtatious baiting of Conor as she manoeuvres to find time and
space to do the deed.

The final scene, however – the contention of Fergus and Conor
against the backdrop of an angry mob baying for the latter's blood –
recalls the late scene in *Macbeth* in which the usurper, faced with
the imminent reconstitution of 'normality', refuses to yield or to
disavow his initial act of treason. Yeats depicts a king who is strong,
wilful, mature and frustrated – fighting back against the 'laws' of
nature and the 'rules' of romantic love. If this is an image derived

from the conservatism of (some of) his sources and from a powerful and radical new philosophy, it is also based in part on the role he imagined for himself when confronted by his own frustrated desires. The image of a powerful king pursuing revenge in the face of conventional love was no doubt more amenable to Yeats than that of the effete poet who had once again been marginalised by a combination of political, religious, social and sexual discourses.

Ultimately, the discourse of power turns on the question of who has the right to describe whom as a traitor. The word has a chilling resonance within revolutionary discourse: the idea that there may be enemies masquerading as friends haunts every politico-cultural programme, whether it be Jewish Apocalypticism of the first century CE, or Irish nationalism of the late nineteenth and early twentieth centuries. The legend of Déirdre and the sons of Usnach includes enough instances of betrayal to satisfy a wide array of allegorists. The fact that Yeats allows the 'villain' to declare an interest in the question of treason emerges from both a local context – the playwright's particular complex of textual influences and personal experience – and a more general circumstance: the radical contingency of betrayal as a political, interpersonal and psychological concept.

Eva Gore-Booth, *The Buried Life of Deirdre* (*c.* 1908, 1916–17)

Eva Gore-Booth was a poet, playwright and philosopher on the one hand, and a political activist and high-profile pacifist on the other. This double life is all the more extraordinary when one recalls that she was raised to neither of these callings: as a younger daughter of a landed Anglo-Irish family during the late nineteenth century her fate was marriage within the tribe or maiden aunthood. The fact that both she and her rather more famous sister Constance (Countess Markievicz) escaped their class and gender destinies testifies to an extraordinary family, but also to the extraordinary times within which they lived: the sisters' experience exemplified the transition from one world – passive, local, agrarian and Victorian – into another – active, internationalist, urban and modernist.

When she moved to Manchester in 1897 to take up residence with life-long companion Esther Roper, Eva Gore-Booth effectively turned her back on her class, her religion, her country and her received gender identity. At various points over the next thirty years she worked for the rights of working-class women and for women's equality in general; she co-founded a journal (entitled *Urania*) dedicated to revolutionising 'natural' discourses of gender and sexuality (Tiernan 2008); she was a declared pacifist at a time (1914–18) and in a place (England) when such attitudes were considered tantamount to treason; and she was directly and deeply involved with the case of Sir Roger Casement, hanged as a traitor by the British government in 1916 for his part in the abortive Easter Rising of that year.[10] She was, in other words, intimately familiar –in terms both of her personal experiences and of her political persuasions – with the nature of 'affinity' and with the multitude of ways and means whereby apparently 'natural' affinities *may be*, and sometimes *must be*, betrayed.

A childhood interest in Irish folklore and literature was encouraged by Yeats, who stayed at the Gore-Booth family home in Co. Sligo on two occasions in late 1894 and who entertained a brief romantic interest in the younger sister (Foster 1997: 144). Gore-Booth retained this interest when she moved to England a few years later; as with so many of her contemporaries, a leaning towards the mythological and the magical was not incompatible with a desire to intervene in the mundane present. Entirely typical, in fact, was the tendency to look to ancient narratives which would be amenable to adaptation in the light of current concerns: as she writes in the (undated) introduction to her play *The Buried Life of Deirdre*:

> The great myths of the world are centres of magnetism to all men; they can never be the property of any individual, however deep his thoughts or subtle his skill. Free to everyone alike, these shapes of ancient beauty are ever ready to bear the brunt of new interpretations and individual experiences. (*c.* 1908: ix)

Thus we find a version of the Déirdre legend which reflects Gore-Booth's complicated experiences and beliefs.

The Buried Life of Deirdre is a play in three acts; this affords the author more scope (compared with Yeats's one-act version) to explore the complex web of desire and action between the principal characters. The play begins with King Conor arriving to claim Déirdre, who, having been raised under his protection by the druidess Lavarcam since birth, has come to marrying age. The importance of betrayal is established immediately, when Conor accuses Lavarcam of 'keeping from me that which is mine. It is treason'

(3). Déirdre enters, having apparently already encountered Naoise when he and his brothers were hunting in the vicinity. She resists Conor's claims, although it's clear that a sense of ownership (and thus of the possibility of betrayal) is already established in his mind. Déirdre fears the 'treachery' (13) of a jealous king; yet, in acting to escape (by eloping with Naoise) she only manages to precipitate further feelings of jealousy and further acts of treachery.

Act II takes place in 'Alba' (Scotland), whither the lovers have fled to escape the King's wrath. Déirdre explains her religious philosophy to a somewhat dim Naoise: basically, her belief in reincarnation and the temporal persistence of all energy (of which more presently) – including all action and all thought – leads her to the conviction that: 'There is not one of us young, not one of us innocent' (28). Déirdre's feelings of guilt are compounded when Fergus – newly arrived as a 'messenger of peace' from Conor – accuses her of '[making] war between those who love each other' (30). Déirdre doubts the truth of the King's forgiveness, however; she is convinced that any act of betrayal will re-emerge in the life of anyone (such as Conor or herself) who has experienced 'the soft voice of treachery' (36) in a previous incarnation. In the final act Naoise and Déirdre return to Ireland, where they indeed encounter acts and accusations of treachery: 'Death to the traitor' (60), cries one of Conor's assassins. After the inevitable slaughter of the lovers, the presiding word is left to the King: 'We none of us understood ...' (62).

It's interesting to contemplate one of the narrative roads not taken by the author of this play: love between strong, independent female figures. With specific reference to Gore-Booth's poetry, Emma Donoghue has shown how a recurring pattern from very early in her career was to rework existing materials from Irish legend with emphasis on female relationships: 'what seems to have appealed to Gore-Booth about the women of Celtic legend was their independence and their focus on other women' (1997: 26). That pattern is repeated in two 'Celtic' plays which predate her Déirdre treatment: *Unseen Kings* (1904) and *The Triumph of Maeve* (1905). The first focuses on a marginal incident from the Cuchulain story: one particular image that it presents – 'of ... two women, walking hand in hand through unimaginable danger' – is, Donoghue suggests, 'central to Gore-Booth's work' (28). She likewise recasts the story of Mève in proto-feminist terms: a powerful queen goes to war to avenge the death of her fellow heroine Déirdre; her daughter

Fionavar dies from grief at the sight of battle; and Mève retires in search of Niamh, the fairy queen of Tír na nÓg, a fitting match for her legendary status.

One might have thought that the existence of a powerful female character in the form of Lavarcam would have afforded the kind of female friendship that the author developed in her two earlier 'Celtic' plays. The older woman is described as 'A druidess and messenger to the King' (xi); no mere serving woman or nursemaid (as in some versions) but occupying an informed and influential role in Conor's court. Déirdre has been 'brought up by Lavarcam in complete isolation and seclusion' (xi), and there are strong bonds of love and trust between the two women. Lavarcam it is who introduces the 'young, innocent maiden' (13) to Mannanān, the deity whose values underpin Déirdre's defiance of the King. After the younger woman's death, Lavarcam refers to Déirdre as 'my beloved' (62); but there's never any sense that the two women can sustain the friendship that has been in place before the commencement of the action. The 'hunter' is present from the second line of the play, and his disruptive presence grows throughout all the early exchanges. The drama turns on a choice between Conor and Naoise; unlike *Unseen Kings* and *The Triumph of Maeve*, female friendship in *The Buried Life of Deirdre* offers no way out of the problems created by men.

This latter point raises another of the contexts within which Gore-Booth's imagination (both artistic and political) operated: the role of gender, especially as it relates to war. Her biographer Gifford Lewis suggests that throughout her life Gore-Booth associated masculinity with 'possessiveness, domination and the mechanical – the "iron fort" of materialism – whereas she connected the feminine with intuition, nature and an ecstatic peace' (1988: 24). Donoghue likewise identifies a dualistic cast of mind, and remarks the contradiction whereby Gore-Booth's 'polarised images of masculinity and femininity seem to show an essentialist view of gender, yet she founded a magazine to help men and women escape from the prison of sex roles' (1997: 17). Such a view must have arisen in part from her own experience, which, as we have observed, rejected the passive, 'indoors' existence that convention had in store for her. It also resulted, however, from her political, philosophical and religious convictions – all of which tended to regard dualism as one of the universe's immutable laws, and pacifism as the only rational response to aggression.

Pacifism was no easy option in London in the winter of 1916, when, exhausted by work and travel, Gore-Booth returned to a play that had been rejected by the Abbey Theatre eight years earlier. Lewis describes *The Buried Life of Deirdre* as a 'World War One protest play in disguise' (1988: caption to plate 19, between pp. 116–17); and certainly there's evidence within the text of Gore-Booth's belief in men's ineluctably aggressive nature. Conor has a developed sense of his own material worth: 'I am the High King of Ulladh', he crows: 'All this forest is mine, and many great lands … Who shall dare rob me of that which is mine by the sacred right of conquest?' (9). Although the discourse of possession by conquest is not one to which Déirdre subscribes, it's the one that will determine her fate in this reality. Conor will betray them, Déirdre argues, because like all men 'he desires, he is jealous, he slays' (34).

The rhetoric of the First World War resonates throughout this exchange between the young lovers:

NAISI: You do not understand, Deirdre. There is no brave man
            who may resist the call of his ancient comrades and the
            need of his native land.
DEIRDRE: Alas, alas, is it only women who are not blind to the
            sorrow that is to come?
NAISI: Would you have me a coward or a woman, Deirdre?
DEIRDRE: Yes, I would have you a coward or a woman, Naisi, if
            you could thus become a seer of truth. (37)

'[It] is the great wrong of the world', the doomed heroine says, 'that one man should slay another' (58). Naoise cannot betray his calling as a warrior, any more than Déirdre can betray hers as a se[ek]er of truth; and yet each regards the other as in some ways a 'traitor' – one for not harkening to 'the need of [her] ancient land', the other for allowing that need to override a more fundamental search for a truth whose earthly embodiment is love.

The concepts of (a) love between women and (b) the inherent nature of the sexes are engaged in *The Buried Life of Deirdre*, but they do not constitute the main interest of the play. Instead, Gore-Booth focuses on the idea of reincarnation – a topic that was very much in vogue in Theosophical circles during and after the 1880s. Theosophy drew on a range of esoteric religious and philosophical systems – both Western and Eastern (including quite centrally Buddhism) – in an attempt to formulate an integrated world view which might encompass the full gamut of human and natural experience. Yeats had been drawn to Theosophy after reading a book entitled *Esoteric Buddhism* sent to him by his aunt in London in 1884 (Foster 1997: 45). It fuelled a penchant for mysticism in the young poet, and became (along with Celticism and many other obscure discourses) one element in the protracted development of his own system of thought.

No doubt Gore-Booth was led to some degree by Yeats's advice and example; she must also have been influenced by a general vogue for mysticism at large in the *fin de siècle*, and by the folklore that she encountered during her Sligo childhood. Whatever the source, her 'Celtic' writings after 1900 reveal a desire to rework existing materials in the light of her developing beliefs – political beliefs, certainly, as indicated above; but religious and philosophical beliefs also. A central pillar of the latter was reincarnation – the idea that souls survive the death of the successive physical forms they adopt. Related to this was the idea (loosely adapted from the concept of *karma*, a central precept of many Eastern religious systems) that one must reap what one has sown – that the current manifestation of a soul *will* encounter, and *will be* obliged to negotiate, the energies released by previous manifestations, be they positive or negative.

Even as she was working for better pay and greater rights for working-class women, Gore-Booth explained her convictions relating to reincarnation (and other beliefs) in a series of books and articles published throughout her life. A key text for present purposes is the book she published shortly before her death entitled *A Psychological and Poetic Approach to the Study of Christ in the Fourth Gospel* (1923). This book represents an attempt to reconcile traditional interpretations of Christ with a range of beliefs developed by the author over the course of her life. One such belief concerns reincarnation, in relation to which she writes that

> [every] spiritual vibration in the self is immortal, therefore the inner spiritual essence of the self, the real Ego in us, of eternal life, cannot die, and continues from one 'generation' or birth to another. Therefore, the new psyche holds, in unconsciousness, the whole history of one's past psychic and spiritual living ... The truth that, in re-incarnation, you always get in the end, what you gave to others in

the past ... is again and again illustrated by the parables of Christ. (1923: 131–3)

One particularly compelling instance of this is provided by the example of Judas. 'Christ would have known', Gore-Booth argues, 'that, in a past life, Judas had been betrayed and murdered treacherously, and that, because of this, he would be tempted by a tremendous subconscious urge to revenge himself, by doing the same action to his past enemy' (272). Christ's achievement was to divert the negative energy onto Himself, to pay the psychical debt that Judas had incurred in a previous incarnation. The power of love makes a decisive intervention:

> Whereas if [Judas] had injured someone else who would not have forgiven him, he would have been confronted in another life ... with the cruelty and treachery of a trusted friend, which he would have been tempted to repay again with cruelty and treachery. And the vicious circle of cruelty, treachery, suffering and vengeance might have gone on for ages. (272)

This is to all intents and purposes the model of psychic energy that is at work in the lives of Déirdre, Conor and Naoise as presented in Gore-Booth's play. Early in the play Déirdre explains:

> I know that I, even I, whom you call a young and innocent maiden, was an old and jealous king. I, too, had a deep grave dug in the forest, and slew my own heart's happiness because of the jealousy of love, and buried her whom I loved in the deep grave under the oak trees. And this deed is the secret of the curse that is on me. The world is growing old, Lavarcam. There is no one young and innocent any more. (13)

Conor's treachery, therefore, is a case of Déirdre getting in the end what she gave to others in the past. Like Judas, she has become ensnared in a web of betrayal stretching across time, a web in which vibrations from the centre continue to be felt along each new woven thread. Unlike Judas, however, she has no Christ to take the burden of the debt she has inherited. She does have Mannanãn, however, a force representing 'the freedom and universality of loving' in contradistinction to the play's other presiding deity, Angus, who stands for 'the possessive and exclusive passion of love' (x). The latter is locked into earthly, corporeal and masculine desires – the ones subscribed to by Conor and Naoise; the former, however – with his emphasis on fellowship, spirit and silence – offers the possibility of escape from the cycle of guilt and betrayal. It is not an opportunity that is taken up on this occasion; the lovers die, Conor is revenged, the cycle continues. Yet the King's acknowledgement of the power of Mannanãn at the end of the play, and his determination to sacrifice to that god on Déirdre's behalf, represents an important step in the eventual mitigation of the original act of treachery. Déirdre and Naoise will love again; Conor will feel the bitterness and the shame of betrayal again; sometime, somewhere, however, in Gore-Booth's imagination, love will bring an end to contention. Those who forgive will be forgiven; there will be silence and stillness.

J.M. Synge, *Deirdre of the Sorrows: A Play* (1910)

Synge's version of the Déirdre legend instantiates a discourse of betrayal as it relates to issues of language, ownership and authenticity. Declan Kiberd, for example, is in no doubt that Synge's effort (unfinished though it was at the time of his death)

> is at once more dramatic and *more faithful* to real life than that of Yeats or Russell ... His play is at all times *true* to the way trapped and terrified people would act under intolerable strains. (1979: 177, emphases added)

The reason for Synge's success (relative to Yeats, Russell and presumably most of the other Déirdre essayists) lay in his familiarity with the original sources:

> The fundamental differences between Synge's play and the other works may be explained by the fact that, unlike Yeats and Russell, Synge did not rely on nineteenth-century English translations. Instead, he went back to the original texts of the legend in the Irish language ... He went back to the *true* source of the tale in oral and manuscript versions in Irish. (178, emphasis added)

According to Kiberd, it is his ability to '[exploit] ... the legend in its native forms' that accounts for 'the unique character of Synge's play – its blend of sentiment and brutality' (178). 'This directness of approach', he concludes, 'is one reason why his play is more faithful to the legend itself and, finally, more exciting as drama' (195).

Both the tenor and the language ('faithful', 'true', 'original', 'native', 'unique') of Kiberd's critical discourse here are interesting; although he does not use the term, it's clear that in this analysis Synge's engagement with the 'original' sources has enabled him to avoid a form of 'betrayal' that contemporary anglophone interpreters like Yeats and Russell were, at least to some degree, guilty of.

Linguistic fidelity, moreover, has segued here into artistic and existential authenticity. Synge's recourse to the earliest versions enabled him to produce a 'more dramatic' play, which in turn is 'more faithful to real life'. Although the critic is careful to avoid either moralistic or crudely evaluative language, there's a clear inference: the power and effectiveness of the contemporary treatment are directly linked with the power and effectiveness of the original story. Interpretations – especially those that rely on earlier translated interpretations – are alienated to a greater or lesser extent from that original power and effectiveness. Such versions may possess their own powers, but they represent in some sense a denial of, or a turning away from, the true meaning resident in the original.

Such a reading leads us down a potentially very dangerous road. For one thing, it reminds us of the fact that the words 'translation' and 'treason' are etymologically linked, as for example in the Italian words *traduttore* and *tradittore* (Cronin 2000: 101). As we saw at length in Chapter 1, there's a duality implicit in the concept of 'treason': a denial of or turning away from one side – which demands the subject's initial loyalty – in favour of another. This duality is echoed in the figurative definition of 'translation' as connoting a sense of movement 'across, through, over, to or on the other side of, beyond, outside of, from one place, person, thing or state to another' (Simpson and Weiner 1989 XVIII: 409). Regarded in a certain way, therefore, every act of translation rehearses this traitorous move from the original to the reproduction, the real to the less real, the organic to the alienated. To employ a different metaphor, the translated text enacts a journey away from home into a foreign country where they do and think things differently – a place where the subject, as a direct result of their movement 'from one place … to another', becomes as it were a stranger unto themselves.

Understood thus, we are obliged to recognise how the spectre of betrayal haunts modern Irish culture – not only its literature but the very fabric of what has become an overwhelmingly anglophone existence. The vast majority of 'Irish' people are likewise implicated in this betrayal – and none more so, Kiberd believes, than the literary critics who use their professional and institutional status to patrol the artificial border between Gaelic and English traditions. Kiberd's description of this situation as 'a gigantic exercise in self-deception' (18) connotes two forms of betrayal: active betrayal (an 'exercise') of a marginalised internal Other who is shuffled aside to make way for noisier or more aggressive forms of 'national' culture; and (self-) betrayal *of* the Subject *by* the Subject who acquiesces with the state's misrecognition of their own meaning.

Of course, Synge did not write his plays in Irish: he wrote them in a highly stylised English which attempted to reproduce the rhythms and peculiarities of the Gaelic language as it had evolved into the present. This was a curious strategy for an avowed opponent of anglophone modernity. As Seamus Deane has pointed out, '[once] the oral tradition is written, it is transformed'; Synge, therefore – for all his insistence upon the value of Gaelic – was implicated in a discourse 'of translation as much as the nineteenth-century rewriters of Irish poetry into English' (1985: 55). Synge, Deane claims, 'wanted a revival of the English, not of the Irish, language' (56). The erosion of Gaelic – and the cultural and psychological losses consequent thereon – thus becomes a metaphysical issue rather than a historical and/or political tragedy. 'Synge aestheticizes the problem of oppression', Deane writes, 'by converting it into the issue of heroism' (60). The issue becomes one of betrayal when the relationship between the individual and the community is recast as a trade-off between the ambivalent rewards of individual freedom and the rituals of convention and establishment.

Synge's artistic vision thus operates in a manner akin to that of a double agent. He was already a 'traitor' in so far as he had seemingly turned his back on a particular cultural (Anglo-Irish) and political (Unionist) inheritance; and yet his supposed embrace of a 'new' identity as champion of a beleaguered Gaelic language masked a deeper allegiance, which was always to Art rather anything so chaotic as 'reality' or so nebulous as 'history'. The 'original' *produces* the version, just as the past *produces* the present and the community *produces* the individual; but in Synge's vision there can be no reintegration, no reconciliation. Each of his heroes and heroines enacts a form of necessary treason, which was in itself a reflection of Synge's own condition as both a political subject and an artist. Deane is left in no doubt as to the implications:

> This Trinity College view of Irish history was extended and enriched by Synge and by Yeats into a myth of union between peasant and aristocrat – leading to the emergence of heroism, spiritual leadership,

still aristocratic in tone, Anglo-Irish in content ... The attempt to recover a new ideal of heroism from the reintegration of the shattered Gaelic culture with the presiding English polity is no more than the after-image of authority on the Anglo-Irish retina. (60)

It's interesting to observe the degree to which these theories are reproduced, challenged or contradicted in a play so centrally focused on issues of political and interpersonal betrayal.

It may be observed at once that Synge's version is conventional in so far as it employs a simple three-act structure which follows the main contours of the legend as it exists in various redactions: (1) Déirdre's retreat on Slieve Fuadh; her meeting and flight with Naoise; (2) the exiles in Scotland, and Fergus's embassy; (3) return to Ulster and death. Although political issues hover around the edges, Synge's treatment (following the eighteenth-century version by Aindrias MacCuirtin) is focused on the tragic love story, and in particular on the psychological organisation of Déirdre's mind. His sources may have been 'original', but Synge elaborated a complex rationale – using dialogue, action, gesture and stage direction – for plot developments that in earlier versions would have had no, or at best crude, motivation.

Certain dominant themes are established early in Synge's treatment. Conor is described as 'a man would be jealous of a hawk would fly between her and the rising sun' (3). A middle-aged potentate used to taking what he wants and having his own way, Conor is a man primed for betrayal; it's no great surprise when – given the examples from nature with which she is surrounded on Slieve Fuadh – Déirdre is drawn towards the young virile hero. As in *Othello*, jealousy is revealed as an emotion which breeds paranoia and destruction, one that in some senses *creates* and *seeks out* the betrayals off which the jealous subject feeds. This leads to the revelation that Déirdre's desire for Naoise is in some senses a function of her status as the object of a powerful old man's desire. For if it was her *fate* to bring death and destruction to Ulster, it was Conor's *fate* to be a jealous king who manufactured a situation in which Déirdre is forced to choose between betraying her saviour and protector on the one hand, or betraying nature and herself on the other.

A related theme established early in the play concerns the nature of truth. Conor's estimation of himself as 'a man has no lies' (14) is countered by Lavarcam's insight: 'It's a queer thing the way the likes of me do be telling the truth, and the wise are lying all times' (9).

Where there's talk of truth, however, there's also always the possibility of denying or betraying truth. Synge introduces the language of 'treachery' during the second act: referring to the concealment of an inimical reality behind a masquerade of amicability, this language relates ostensibly to Conor's intentions in inviting the exiles back to Emania. Such language appears at various points throughout the remainder of the play: the spy Owen talks of 'plots and tricks and spies' (59); Naoise's brothers are 'betrayed and broken' (81) while he contends with the King; most damningly, Fergus describes Conor towards the end of the play as 'a thief and traitor' (95). This discourse, however, represents merely a localised rendition of a more fundamental discourse of truth operating throughout the play – one focused (as Una Ellis-Fermor recognised in an early response) on the two great truths that order human existence: love and death (1939: 180).

Perhaps the principal question facing any modern writer attempting to retell this ancient story concerns the issue of motivation: *why* do the exiles return to the place of danger? The older versions make much of the brothers' homesickness and of their implicit faith in Fergus's trustworthiness as an emissary of peace and forgiveness. Déirdre's forebodings of doom and her laments for Scotland also feature in most of the early Gaelic versions. While touching on all these ancient plot elements, Synge's major innovation was to make the lovers decide to return to Ulster of their own accord. They do so, ultimately, in order to avoid the diminution and eventual disappearance of their passion. Synge's modernity leads him to doubt the enduring viability of any emotional commitment – as Déirdre says:

> It's lonesome this place, having happiness like ours, till I'm asking each day will this day match yesterday, and will to-morrow take a good place beside the same day in the year that's gone, and wondering at all times is it a game worth playing, living on until you're dried and old, and our joy is gone for ever. (41–2)

Likewise, Naoise has experienced 'a dread upon me a day'd come I'd weary of her voice ... and Deirdre'd see I'd wearied' (51). A number of characters have already touched upon this likelihood: Owen speaks of 'Naisi getting a harshness in his two sheep's eyes and he looking on yourself' 46); while Fergus warns Naoise against 'lingering until the day that you'll grow weary, and hurt Deirdre showing her the hardness will grow up within your eyes' (50). It's their unwillingness to betray the 'truth' of their love – to keep, as Naoise puts it, 'a watch on love had no match and it wasting away' (57) – that compels Déirdre and her lover to leave Alban, and to place themselves in the power of a man whose jealousy and vengefulness have already been established.

The elopement of Déirdre and Naoise represented in itself an act of betrayal: political in the case of the latter (the warrior's denial of his king); interpersonal in the case of the former (the ward's denial of her protector). After seven years, however, they have found themselves in a position where to remain in exile would be a betrayal of their love – indeed, of their very selves. Love degenerating into complacency and perhaps even aversion: that would be a poor end to the story of passion in which the young lovers had been involved. Therefore they return to Conor's inevitable betrayal – 'to a grave was scooped by treachery' (50). Even then, treachery stalks the lovers to the grave: referring to their final exchanges, Kiberd remarks the brutal irony whereby the lovers 'lapse, before death, into that very disharmony which the sacrifice of their lives was designed to avoid' (1979: 187–8).

Betrayal, as we have observed elsewhere, is a weed that grows voraciously in the soil of human interaction; given that interaction of one kind or another is the very essence of human culture, it's inevitable that betrayal should feature so strongly in all forms of cultural practice. As an Irishman and as a nationalist Synge was extremely concerned with the fate of the Gaelic language, and at the ways in which it had been betrayed by inimical forces into near-obsolescence. All 'Irish' culture in the English language was to some extent complicit with that act of betrayal; his command of the language, and his willingness to consult 'original' sources as the bases for his work was thus an attempt to ameliorate the betrayal in which he himself – as a translator and as an English-language writer – was implicated.

Like Yeats, Synge's career was dedicated to the discovery and development of an 'Irish art' worthy of the name, and (he would have argued), as a consequence, to the realisation of a modern nation-state that would in turn be worthy of such an art. This, as we have seen, necessitated a complex psychology, one in which feelings (and accusations) of betrayal – both cultural and political – were a constant presence. As an artist, however, Synge was concerned also with another, deeper level of betrayal – one that was no doubt very much on his mind as he worked at his play during his final illness:[11] the act of betrayal represented by death. Death connotes a form of betrayal – of love, of passion, ultimately of life itself – that the artist in general, and this artist in particular, is uniquely equipped to comprehend.

Considered in its most fundamental terms, *Deirdre of the Sorrows* is a dramatisation of the complex negotiations between love and death. In Synge's discourse, the question of Irishness and the Irish language tends to slip between the crack that emerges between the desirability of the one (love) and the inevitability of the other (death).

James Stephens, *Deirdre* (1923)

We turn aside from drama for the final treatment of treason and betrayal in this case study. The eponymous novel by James Stephens prepares us – both in terms of its publication date, but also (and more significantly) in terms of its generic attributes – for the focus on the modern Irish novel in Part II of this study.

Stephens was already a successful writer when he decided (in 1917) to undertake a Herculean task: to rewrite the ancient Gaelic epic known as the *Táin* in novel form. The plan was to compose a suite of novels focusing on key aspects of the cycle, thereby building up a modern version of one of the foundational narratives of Irish culture. In the event, Stephens only wrote two of the intended five volumes – *Deirdre* (1923) and *In The Land of Youth* (1924) – before abandoning the project.

In so far as it offers a mixture of the realistic and the mythological – or what Augustine Martin (1977: xii) calls 'actuality and dream' – *Deirdre* is typical of its author's career up to that time. Individual texts may lean towards one or the other: that is, realism – such as *The Charwoman's Daughter* (1912a) or *Hunger* (1918); or the fantastic – such as *The Crock of Gold* (1912b) or *The Demi-Gods* (1914). Stephens's characteristic method, however, was one in which the real and the fantastic inhere within each other. The result was a richly evocative style that was truly carnivalesque in its ability to orchestrate a range of voice zones and discourses. This accounts in some measure for the pleasure of Stephens's writing: the various voices are constantly interrogating one another in his work at the level of idiom – often, indeed, at the level of the individual signifier – and this demands an active response from the reader in order to be able to identify and appreciate the nuances of interconnected meanings.

Inasmuch as he was willing and able to engage with a range of aesthetic practices, Stephens was in many ways an exemplary writer of this period of Irish cultural history. In some ways, indeed, he bridges the gap between the two great impulses of early twentieth-century Irish writing: the revivalism of Yeats and the modernism of Joyce. Yeats was instrumental in his 'protégé' (Foster 1997: 486) receiving a Royal Irish Academy award for *Deirdre*, but his association with the famous poet exposed Stephens to the censure of dominant nationalism: his novel was described by the *Irish Monthly* as 'sheer filth to all who hold an ideal of chaste manhood and womanhood' (quoted in Foster 2003: 267). Stephens was also friendly with Joyce, who proposed various collaborations, including his fellow Dubliner's completion of *Finnegans Wake* in the event of his own death. This association likewise implicated Stephens in a treacherous attitude towards Ireland – 'treacherous', that is, when observed from the perspective of prevailing Catholic nationalism.

In their different ways, both Yeats and Joyce were concerned to provide Ireland with an 'epic' vision – one that might sustain the country in the dangerously alienating modern world. Stephens's projected five-novel cycle based on the ancient Ulster Cycle might be regarded – as much as *Ulysses*, *The Tower* or *Finnegans Wake* – as a similarly 'epic' endeavour: to provide a coherent vision of Irishness past and present, one that would draw on the former in order to aid survival in the latter.

In broad terms, Yeats's (poetic and dramatic) vision was essentially tragic, while Joyce's (novelistic and narrative) was essentially comic. Stephens, as already observed, was drawn to both these impulses, and indeed made a virtue of being able to slip easily between different discursive narrative zones in order to surprise the reader and to involve them in the meaning-making process. The various narrative forces within *Deirdre* are constantly mitigating one another, pulling the reader between different levels and forms of interpretation: comic and tragic, historical and contemporary, political and personal, archetypal and psychological. The effect, moreover, is underpinned by the subject matter – that is, a tale of political and interpersonal treachery in which overt allegiance is constantly qualified and mitigated by covert desire.

As remarked earlier, there had been many English prose versions of the legend of Déirdre and the Sons of Usna throughout the modern era. The history of this tradition is shadowed by the evolution of the novel – a highly specialised form that is itself (as we shall observe throughout the remainder of this book) finely calibrated in relation to the socio-cultural development of the various national formations in which it emerges. Extended prose versions were, of course, available: P.W. Joyce's 'The Fate of the Sons of Usna' (1879), for example, is approximately 7,500 words long, and is divided into quasi-novelistic 'chapters'; Lady Gregory's version (1902) is about twice as long, and reproduces some features of established novel-writing practice, such as dialogue and narrative reflection. Stephens was the first to attempt a properly 'novelistic' treatment of the story, however (Martin 1977: 140); and if this afforded him greater scope for character development, plot nuance and psychological motiv-ation, it also set him particular problems. For, given the status of the novel as an artistic practice locked into particular social values, it's not surprising that the issues of betrayal which beset the characters at the level of content should be reprised and renegotiated at the level of form.

Stephens produces a version of the Déirdre legend which is amen-able to the genre in which it is conveyed and to the period in which it was written. The novel is clearly focused on two of its author's recurring concerns: sexual jealousy and the contention of the sexes. The former in particular is, as Augustine Martin avers, 'the most persistent theme in Stephens's fiction' (1977: 144). These themes are broached in the first instance by the relationship between King Conor mac Nessa and his wife Queen Mève. The presence of the latter seems anomalous at first, as she has no real part to play in the story. As Martin elsewhere pointed out (1965: 29), however, the Connaught queen was to feature strongly in the later texts in the projected series; she is introduced here by Stephens, therefore, in order to provide backstory and to establish some elements of her personality. More than this, however, her desertion of Conor early in the text provides a psychological impetus for the ensuing narra-tive: the King is diminished – in the eyes of his people and in his own esteem – by Mève's 'betrayal', so he comes to place an inordin-ate emphasis on possession and mastery of Déirdre. If he had not been so damaged by the older woman, the inference is, he might have been better able to forgive the younger one.

The rightful King of Ulster is Fergus mac Roy, who, we learn, has been usurped by Conor (aided by his mother Nessa) through a combination of deceit and diplomacy. Fergus is now one of the King's most trusted warriors; that trust, however, is one-sided. For having been the perpetrator of a betrayal, the 'king' finds himself prey to suspicions of treachery. More than this, however, the presence of Fergus serves as a constant reminder of Conor's compromised integrity as well as the essential illegitimacy of his rule. As the narrative has it: 'He looked lovingly and mildly on Fergus because he hated Fergus and had wronged him so bitterly that he must wrong him yet more in justification' (6). Lavarcam's description – 'Conachúr loves him on the surface, but he hates him in the bone' (125) – perfectly encapsulates the psycho-spatial disposition of treachery: the reality (hate) subsisting below the appearance (affinity).

As both a man and a ruler, therefore, Conor is disposed towards betrayal. This disposition, moreover, extends to the society over which he rules. Thus, Lavarcam – who in other versions was a nursemaid, a companion, a conversation-woman, a druidess and other variations on the wise woman – is here a 'household spy' (19): someone, in other words, who processes all information and all relationships (including that with her beloved Déirdre) in terms of a covert affiliation to the King. Mève has her own personal spy – mac Roth – who is Lavarcam's master in terms of espionage, and who expedites his mistress's escape from Emania. The atmosphere of treachery, moreover, extends to the next generation. When she hears the story of Mève's flit, Déirdre is impressed by the older woman's wilfulness in the face of the King's power, and this provides a spur for the pursuit of her own desires when they begin to make themselves felt. Naoise, whose 'personal loyalty to Conachúr was such that he would not dwell even in imagination on that which belonged to the king' (79), finds himself brought around by degrees to just such an act of betrayal – an act that is at once both political (he is Conor's bondsman) and interpersonal (he is the King's nephew). He achieves this by an act of renunciation (145), and in the name of a relationship that is seemingly more natural (in terms of temper, age, social standing, etc.) than the putative one between the King and Déirdre.

The instances and the accusations of betrayal multiply as the plot develops and the stakes rise. From a starting position in which 'their experience of treachery [is] so small' (71), Déirdre and Naoise are educated by degrees into the reality of betrayal – what might be described as 'the experience of the world' or simply 'the experience of experience'. Over the course of the narrative they learn that merely *to be* in the world, *to desire* and *to be desired*, is to be confronted sooner or later by the inevitability of treachery. Each character is infected by the disease that Conor has loosed in Ulster. Despite his determination to live a life bound by honour, Fergus finds himself implicated in the King's revenge: 'He is a traitor, that Fergus', says Déirdre when she learns of his embassy; 'He is being used by the king to betray us' (211). Lavarcam is guilty of 'treachery' (234) towards the King when she lies to him on the subject of Déirdre's beauty. Buinne describes Conor as a 'traitor king' (249) shortly before he himself betrays the sons of Usnach and, by inference, his own father.

The exchange between the King and Fergus's other son goes to the heart of the matter:

> 'We have you, Iollann!' said Conachúr. 'Traitor to your king!' he growled.
> 'Traitor to your friends,' Iollann retorted. (266)

Two discourses confront each other here: one claims loyalty in the name of political authority, the other in the name of interpersonal allegiance.[12] Each claims precedence and anteriority in relation to the other. Each may preside over the other only by an act of performance – a claim, a statement – which has no basis in reality, no natural authority or precedence to which it may appeal.

Questions of sovereignty, authority and loyalty were part of the fabric of Irish life in the early 1920s when Stephens was conceiving his five-novel series and writing this initial part. The Treaty negotiations had forced ideologues on all sides to focus on practical issues of power and authority. Whence did nationalist rights derive, and where did that power extend to? The broad front that had sustained the revolutionary movement since 1916 was just about to be tested (and found wanting) by the reality of executive power, limited though it was. The image of a vengeful monarch was a particularly loaded one: what was the status of an 'Irishness' that remained in thrall to the British Crown? Could the quality of Irishness be 'strained' to that extent, even as a stepping-stone to full independence? Whatever else it was, the Civil War (June 1922– April 1923) represented a stand-off between competing accounts of authority and morality, each of which regarded the other as in some way and to some degree traitorous in relation to its own narrative.

As always, questions concerning the ways *in* which, and the extent *to* which, such matters find their way into artistic texts remain difficult to frame, let alone answer. In a study that claims an indelible link between literary concerns and the wider socio-cultural climate, however, such questions persist. That's the principal task of Part II; in the meantime, and by way of conclusion here, it's worthwhile signalling once again the extent to which issues of treason and betrayal are implicated in the formal constitution of the novel itself. Clearly, Stephens's text connotes a different aesthetic experience from those provided in the dramatic texts of Yeats, Gore-Booth and Synge: although telling ostensibly the same story (with the differences in emphases, structure and motivation that we have noted), the novel operates according to markedly different narrative systems and protocols. This emerges most clearly in relation to the narrator's attitude towards language – that most fundamental and yet potentially treacherous of the novel's tools.

At one point in the story, the narrator attempts to describe the two principal characters as they appeared to each other. He is forced to admit defeat, however; the love of Déirdre and Naoise simply cannot be rendered in language. Poetry or music might be up to the task, he concedes, but 'words cannot stand the trial' (70).[13] Some things, it appears, 'cannot be unveiled in speech' (71). The poets employ allusion, simile and metaphor, using images from nature to try to convey the *kind* and the *strength* of an emotion such as love; or they try to describe the resulting emotional states: abasement, sadness, despair. Such usages only 'approach perfection' (71), however, they never 'achieve' it. This is because of the nature of language itself – the novelist's medium – which is in essence a melancholy, superannuated, *late* phenomenon, always attempting to describe the indescribable, to convey the unconveyable.

Language in this sense always acts treacherously towards that which it attempts to represent; and both the narrator and the reader are implicated in that betrayal. The narrator, as it were, invites the reader into a compact of treason vis-à-vis the story; and this compact echoes (in this instance) the acts of betrayal perpetrated in the story itself. This betrayal, moreover, remains necessary inasmuch as one must differentiate between the telling of the story and the 'real' events – however fantastic, however removed in space or time – on which the story is based. Stephens's narrator recognises this and, with his metafictional reflections on the limits of language, subtly reminds the reader of their complicity.

Chapter 15 of Stephens's novel focuses on the thoughts and actions of the eponymous heroine as she flees her childhood home late at night in order to escape her fate as Conor's bride, and to find Naoise, the man on whom she has set her heart. Déirdre experiences a wide range of emotions during this journey: anger, despair, fear, nervousness, hope. The nocturnal flora and fauna through which she moves seems to offer tacit support for her actions. The weather, also, is on her side, with giant clouds providing cover from the moonlight which might otherwise have exposed her. Nature, it seems, acquiesces in the 'natural' alliance of these young lovers. But Déirdre's excitement grows as she reflects on her actions:

> She was sure that this time he would speak to her, and that whatever he said would be wiser and sweeter and stranger than any words she had yet listened to; and she wondered, without thought, what his magical utterance would mean and how it could possibly be replied to; knowing yet that her replies were already formed, and that the only word she need utter until she dies was the word 'yes'. (96–7)

Many of the formal and conceptual aspects of this passage recall the end of Molly Bloom's famous soliloquy from *Ulysses*, published a year earlier: the strain on conventional punctuation; the proliferation of 'and' as a clausal link; the anticipation of the lover's words; and, most tellingly, the resounding 'yes' with which the passage ends. I'm not, of course, claiming any direct link between the two texts: I would maintain, however, that their shared concern with Irish identity implicated Stephens and Joyce in similar activities (novel-writing), and a shared focus on the role played by betrayal in the formation of that identity.

Part II

I gave up treachery for Lent
And forced myself to meditate
On what sincerity meant.
I gazed long and long at the Irish Free State

Seeking a sincere man or woman.
Sincere. Sin seer. Won't do. I couldn't find
A single soul in the whole island
Whom I could, with all my heart and mind,

Dub sincere. But I tried, I tried, I really tried
Because I am a sticky lad
Once I get something into my head

But I failed, I failed, I really failed, and I sighed
Briefly before releasing the Judassmile
With 'I think I'll return to my old style.'

Brendan Kennelly, The
Little Book of Judas, 188–9

3

'Trust Not Appearances': James Joyce's *Ulysses* (1922)

Language is a farce.
The fascist flesh rules you and me.
No words can shape the curse.
I lock my lips on nothing and go free

To mope at street corners
Give pet names to stars
Ruminate on the factors
That influence the blood of traitors.

Brendan Kennelly, *The
Little Book of Judas*, 199–200

Introduction

On 22 March 1907 James Joyce published an article entitled 'Il Fenianismo: L'ultimo Feniano' (translating as 'Fenianism: The Last Fenian') in a journal published in Trieste (where he was then living) entitled *Il Piccolo dello Sera*. Joyce wrote the article at the invitation of the journal's editor, Roberto Prezioso, to whom he was teaching English and whom he considered to be a good friend and supporter. In that article the exiled Irishman invoked one of his favourite themes: the inevitable betrayal of those who had dedicated themselves to the winning of political freedom for Ireland. In respect of the failed Fenian insurrection of 1867, Joyce asked: 'Why this collapse of such a well-organized movement? Simply because in Ireland, just at the crucial moment, an informer appears' (2000: 139).

A few years later, Joyce accosted Prezioso in a Triestene square and accused him of trying to seduce Nora Barnacle, Joyce's partner since 1904.[1] The Italian was devastated, especially as he believed that his extremely tentative advances had been made with the knowledge, if not the tacit encouragement, of his Irish friends. On the contrary, Joyce was mortally insulted, although it's not clear from any account whether he was more offended with this instance of a friend's betrayal or with the idea of himself as a cuckold. In any event, Prezioso was summarily dismissed from the Joycean circle, although the tears of humiliation he wept during the Irish writer's onslaught left a deep imprint on all parties.

James Joyce is the only Irish author I have discovered during the course of this study who has an index entry for 'betrayal' in his standard biography (Ellmann 1959: 819); with the inevitable exception of Shakespeare, he may be the only author in literary history to be so endowed. Indeed, Richard Ellmann's exemplary study established betrayal at the core of Joyce's life and art, and it's true to say that much of the critical discourse attending his work has been inflected to some degree by this subject. As the two instances cited above suggest, moreover, this engagement has been multi-focused and multi-disciplinary – political, historical, psychological, aesthetic, linguistic, racial, and so on. Just as he was the precursor of so much else that would engage subsequent critical attention, Joyce it is who establishes betrayal at the heart of modern Irish experience, and it would be as well to acknowledge now that this study is conducted significantly in the wake of his example.

The causes of Joyce's fixation with treason and betrayal are no doubt many and various,[2] but one key factor was certainly the fate of Charles Stewart Parnell. An austere Anglo-Irish Protestant, Parnell was deposed as leader by his colleagues in the Irish Parliamentary Party after his citation as co-respondent in a divorce case in December 1889.[3] This blow was felt keenly in the Joyce household, where it was regarded by paterfamilias John as an outrageous act of betrayal, and where it inspired his nine-year-old son to compose a poem entitled 'Et Tu, Healy', in which the precocious writer likened the relationship between Parnell and Tim Healy – trusted lieutenant and chief agent of the fall – to that (as portrayed in the Shakespeare play) between Julius Caesar and his friend Brutus.

It was at this point, Ellmann explains, that 'the word betrayal became a central one in Joyce's view of his countrymen' (1959: 32). That sense of betrayal, however, was not only political. Parnell's great sin, after all, was to be implicated in a series of personal relationships which undermined the institution of marriage; and his

reputation crumbled in the face of contemporary Irish Catholic attitudes towards adultery, which history tells us were orthodox and
stringent (Foley 1997; Inglis 1998: 23–49). No one knew his own
constituency better than Parnell; no one appreciated better than he
the fragility of the broad political front which had been so pains-
takingly established during the 1880s in the name of Home Rule.
In a sense, he 'betrayed' that constituency when he entered into an
affair with Katherine O'Shea; in a sense he betrayed his own cause
when he engaged in activities so repugnant to those upon whose
support the cause of Home Rule relied. Reading backwards from
Joyce, furthermore, we might say that in yet another sense Parnell
may have betrayed himself if he had failed to act upon his desire for
the woman he loved.

The fall of Parnell, then, instantiates a matrix of traitorous
impulses and actions – some political-cultural, some subjective and
interpersonal; and it's clear, as remarked above, that such a matrix
was a crucial component of the artistic vision of James Joyce. *Ulysses*
represents the cornerstone of that vision, and it comes as no surprise
to find the shade of Parnell floating through the pages of that novel.
In fact, *Ulysses* is haunted by many ghosts – personal, political, aesthetic – each of which represents a dimension of what one critic
refers to as Joyce's 'pathological obsession with betrayal – an almost
voluptuous desire to be betrayed' (O'Connor 1990: 343). But in
order to appreciate how betrayal comes to occupy such a central
position within one of the key texts of twentieth-century literature
we have to follow a circuitous path through the history of the novel
(in Ireland and elsewhere), along the way taking in Joyce's earlier
artistic output as well as a famous incident in the author's own life.

Adultery and the novel

In his 1979 study *Adultery and the Novel* Tony Tanner exam-
ined the overlapping trajectories of the novel form, the bourgeois
society in which it emerged and flourished, and the institution of
marriage which operated as the ideological mechanism whereby
such societies were validated and reproduced. There's an obvious
reciprocal link, Tanner suggests, between the emergence of the
modern family and the emergence of a narrative form which takes
the family as its principal focus. Implicitly linked with discourses
of property-ownership and inheritance, marriage represents a

contract whereby patrilineal law – the basis of bourgeois society – is underwritten. At the same time, that particular form of social organisation implicitly endorses narrative forms which appear to ensure its own normality – which is to say: marriage and the family. Society, marriage and the novel thus enter into an alliance of interests and expressions.

Tanner discovers the roots of the adulterous novel in Rousseau's *Julie, ou La Nouvelle Héloïse* (1761), and in Goethe's *Die Wahlverwandtschaften* (1809). The exemplary articulation, however, remains Gustave Flaubert's *Madame Bovary* (1856). In Emma Bovary's tortured, self-delusional emotional career, in her oscillation between a state of virtuous marriage and a state of banal adultery, Tanner discerns the primary ideological motor of the nineteenth-century novel. The figure of the adulterous woman, whose desires outstrip the limitations of bourgeois marriage and who is forced to pay with her life for succumbing to adulterous desires, was to be revisited in texts such as *Thérèse Raquin* (1867) and *Anna Karenina* (1878). And it was this tradition, and in particular the concept of a human desire that was at odds with the social disposition of desire (which is to say, marriage), that was to prove influential upon James Joyce when he came to create his own fictional world.[4]

A crucial problem emerges in relation to this affinity, however. The institution of marriage operates with reference to *repeated* instances of the *same* contract: a particular couple rehearses the same emotional commitment again and again until death.[5] The novel, however, depends upon conflict and disruption to drive the narrative forward; and much of the time, conflict and disruption take the form of an assault upon the most obvious, and at the same time the most available, expression of bourgeois values: marriage. Furthermore, while the novel apparently works to obviate this threat, its evocation in fact undermines the ideology of marriage as an expression of 'normal' social relations. As Tanner writes:

> Apparently complicit with the sanctity of the family, the centrality of marriage, and the authority of the Father, the novel has, in fact, in many cases harboured and deviously celebrated quite contrary feelings. Very often the novel writes of contracts but dreams of transgressions, and in reading it, the dream tends to emerge more powerfully. (1979: 368)

The history of the novel in the nineteenth century alerts us to the absolute centrality of adultery as a constitutional element of the genre.[6]

To revisit the metaphor introduced above in relation to Parnell and *Ulysses*, we might say that adultery 'haunts' the nineteenth-century novel, although it does so in different ways and to different degrees in the various national traditions. Although English fiction after Richardson is obsessed with the role of marriage in securing patrilineal law, for example, adultery *per se* does not feature particularly strongly. The *idea* and the *possibility* are broached constantly: in the troubled relationships between Catherine Earnshaw and Heathcliff, Jane Eyre and Edward Rochester, Becky Sharpe and George Osborne, Dorothea Casaubon and Will Ladislaw, Bathsheba Everdene and William Boldwood, and so on. Despite this, the English novel by and large tends to steer clear of explicit instances of adultery, preferring to develop elaborate, frequently melodramatic, plot devices that avoid the final sexual liaison that would constitute an act of legal adultery. It's as if the English novel is content to approach the gates of adultery, but not to enter therein.

The 'ghost' metaphor is apt if one considers the extent to which issues of inheritance, paternity and indefeasible desire permeate the tradition of Irish gothic fiction.[7] We shall be revisiting that tradition, and its implications for an understanding of betrayal, in future chapters. In the meantime, we find that contemporary Irish realist fiction is likewise concerned with the legal and moral status of marriage, but for different reasons and to different ends. In his book *Catholic Fiction and Social Reality in Ireland, 1873–1922* (1997), James H. Murphy discusses the 'devotional revolution' which overlapped with Joyce's early life in Ireland, and how such a phenomenon may have impacted upon contemporary narrative fiction. Whatever its causes, he avers, the devotional revolution had the effect of placing Catholicism and the family at the centre of Irish cultural experience. Essentially an expression of the lower middle class from which Joyce emerged, this emphasis was opposed to two contemporary impulses: one – that of a Protestant ascendancy class – which sought comfort for its increasing economic and political marginalisation through the imagination of a heroic Celtic history; and the other – that of a Catholic intelligentsia – which, finding itself at odds with the mores of the Catholic centre, 'valued self-realization and the liberty of the individual' (1997: 149).

The emphasis on family amongst that section of the community which was moving towards hegemony worked to fetishise the institution of marriage, and to demonise those practices which undermined it: divorce and adultery. In *Irish Novels 1890–1940*, John Wilson Foster points out that the first of these – divorce – was simply too far off the Irish radar to be much of a problem.[8] The bulk of contemporary Catholic opprobrium, therefore, was reserved for practices which appeared in some form or other to undermine marriage and family – the cornerstones of national morality. He notes the 'hostility to adultery or even second marriages contracted out of true love' (2008: 267) characteristic of life in Joyce's Irish youth; but he notes also those many novelists – Catholic *and* Protestant, Irish resident *and* exiled – who attempted to broach a range of issues which implicitly questioned the moral economy of contemporary Ireland: unhappy marriage, unfulfilled desire, unrealised ambition.

Certainly, Joyce's work may be approached in terms of these local issues and debates. Murphy, for example, suggests that 'the confrontation between Simon Dedalus and Casey, on the one hand, and Mrs Riordan, on the other, over the fall of Parnell' (in the opening chapter of *A Portrait of the Artist as a Young Man*) represents the *locus classicus* for the contemporary intellectual's rejection of Catholic Ireland (1997: 145). And Wilson Foster notes that

> [a] major preoccupation of Joyce is the nature of the Blooms' marriage, and although its secret and rich infidelities of thought and deed make it an unusual union among the legion of fictional marriages in the 1890–1922 period, *Ulysses* can nevertheless be added, in that respect, to the long list of marriage novels of the time. (2008: 495)

This may be so: at the same time, it's clear that Joyce looked neither to Ireland nor to England for his primary literary references, but to Paris, Rome, Moscow and Oslo. And there he found in abundance a willingness to engage with the clash between protean human desire and the social conventions (including marriage) that had evolved to organise and restrict desire.

Joyce's artistic ambitions, as well as his moral vision, were profoundly influenced by the contemporary writer he most admired: Henrik Ibsen. In plays such as *Ghosts* (1881), *Hedda Gabler* (1890) and *When We Dead Awaken* (1899), Ibsen dramatised, with increasing insight and subtlety, the confrontation between individual desire and social convention, especially as it pertained to established gender relations. Joyce utilised these influences in his one surviving play, *Exiles* (1918), of which more presently; but he was also to carry Ibsen's influence into his own favoured medium – narrative fiction – and to incorporate it alongside the novel's inheritance as a genre whose very existence depended to a defining extent on the institution of marriage and, more pointedly, on the implications of threatening or undermining that institution.

Betrayal before *Ulysses*

If the lost 'Et Tu, Healy' speaks of Joyce's aptitude for betrayal, so too does the juvenile essay 'Trust Not Appearances', written during his time at Belvedere College.[9] Although this short piece represents nothing more than an entirely conventional, somewhat callow, meditation on the discrepancy between outward appearance and underlying reality, regarded from the perspective of its author's subsequent career it assumes a compelling resonance. For it was precisely the relationship between appearance and reality that was to exercise Joyce so much in *Ulysses*; and it was the search for a style and a technique with which to render that inscrutable relationship that was to occupy the remainder of his career. Particularly interesting is the youthful author's use of the word 'traitor':

> Still however, there is a 'something' that tells us the character of man. It is the eye. The only traitor that even the sternest will of a fiendish villain [*sic*] cannot overcome. It is the eye that reveals to man the guilt or innocence, the vices or the virtues of the soul. This is the only exception to the proverb 'Trust not appearances'. (2000: 3)

And so: the person harbouring inimical intentions behind a mask of amicability is exposed by a flaw in their own body. The traitor's eye is thus doubly alienated: once, as a part of the traitor's otherness vis-à-vis the realm of 'the same' (it 'belongs' to the traitor), and once again vis-à-vis the traitor's own hidden intentions (it betrays the traitor). It's not possible to say if this complex proposition is the result of confusion on the part of the teenage writer, or whether it's a prescient insight into the duplicitous nature of representation.[10] In either case, it anticipates the moral and aesthetic complexities of *Ulysses*, a novel in which the uncertain relationship between appearance and reality features so centrally.

The idea of betrayal is taken up with greater or lesser emphasis in all Joyce's subsequent creative writings. *Dubliners* is populated by a series of characters (themselves representative of an entire race) who inhale the atmosphere of betrayal which is at large within Irish society. In the poem recited in 'Ivy Day at the Committee Room' (completed, according to Ellmann, by 1 September 1905), Parnell is likened to Christ betrayed:

> He dreamed (alas, 'twas but a dream!)
> Of Liberty: but as he strove
> To clutch that idol, treachery
> Sundered him from the thing he loved.
>
> Shame on the coward caitiff hands
> That smote their Lord or with a kiss
> Betrayed him to the rabble-rout
> Of fawning priests – no friends of his. (1914: 104)

The Jesus/Judas relationship is revisited seven years later in 'The Shade of Parnell' (his own translation of an article originally published in Italian as 'L'Ombra di Parnell'), when Joyce wrote:

> Of the eighty-three deputies, only eight remained faithful to him ... The sadness that devastated his soul was, perhaps, the profound conviction that, in his hour of need, one of the disciples who had dipped his hand into the bowl with him was about to betray him. (2000: 196)

The allusion to Christ's betrayal by Judas carries all the weight of Christian prejudice, freighted even more with the confessional Catholicism that was coming to prominence in late nineteenth-century Ireland. But Parnell's case is merely an exemplary public instance of a much more entrenched malaise.

The longest story in *Dubliners* begins to approach the adulterous territory mapped out in the European novelistic tradition of the previous century. 'The Dead' is a tale of bourgeois insecurity, set in a milieu not dissimilar to that familiar from the work of Flaubert, Tolstoy and Zola. Gretta Conroy has not been sexually unfaithful to her husband Gabriel; yet he suspects that the story she tells him late one evening after a Christmas party, about her relationship with a young man from her Galway youth, may have cuckolded him in spirit if not in fact. Gabriel is another of Joyce's typical Dubliners – emotionally constricted, mistaking lust for passion and self-consciousness for deliberation. He loves his wife, but more as a reflection of himself and his own achievements than out of any grand passion. Bourgeois marriage has brought comfort but has in some senses drained their relationship, leaving it as little more than a collection of verbal and physical gestures. Treason and betrayal stalk the evening in the form of Lily the maid, Bartell D'Arcy, Molly Ivors and the abandoned lass of Aughrim. The recollection of Michael Furey, her former suitor, awakens a memory of true passion in Gretta that leaves her vain, brittle husband fearfully exposed; at the same time, she herself may be guilty of betraying the present in her fetishisation of an unrecoverable past (Ingersoll 1993). It doesn't matter that Furey is dead, or that the relationship of the young lovers was never physically consummated: Gabriel's identity – as husband, lover, father, man – has been thoroughly undermined. That threat extends to the institution of Irish Victorian marriage and all its social corollaries: power, ownership, property, inheritance.

'The Dead' may broach the concerns of the adulterous novel, but its Irish setting inflects that genre in particular ways. Dublin's relatively small size and its constricted society mean that either spouse would struggle to conduct a secret affair, should their inclinations tend in that direction. At the same time, divorce – forbidden by Catholicism and economically unviable – is no option at all. More importantly, Ireland's status as a dependent society possessed of independent aspirations alters the status – and thus the meaning – of those discursive properties and effects mentioned above. To put it bluntly, the notions of power, ownership, property and inheritance function differently in a colonial society – even more so in one that is launched, however partially, however provisionally, on a programme of decolonisation. If its amalgam of national-social and intra-personal transgression is one reason why the Parnell affair resonated so strongly in contemporary Irish life, it's also why Joyce's sustained assault on received notions of marriage, gender and sexuality represented such a threat to the entire colonial nexus: British *and* Irish, coloniser *and* colonised.[11]

In *A Portrait of the Artist as a Young Man* (1916), the emphasis is on the evolution of the Irish writer's mind, and in particular the role of language in that process. In a number of early incidents and exchanges, the child Stephen Dedalus encounters the implicitly duplicitous nature of language:

– Tell us, Dedalus, do you kiss your mother before you go to bed?
  Stephen answered:
– I do.
  Wells turned to the other fellows and said:
– O, I say, here's a fellow says he kisses his mother every night before
he goes to bed.
  The other fellows stopped their game and turned round, laughing.
Stephen blushed under their eyes and said:
– I do not.
  Wells said:
– O, I say, here's a fellow says he doesn't kiss his mother before he
goes to bed.
  They all laughed again. Stephen tried to laugh with them. He felt
his whole body hot and confused in a moment. What was the right
answer to the question? He had given two and still Wells laughed.
  (1916: 11)

Three issues – each linked with a discourse of betrayal, each to pre-
occupy Joyce throughout the remainder of his career – emerge here
in incipient form. Firstly, Stephen observes the ability of language
to contain meanings other than the one that is apparently 'right'
in any given context. Language is inherently treacherous, it seems,
possessed of secret meanings that can work against the speaker's
intentions. Although a great lover of language, Joyce was also
notoriously wary of its potential deceitfulness – of the possibility
that an interlocutor was implying (consciously or not) something
other than they actually said. One might speculate that such hyper-
sensitivity was a result of Joyce's enculturation in a city in which, for
a variety of historical reasons, language-use was extremely complex
and subtle social practice.[12] In any event, the treacherous nature of
language became a cornerstone of Joyce's imagination, feeding an
underlying suspicion of all forms of human intercourse. His work is
replete with characters who suspect their interlocutors of duplicity
in some degree or form.
  Secondly, Stephen is ragged for kissing (or not kissing) his mother;
the reader is thus invited to acknowledge the overt linkage between
language's polysemous status and the underlying reality of poly-
morphous sexual desire. Stephen's relationship with his mother, and
its impact upon his ability to relate to other females, recurs throughout *Stephen Hero*, *A Portrait* and *Ulysses*; and in exploring the nature
of that relationship it's clear that Joyce was also exploring aspects
of his own sexual identity. Stephen's 'natural' relationship with his

mother is denaturalised in the extract quoted above; his self-consciousness vis-à-vis that relationship (should he kiss her or not kiss
her?) introduces a measure of perspective which paves the way for
the transfer of his desire onto substitute figures – prostitutes, Emma
Clery, the bird-girl, etc. It's the first in a series of betrayals which
will reach its climax in Stephen's refusal (as reported in *Ulysses*) to
kneel at the bedside of his dying mother. For Joyce himself, it would
seem that a complicated relationship with his mother had implications for the sexual relationship he developed with his life partner
Nora Barnacle, as well as for the life of exile that he chose.

Thirdly, the ability of verbal phenomena to precipitate changes in
the subject's physical disposition ('He felt his whole body hot and
confused in a moment') instantiates a dualistic discourse in which
outside and inside are seen to be locked in a constant exchange of
influence and effect – one, moreover, that is frequently treacherous
in its nature. *A Portrait* tracks the maturation of Stephen's mind *and*
body; much as he might like to differentiate the two processes, the
reader observes (along with the author) their ineluctably dialectical
condition – which is to say, a final inalienable inter-reliance which the
young man, for all his 'artistry', must learn to appreciate. Such a view
led on the one hand to Joyce's emphasis on the importance of sex for
humans – in which opinion he was at odds with a Catholic doctrine
which stressed procreation, not pleasure, as the object of sex. At the
same time, the frequently duplicitous relationship between mind and
body, the never-ending struggle for balance between these forces,
fed Joyce's conviction that betrayal was at the heart of the subject's
experience. We all exist in the presence of betrayal (*our* mind, *our*
body); no wonder, then, that betrayal represents such a force when
it comes to ordering the relations *between* people.

Later in the novel, Stephen reiterates the Joycean line regarding the inevitability of treachery in Irish political history. In conversation with the nationalist Davin (modelled on Joyce's student
acquaintance, George Clancy), Stephen says:

> – No honourable and sincere man … has given up to you his life and
> youth and his affections from the days of Tone to those of Parnell but
> you sold him to the enemy or failed him in need or reviled him and
> left him for another. (170)

A Portrait works to demonstrate how the three discursive effects
described above are related to the failure of Irish revolutionary politics so bitterly (if rather rhetorically) described here.

The next chapter in Joyce's exploration of the daunting complexity of human relations, and more particularly of the role that betrayal played in those relations, was his play *Exiles* (1918).[13] It's a piece that raises many questions: why does the returned exile Richard Rowan encourage his wife to commence an affair with his best friend, Robert Hand? Would Rowan be more offended by the betrayal of his friend or his wife? Is there something uniquely treacherous about the 'double betrayal' (Lawson 1988: 16) represented by the affair between a wife and a friend? Does he wish to establish some kind of *ménage à quatre*, with Robert's cousin Beatrice as the final member? Or perhaps he wishes to offset the guilt he feels at his own infidelities, imaginative and otherwise? Is he trying to evacuate the inevitability of deception by becoming its agent? Is it a blow against bourgeois morality? Is he looking for material for his next novel, or does he wish to indulge the sexual stimulation he experiences when imagining his wife having sex with another man?[14]

In the play itself, as well as in his working notes, Joyce touched on many of the central issues and ideas relating to betrayal broached so far in this study: *Othello* (which he regarded as an '[incomplete] contribution to the study of jealousy' (1918: 101)); *Madame Bovary* (which he understood to have '[shifted] the centre of sympathy ... from the lover or fancyman to the husband or cuckold' (103); the 'breaking' of '[the] two greatest Irishmen of modern times – Swift and Parnell ... over women' (112)). In the strained friendship between Richard and Robert, moreover, there are clear allusions to the Jesus/Judas nexus:

ROBERT (*gravely*):	I fought for you all the time you were away. I fought to bring you back. I fought to keep your place for you here. I will fight for you still because I have faith in you, the faith of a disciple in his master. I cannot say more than that. It may seem strange to you ... Give me a match ...
RICHARD (*lights and offers him a match*):	There is a faith still stranger than the faith of the disciple in his master.
ROBERT:	And that is?
RICHARD:	The faith of a master in the disciple who will betray him. (31)

We know that it was Joyce's custom to displace what he suspected to be the flaws in his own character – egotism, narcissism, intolerance,

prejudice, crankiness – onto his fictional avatars (Stephen Dedalus
and Gabriel Conroy, for example). Richard Rowan's ridiculous
Christ complex is another version of this pattern. Nevertheless, the
image of himself as a 'master' apt for betrayal by one (or indeed
a conspiracy) of his 'disciples' provides an important clue as to
Joyce's imagination. In the casual treacheries depicted in the pages
of *Dubliners,* especially in Gabriel Conroy's mortified reaction to
his wife's confession; in Stephen Dedalus's growing appreciation
of the various roles played by betrayal in Irish history and in his
own maturation; in the tortuous, counterintuitive complexities
of human desire explored in *Exiles*; in all these texts Joyce was
preparing the ground for the microscopic analysis of betrayal and
Irish identity he undertook in *Ulysses.* But there was still one more
key factor waiting to be brought to bear: intense sexual jealousy.

Intrigue in Dublin, July/August 1909

On 29 July 1909 James Joyce stepped off a train at Westland Row
station in Dublin. With him was his son, Giorgio, who had just
celebrated his fourth birthday, and there to meet them was Joyce's
father and all his sisters. The exile had returned to the city of his
youth in order to attend to issues arising from the publication of
Dubliners, to inquire into the possibility of a job and to introduce
Giorgio to his Irish family in Dublin and Galway. It was to be a
memorable trip.

Joyce had been living in Trieste (then a part of the Austro-
Hungarian Empire) with his partner Nora Barnacle since March
1905; they had been joined there by Joyce's brother, Stanislaus,
in October of that year. The Joyces had two children whilst living in Trieste: Giorgio (26 July 1905) and Lucia (25 July 1907).
Besides writing occasional articles for influential friends such as
Roberto Prezioso, Joyce eked out a living teaching English at the
Berlitz School and taking private students.[15] During this time he
gave himself over with alacrity to the role of exiled artist, continuing to correspond copiously, to write and to try to get his work
into print. As Richard Ellmann and Brenda Maddox reveal in their
respective biographies, however, much of Joyce's time during the
early years in Trieste was taken up with Nora and with the issues
that her very presence in his life posed: the nature of domestic life
and, more pressingly, the importance of gender and sex in human
experience.

These concerns were to react in spectacular fashion with Joyce's ultra-suspicious nature when he returned 'home' for the first time in nearly five years. Stanislaus was supposed to make the trip, but Joyce – perhaps feeling the need to face some of his demons – pulled rank and set off with his son. As Ellmann writes:

> It was time for Joyce to go to Jerusalem, which for him was Dublin. What had happened to his own betrayers? What new crisis could be brought about by his return to the scene of their betrayals? ... The next six weeks were to provide him with material central to two books, though he did not anticipate that the acquisition would be so painful. He plunged deeper than ever before into the black pool of Dublin. (1959: 275)

The defining events of that trip are well known. Joyce met Oliver St. John Gogarty, but refused to be drawn into nostalgic bonhomie, or to pretend that the old offences (whatever they were) had been forgiven or forgotten. With everyone he met from the old life, in fact – Francis and Hanna Sheehy-Skeffington, George Russell, John Eglinton, Con Curran – he was prickly, cool and condescending. Dublin had betrayed him, and everyone who lived there was implicated in that betrayal; Nora had saved him, and he walked the streets of Dublin safe in the knowledge that her total, committed love afforded him a licence to be as 'honest' as he wished in respect of his former acquaintances.

This was the context in which Joyce was psychologically mugged by Vincent Cosgrave at some point on 6 August. The latter had been a member of Joyce's university circle, known for his quick wit and dissipated habits. Joyce portrayed him as the character Vincent Lynch in both *A Portrait* and *Ulysses*, and had one grievance against him: Cosgrave had declined to intervene when Joyce was beaten up in St Stephen's Green in June 1904 (shortly after his first meeting with Nora) by the offended escort of a woman he had addressed.[16] Back in Dublin after five years abroad, Joyce was willing to forgive (though not forget) this minor betrayal, and happily spent time with Cosgrave during the first week of his sojourn. On this occasion, however, the latter claimed that he and Nora had spent time with each other after 10 June 1904 – *after*, that is, her first meeting with Joyce. On those evenings when she said that she could not see Joyce because of work commitments, Cosgrave declared, she had in fact been walking out with him, and they, too, had experienced a degree of intimacy.[17]

Joyce believed him in the first instance, and rushed home to write two impassioned letters to Nora in Trieste, in the first of which – amidst protestations of sorrow, mortification, bitterness and despair – he accused her of disloyalty. After a few hours of reflection he wrote a second letter questioning Nora as to Giorgio's paternity, whilst repeating the accusation of deception.[18] The next day he shared his anguish with another old university friend – J.F. Byrne (the Cranly of *Stephen Hero* and *Portrait*) of 7 Eccles Street – who managed to convince Joyce that Cosgrave's claim was 'a blasted lie' (Ellmann 1966: 235; 1959: 281) inspired by jealousy, possibly part of a plan (and possibly co-hatched with Gogarty) to revenge himself on a former friend for various perceived offences. As Ellmann points out, the inference of conspiracy appealed to Joyce because the presence of betrayal, while retained, was removed from his common-law wife – the person in whom he had invested all his trust – and located instead within individuals whom he suspected to be, if not already possessed of, then certainly capable of, ill will towards himself.

Joyce's almost immediate invocation of the issue of his son's status is a classic reflex, and accords with all that was noted in a previous section relating to the absolute importance of paternity in nineteenth-century culture. Joyce here was a victim of the legal truism – noted by Freud in a short essay entitled 'Family Romances' (published coincidentally in 1909) that *pater semper incertus est* (the identity of a child's father is always in question) while the mother is *certissima*.[19] More fundamentally, the concern with paternity, as Mark Patrick Hederman has pointed out (1985), interfaced significantly with the issue of Joyce's relationship with his own parents, with his interest in Thomist aesthetics and with his theories relating to the 'family romance' underpinning the work of William Shakespeare – all of which were to feature strongly in *Ulysses*.

If it's straightforward enough to understand Joyce's acceptance of Byrne's explanation, it's less easy to understand why the former's chief biographer accepted that explanation so readily and so consistently. As Brenda Maddox, Nora's biographer, points out:

> It is clear that Byrne reassured Joyce on the basis of speculation rather than information. Byrne did not know that Cosgrave's story was true or not; he himself had never even met Oliver Gogarty. His words to Joyce were emotional first aid, spoken to calm a friend as a parent might offer a child a less painful explanation for an imagined result. (1988: 125)

Maddox goes on to point out that Byrne revised his story in later life (in a letter written to Ellmann in 1957), to the effect that Cosgrave probably did enjoy 'carnal knowledge of Nora *before* he introduced Joyce to her – *not* afterwards' (Maddox 1988: 128, original emphases). Joyce's horror, after all, was occasioned both by the possibility that Nora was not a virgin when she first gave herself to him, but also by the inference that Nora had been seeing another man *during* the period when he was in the process of committing himself emotionally and sexually to her. In Joyce's mind, it would appear, the latter was at least as important a source of betrayal as the former. Maddox concludes: 'The chances are high that there was some truth in the tale Cosgrave poured into Joyce's ear ... and that Joyce fashioned them into the story that he craved to hear.'[20]

Of course it's not possible to know the truth of Cosgrave's claims; that he was acquainted with Nora, and that he featured in some of the earliest letters between her and Joyce, is certain.[21] In the absence of proof one way or the other, the emphasis must fall on Joyce's *reaction* to what he believed happened, rather than on speculation about what *really did* happen. And from that perspective, it's clear that the events of early August 1909 had a profound effect on him, both emotionally and artistically. Amongst other things, the novel he spent the next decade writing represents an experiment in understanding the one (his emotional response) in terms of the other (his artistic response).

Joyce's experience, as represented in his letters and imaginative writing, points to the fact that having once experienced the power of interpersonal betrayal (whether actual or imagined), he became fascinated by it. It's probably not going too far to say that he became addicted to betrayal, or at least to the emotional charge associated with it. As Maddox puts it: 'He had a need to feel deceived ... for which world literature is the richer' (1988: 129). John McCourt writes of 'Joyce's need to feel at first hand the betrayal which so attracted and appalled him, and which he made so central to *Ulysses*' (2000: 82). This manifested itself in the first instance in his domestic life, as soon after his return to Trieste in 1909 Joyce began to encourage Nora to flirt with attractive men such as Roberto Prezioso. Maddox sees this as a possible indication of troilism – 'a psychological vagary ... in which a homosexual desire for someone is expressed in sharing, or dreaming of sharing, a partner' (1988: 156). There was, moreover, a precedent from an earlier stage in the relationship: on 26 August 1904, the night before he famously sang on the same bill as John McCormack, Joyce sent a short letter to his new girlfriend:

My dear Nora. I hope you will accept these [tickets]. Mr Cosgrave will meet you at 7.30 tomorrow (Saturday) evening ... What a long time since I have seen you! (Ellmann 1966: 48)

At one level, this is merely an innocent moment snatched from the everyday activities of a group of busy young people. At another level, and regarded in the light of his subsequent obsessions, we observe Joyce engineering a situation in which his friend and girlfriend can be together in his absence. The reference in the closing sentence to the deferment of the 'real' relationship is particularly interesting: mentioned in such close proximity to each other (in a very short letter), it's as if Joyce was making a subconscious connection between Cosgrave's presence and Nora's unavailability.

The suggestion of troilism is interesting (Joyce was aware of the complex), and it may indeed be possible to link Cosgrave and Prezioso (and Robert Hand) in this regard. From our perspective here, it's more useful to regard Joyce's behaviour after August 1909 as a symptom of his growing addiction to the intense emotional energies associated with betrayal. The idea of cuckoldry gave Joyce an opportunity to indulge a range of fantasies relating to Nora's emotional and physical infidelity. In the meantime, Prezioso's tentative advances earned him a verbal assault from Joyce playing the dual role of dishonoured husband and betrayed friend.

We've already noted the extent to which *Exiles* may be regarded as an attempt to work through Joyce's complex response to the possibility of betrayal. There's no doubt that *Ulysses* is launched upon the same emotional/artistic trajectory; or that it represents an attempt on the part of its author to come to terms with the existence of betrayal as a constant presence with interpersonal relations. Neither is there any doubt that the latter fact is closely enmeshed with the national cultural formations within which individuals live out their lives.

In this context, Leopold Bloom's response to the fact of his wife's infidelity represents in some respect Joyce's artistic idealisation of his own conflicted attitude towards interpersonal and national betrayal. In the fictional world created by Joyce, at some time after 4.00 p.m. on 16 June 1904, Molly Bloom has sex with

Blazes Boylan in the bedroom of a small house in north inner-city Dublin. Despite his attempt to '[think] no more about that' (1922: 147), her husband is aware of this: thus, whereas Joyce the author lived only in the shadow of Nora's potential infidelity, Leopold Bloom the character has to face up to the reality of being a cuckold. This 'reality', moreover, is 'shadowed' throughout the day by other instances of betrayal, variously encountered in the words and deeds of Jesus Christ, the Citizen, the Croppy Boy, Stephen Dedalus, Robert Emmet, Henry Flower, Anne Hathaway, Judas Iscariot, Lily Langtry, Vincent Lynch, Buck Mulligan, Kitty O'Shea, Charles Stewart Parnell, William Shakespeare and a host of other characters. As Richard Brown writes: 'Joyce gathered and carefully incorporated into his writings the minutiae of adulterous intrigue' (1985: 39).

Beyond this again, and returning to some of the issues introduced in the earlier part of this chapter, there's a sense in which Joyce's entire modernist enterprise engages with a discourse of betrayal in respect of the national cultural history within which he was operating. That betrayal is embedded in *Ulysses* at a deep structural-linguistic level, and it's to that level that I wish finally to turn.

Ulysses

In so far as it's an extended anecdote relating to marital infidelity amongst the *petit bourgeoisie*, then, *Ulysses* may readily be located within the trajectory of nineteenth-century European fiction.[22] Inasmuch as it universalises, internalises and ironises the emotional energies associated with that act of infidelity, however, Joyce's novel is very much a modernist rejoinder to, or development of, that tradition. To finish off with, let's observe that development in action.

The following passage appears in the twelfth chapter of *Ulysses*, the one entitled 'Cyclops' in all schemata:

> – The strangers, says the citizen. Our own fault. We let them come in. We brought them. The adulteress and her paramour brought the Saxon robbers here.
> – Decree *nisi*, says J.J. (1922: 310)

This snatch of conversation takes place in a pub on the north bank of the Liffey soon after 5.00 p.m.[23] A number of characters featured throughout the book are present, and at least three conversations are taking place simultaneously: Bloom is talking to Joe Hynes about an advertisement; the failed lawyer J.J. O'Molloy is discussing a recent case with Hynes, Ned Lambert and Alf Bergin; and the citizen is discoursing to the room in general on what appears to be his perennial topic – perfidious Albion.

'The adulteress and her paramour' refers to an infamous episode in Irish history, when in the year 1152 Diarmait mac Murchada (Dermot Mac Murrough), King of Leinster, abducted Derbforgaill (Dervorgilla), the wife of a rival, Tigernán Ua Ruairc, King of Bréifne. After he was deposed (in 1166), mac Murchada sought help from the King of England, Henry II, in order to recover his kingdom, thus supposedly initiating British involvement in Irish affairs.[24] The first incursions were actually led by a French-speaking Norman baron based in Wales named Richard fitz Gilbert (Strongbow); but the citizen is not about to let such historical details get in the way of his extended indictment of 'the Saxon robbers'.

Although separated by 750 years of Irish history, the parallel between the two cases is clear, and intended to be so: Blazes Boylan plays the part of mac Murchada the aggressive interloper, while Bloom and Molly reprise the roles of Ua Ruairc the cuckolded husband and Derbforgaill, his 'dishonoured wife'.[25] Knowingly or not, the citizen emphasises the symbiotic connection between political treason and interpersonal betrayal which is one of the central themes of *Ulysses.* Modern Irish history begins, in this sense, with a series of betrayals, and all subsequent acts and personages are tainted by this original sin.

At this point, J.J. O'Molloy interjects a legal phrase: 'Decree *nisi*'. This may be part of a conversation relating to 'that Canada swindle case' (308) which he had been conducting with Lambert, Bergin and Hynes, before the latter gets diverted by Bloom. (The fact that it is a *swindle* case – that is, concerning deceit and deception – and that the judge who tried it is susceptible to a fabricated hard-luck story, is not coincidental.) Alternatively, O'Molloy could be making an ironic comment on the mac Murchada/Derbforgaill/Ua Ruairc case. The Matrimonial Causes Act of 1857 established the pattern whereby a decree *nisi* could be granted once a court was satisfied that the grounds for divorce had been proved, although remarriage was not possible until after the granting of a decree absolute, six months later. O'Molloy may or may not have been aware of medieval Ireland's complex and sophisticated attitude towards divorce.[26] If regarded as a response to the citizen rather than to an uncited comment from Bergin or Hynes, O'Molloy's interpolation is ironic in so far as it engages distant historical events and persons in terms of contemporary legal discourse. And as such, it could be regarded as yet another instance of the parodic intertextuality (including inflated legalese) adopted by Joyce as the prevailing style of 'Cyclops'.

O'Molloy is commonly known by the initials of his Christian names – J.J. – a common practice in Ireland. We note, however, that these initials replicate those of the author of the novel in which this character appears: James Joyce. How would it be if we regarded this passage as 'James Joyce' weighing in with a comment – 'Decree *nisi*' – relating to the provisional nature of any judgement? How would it be if we refused to regard 'says' as typical of the local narrator's Dublin idiom, but as a usage of the continuous present tense which represents the author's gloss on his own work? In this interpretation, '– Decree *nisi*, says J.J.' would translate as something like: 'In this novel James Joyce insists upon the provisional nature of all attempts to articulate meaning.'[27]

Now, it's clear enough that 'J.J.' refers to the fictional character with whom the reader is already familiar: first introduced in 'Aeolus' (120–1), he has been present for much of this scene, he is wont to offer legalistic pronouncements and the narrator of this chapter – despite 'his customary scorn' (Blamires 1966: 130) – refers to him throughout as 'J.J.'. And yet the name constitutes enough of a coincidence to warrant consideration, however brief or dismissive; for even if no other reader has ever remarked it, the fact that I did means that the possibility – however eccentric, however implausible – was always there: a secret lying dormant in the text waiting to be revealed.

The point is not that it *is* or *is not* J.J. O'Molloy, it *is* or *is not* James Joyce, who 'really' speaks. Rather, it is that, in a chapter emphasising rhetoric and perspective, this is another means whereby the text signals to the reader the fact that language possesses signifying potential above and beyond that intended by the language-using subject, whether character or author. Language possesses secrets, in other words, and this fact implicates all language users (everyone, in other words) in a constant process of concealment and revelation. Nobody can say just one thing, for the medium through which they might attempt to articulate 'just one thing' is itself dialogic – always already pregnant with other potential meanings.

This insight is of central significance to Joyce's intentions here and throughout *Ulysses.* The critic David Lloyd has discussed the context within which this particular novel was conceived and written, pointing out that 'not only the anti-representational tendency in Irish literature but also the hybrid quality of popular forms constantly exceed the monologic desire of cultural nationalism, a desire which centres on the lack of an Irish epic' (1993: 89). Because 'the principal organizing metaphor of Irish nationalism is that of a proper paternity, of restoring the lineage of the fathers in order to repossess the motherland'.[28] Joyce's fearless and relentless exploration of adultery in *Ulysses* represents a scandalous threat to contemporary nationalist discourse. At a more fundamental level, however, his deployment of an 'adulterated' narrative style flies in the face of nationalism's anxious search for authentic expression.[29] This is because of the multiplicity of available voices which the novel makes available, and the ease with which they can be 'quoted'. With direct reference to the passage in question, Lloyd continues:

> For the nationalist citizen, the identity of the race is adulterated by 'la belle infidèle' and, as in the old expression, the restoration of that identity by translation (*traditore*) is haunted by the anxiety of betrayal (*traduttore*). This chapter, that in *Ulysses* in which issues of nationalist politics and culture are played out most intensely and in which the various elements of Irish culture are most thoroughly deployed, circulates not only thematically but also stylistically around adulteration as the constitutive anxiety of nationalism. For while the citizen is militant against the hybridization of Irish culture, the chapter itself dramatizes adulteration as the condition of colonial Ireland at virtually every level. (106)

This, then, brings us to the heart of Joyce's lifelong obsession with political and interpersonal betrayal. The reciprocal relations between these two apparent inevitabilities infused his imagination and his work from early in his life. Modern Irish history represented a search for an authentic voice in which a 'proper paternity' could be affirmed; such a search, however, was always haunted by the possibility of deception and failure – the mocking alliance of the bastard and the betrayer. In his fear at succumbing to the inevitability of betrayal, Joyce himself adopted the role of traitor, deploying his mastery of language to expose the machinations of nationalist rhetoric. In this respect we might say that in relation to contemporary Irish cultural nationalism, Joyce *was* himself the traitor that he so feared; or, to deploy another figure, he was the legitimate son who cast aspersions upon his own legal status. And yet, it was always in the name of *another* Ireland, a *better* Ireland, that Joyce undertook his deconstructive work.

This paradox extended to his personal relationship with Nora Barnacle, and to his general understanding (as represented in his writing) of the politics of desire. Joyce's search for a soul mate – one in whom he could trust implicitly – led him to Nora and to a difficult, unconventional life across Europe. That trust was temporarily shattered in August 1909 when he was led to believe that she had deceived him, and was continuing to do so. And yet, there is that in his subsequent letters and behaviour which reveals his fascination with the idea of Nora and him betraying each other in some manner or degree. In this, Joyce was perhaps acting hysterically, seeking to pre-empt a pattern his unconscious had convinced him was both inevitable and universal. In any event, revisited and reworked throughout his *oeuvre*, this fascination is played out most visibly in the pages of *Ulysses*, where Leopold and Molly Bloom work through the dynamics of interpersonal fidelity and betrayal, from casual white lies (blackberry juice on a bed sheet as 'proof' of *virgo intacta*, for example) to the most resonant cultural echoes (*Othello*, *Hamlet*, Parnell, Derbforgaill, etc.).

Molly Bloom's affair with Blazes Boylan represents an attempt to empower herself in one of the few ways that would have been available to her. It implicates this lower-middle-class Dublin housewife in a network of resistance to what Timothy P. Foley describes as 'bourgeois society's official self-knowledge' – that the late nineteenth-century Irish woman was the exemplar of 'self-abnegation and self-sacrifice' (1997: 35). At the same time, it affords Molly an opportunity to rewrite what sociologist Annette Lawson, in her book *Adultery: An Analysis of Love and Betrayal*, entitles 'The Myth of Me' – as a pro-active, attractive sexual agent.[30] Her husband, meanwhile, displays levels of 'tolerance and emotional equilibrium' (R. Brown 1985: 19) in respect of his partner's infidelity that were signally absent in his creator. *Ulysses* is ideological in many ways, but none more so than its depiction of the central male character's resigned attitude towards the transference of the central female character's sexual attentions to another. An ordinary Dublin man, Bloom cannot afford the luxury of tears and grand gestures; given the times, given his position, his age, his background and his temper, he does what he has to do. It may be that Bloom's attitude represents Joyce's response to the unapproachable and ultimately insoluble mystery of Nora Barnacle's activities in the summer of 1904.

As stylistic adulteration is to nationalist discourse, so adultery is to marital fidelity; each inheres within the other, each is a function of the other's very possibility. Thus Joyce sets the agenda for the Irish novel in the coming century – an artistic practice in which questions of political and interpersonal betrayal (and the relations between these) will feature seminally.

4

The landscape of betrayal:
Liam O'Flaherty's *The Informer* (1925)

> Who would have dreamed
> Seeing you reeling
> The streets of Dublin
> Hurting yourself
> As if you were the only man
> You could never forgive
> That your words would tell
> Young men and women
> How to live?
>> Brendan Kennelly, *The*
>> *Little Book of Judas*, 96–7

Introduction

The extensive differences between James Joyce and Liam
O'Flaherty – in terms of their experiences, their personalities and
their literary imaginations – should not blind us to some striking
parallels between *Ulysses* and O'Flaherty's most famous novel.
Each is set in inner-city Dublin; the action of each takes place
within one day (the first lasting eighteen hours, the second twelve);
each features a central male character depicted in close physical
and psychological detail; this character is, moreover, an outsider,
alienated to some degree from the community to which he ostensibly belongs. Like Leopold Bloom, Gypo Nolan wanders through
the city drinking, eating, encountering 'friends' and enemies, visiting brothels, contemplating the unsatisfactory nature of his life and
how he might go about changing it. In so far as this is the case,
Gypo is also a modern Odysseus, trying – like Bloom, like everyone – to make his way through a difficult and dangerous landscape
towards a place that feels like home.

The respective authors also shared at least two important traits which decisively influenced their literary visions in terms of style and subject matter: each experienced different aspects (comprehended in terms of class and intellectual milieu) of Irish life, and each had extensive experience of living outside the country. The first aspect, for Joyce, encompassed his family's fall from middle-class grace during the 1890s, and his thorough grounding (under the tutelage of his father) in the lower echelons of Dublin life, including, most significantly, its language. Joyce's unique literary imagination – underpinned by his familiarity with a broad swathe of the late Victorian Irish class spectrum – was extended still further by the discrepancy between his lifelong engagement with Ireland and the fact of his more or less permanent exile after the age of twenty-two. O'Flaherty moved in the opposite direction in the first instance – from the (rural) poverty and ignorance of his upbringing on Inishmore to a maturity characterised by full intellectual engagement. And as with Joyce, the latter experience was reinforced by the perspective gained from extensive travel and periods of domicile outside Ireland.

One other shared interest, obvious from the title of O'Flaherty's novel, is betrayal. Gypo Nolan is the eponymous 'informer' – a word conjuring up 'a horror to be understood fully only by an Irish mind' (O'Flaherty 1925: 47). What that 'horror' was, whence it derived, its psychological structure and its contemporary contours, are the subjects of O'Flaherty's story. And it's this sense of a novelist attempting to get to grips with the universal experience of betrayal in a peculiarly Irish context which, more than anything else, links *The Informer* with *Ulysses*.

Political contexts

O'Flaherty's life and experiences between 1896 (when he was born) and 1924 (when he wrote the novel) prepared him for the images of treason and betrayal that he depicts in *The Informer*. Those experiences included a relatively impoverished upbringing on Inishmore; identification, and subsequent disillusionment, with the Catholic Church (although not necessarily the faith); over two years of front-line experience in the army of Ireland's traditional enemy in the most terrible war in history, for which he 'was regarded as a pariah and a fool and a renegade' (O'Flaherty 1934: 21); a year of (successful) physical and (incomplete) mental convalescence; two years of global wandering; growing fascination with the world-wide revolutionary movement; and return to a country that was 'divided and factionalized' (Hart 2003: 20) by its own response to that movement.

O'Flaherty had developed an interest in class politics whilst still a soldier fighting with the Irish Guards on the Western Front (O'Flaherty 1930: 71). During his travels in North America after the war he joined both the Wobblies (Industrial Workers of the World international union) and the Communist Party. Nationalism and republicanism he came to regard (along with Christianity) as diversions, in essence collusive with the bourgeois imperialist practices they ostensibly opposed. In so far as the Irish revolution retained any validity at all, O'Flaherty's affiliations remained much more with James Connolly than with Patrick Pearse, and he returned to Dublin in late 1921 determined to expedite the Irish wing of a proper international class-based revolution.

In Ireland O'Flaherty found a political situation that was daunting in its complexity. He set to work with energy and commitment: taking an active role in the fledgling Communist Party of Ireland (CPI), helping to edit and sell the party's newspaper, *The Workers' Republic*, and supporting attempts by workers throughout the country to improve their lot. Eventually, having become frustrated with an apparent lack of revolutionary energy, on 18 January 1921 O'Flaherty (along with approximately 200 unemployed Dubliners) seized an important building in the city in the name of an Irish Soviet Workers' Republic (O'Flaherty 1934: 22). This occupation (unpopular for one reason or another with just about every strand of contemporary opinion) ended after four days, and O'Flaherty fled the city. He returned just in time to witness the commencement of the Civil War, and to participate briefly in the CPI's strategic engagement with that conflict. Once again he fled, this time to Liverpool and thence to London, where he would remain until 1924, and where he would begin his career as a writer.[1]

The latest, most committed and best-organised phase of Irish anti-colonial activity took place against the backdrop of an international revolution dedicated to the overthrow of capitalism, as well as the emergence of potent reactionary elements determined to resist any such assault. All these forces coalesced to produce a perfect revolutionary storm in Ireland in the years between the Great Lock Out of 1913 and the fall-out from the Civil War a decade or so later. And it was because of this that questions of nationalism, republicanism and communism (and latterly fascism) became tortuously enmeshed in contemporary Irish political discourse – in Peter Hart's description 'a many-sided struggle' (2003: 9) productive of a situation in which every thought, word and action was burdened with super-sensitive significance. In such a situation, everyone was a potential traitor as well as a potential victim of betrayal.

This situation was all the more perturbing because of the profound resonance of the idea of 'betrayal' in modern Irish history. Irish agitation against British power had always been monitored by spies and informers, but that process had become fully organised after the rebellion of 1798 and Emmet's abortive rising of 1803. By the late nineteenth century Dublin Castle had developed an elaborate system for recruiting and handling informants from amongst the 'enemy' community – people who, because of their upbringing, their religion and their apparent political persuasions, were accepted within the various organisations working to resist British dominion. Despite extensive measures to retain its secrecy, the Irish Republican Brotherhood, for example, remained vulnerable to the network of informers who had wrecked the abortive rebellion of 1867 (Ó Broin 1976: 3, 6). The story of the Invincibles, likewise – the rogue Fenian cell responsible for the murder of two high-ranking British officials in Dublin's Phoenix Park on 6 May 1882 – was (as we'll observe in Chapter 7) riddled with treachery before, during and after the event.

As noted in the previous chapter, it was the ubiquitous presence of the informer that led James Joyce to reject the possibility of armed rebellion as a viable response to colonial domination. If his scepticism drew him away from the possibility of successful (or necessary) physical resistance, however, Joyce did at least share a general Irish opprobrium towards the figure of the informer. Discussing what he describes as 'an atavistic hatred of informers' amongst republicans, Kevin Toolis argues that

> [on] the bloody stage of Irish history, the informer is the villain, a cultural bogeyman who has played his part in the downfall of endless fine and noble patriots. The informer is the Judas within, the betrayer, the fountainhead of all Irish misery and a convenient scapegoat for centuries of glorious failure. (1995: 194)

If nationalist/republican revolution was bedevilled during the modern era by informers,[2] then so too was the relatively recent international communist movement. The full force of Stalinist paranoia had yet to emerge, but developments since the nineteenth century across a wide range of contexts had already proved that treachery was woven into the warp and woof of the revolutionary imagination. Even setting aside the forces of counter-revolution, the relations between communists, socialists, anarchists, syndicalists and various other anti-capitalist ideologies made for a situation in which treachery – actual, imagined, suspected, implicit – was bound to thrive. As with Irish republicanism, the idea of 'betrayal' was anathema to all parties; yet there were in practice so many parties claiming allegiance – claiming, that is, the sovereign right to define what might and might not be defined as 'treacherous' – that it was seemingly impossible to engage with revolutionary discourse and not to feel betrayed or (and at the same time) to be regarded as a traitor.[3]

Literary and cultural contexts

Besides the practical element of finding a career that would sustain him in the long term, O'Flaherty turned to writing in 1922 in order to try to come to terms with his political disillusionment, and to develop a philosophy that would enable him to survive in the modern world. This was a timely project, because, whether aware of it or not, O'Flaherty took up his pen during a period of intense speculation regarding the form and function of literature in the modern era. These debates were themselves thoroughly informed by issues which both presaged and reflected the theme of betrayal invoked in his most famous novel.

O'Flaherty is sometimes regarded as a purveyor of Irish naturalism, cast in opposition to the twin poles of Celtic Romanticism and anti-mimetic modernism *à la* Joyce.[4] When his work began to appear, O'Flaherty was identified as a 'new realist' of the school of Joyce and O'Casey – those who had, apparently, set out their stall against the romantic mysticism of the Celtic Twilight, choosing instead (as a contemporary reviewer put it) to '[explore] the slums of our cities, the slums of the soul' (quoted in Sheeran 1976: 90). O'Flaherty's class consciousness certainly drew him towards the same lower echelons of Irish society addressed in the work of Joyce and O'Casey. His public identification with communism, however, rendered him a figure of suspicion and resentment in counter-revolutionary Ireland, and this had an impact upon the context within which his work was read, as well as the value accorded it. In a letter of 1931, for example, the Free State minister Desmond Fitzgerald wrote: 'I think if you eliminate Bolshevism and muck-raking from Liam O'Flaherty, you have a very unimportant writer left' (quoted in Regan 1999: 283) The assumptions underpinning this response from a non-professional literary critic are revealing: the value of the writing (its importance or lack thereof) is directly linked to the political ideology with which the author is associated. Politics and literature are thus implicitly linked in a way which would have gratified the ideologues of *Prolekult* and the *Reichskulturkammer*: only the emphasis was different.

At the same time, the allusion to 'muck-raking' carried connotations of sordidness and obscenity – some of the (modern and foreign) qualities that those in control of counter-revolutionary Ireland were determined to eradicate from national life. Keen to consolidate its monopoly on the moral conscience of the new state, the Catholic Church had moved very rapidly to a position of national prominence in the years after the Civil War. With representation throughout all the cultural, civic and executive strata of society, the Church ensured itself a strong position from which to resist what it regarded as the moral degeneracy promulgated in the work of authors such as James Joyce and Liam O'Flaherty.

In short, O'Flaherty's work became subject to the strictures of a full-scale moral panic identified, and to a large degree engineered, by the twin forces of the Catholic Church and the Free State. John M. Regan writes:

> Though there is no evidence to suggest that post-revolutionary Irish society was confronted by a crisis of morality the Church created a culture of moral paranoia where sin and the devil were ever-present and ever-invisible forces for the corruption of native youth and innocence. Sin within the culture of imperilled morality became in the first instance synonymous with modernity and representations of modernisation. The case against communism was primed on the same ground. It was a profound corrupting influence, invisible, and for that all the more potent. (1999: 282–3)

The Anglo-Irish Protestant writers of the Celtic Twilight had been indicted in terms of their religion and their ethnicity; the writers of the post-Twilight era – especially 'spoiled' Catholic ones such as Joyce and O'Flaherty – were now being indicted in terms of their moral and political proclivities. Both these literary impulses represented in some senses a betrayal of Ireland, of the *real* Irish identity in whose name the bourgeois nationalist revolution had taken place and which was now ready to come into its own in a state engineered in its own image. The irony of both Joycean modernism and post-revolutionary Irish naturalism, of course, was that they emerged and developed in the name of a 'realism' that was opposed to the blithe unrealities sustaining the new state.

'Betrayal' featured as a seminal element within another contemporary discourse, one with implications for both the literary and philosophical aspects of O'Flaherty's work. In 1927 the French philosopher Julien Benda published a short book entitled *La Trahison des Clercs*, which appeared in translation the following year in Britain as *The Great Betrayal*, and in the United States as *The Betrayal of the Intellectuals*. In this book Benda argued that since the nineteenth century Europe's intellectual classes had 'betrayed their duty, which is precisely to set up a corporation whose sole cult is that of justice and truth' (1927: 41). These 'clerks' had abrogated an age-old mission: resistance to, and mitigation of, the inevitable drive towards 'realism' on the part of 'laymen' – by which he meant the vast majority of any given society concerned to address considerations that were principally local and material in nature. Regarding the modern world, Benda observed a

> mass in whom realist passions in its two chief forms – class passion, national passion – has attained a degree of consciousness and organization hitherto unknown, [and a] body of men who used to be in opposition to the realism of the masses, but who now, not only do not oppose it, but adopt it, proclaim its grandeur and morality; in short, a humanity which has abandoned itself to realism with a unanimity, an absence of reserve, a sanctification of its passion unexampled in history. (143)

The betrayal of the clerks during the nineteenth century had underpinned what Benda described as 'the intellectual organisation of political hatreds' (21); this had in turn contributed to the inevitability of large-scale industrial war – such as the one that had recently concluded, as well as the one that (Benda suspected, correctly as it happened) was soon to commence.

Benda cites artists (including poets, novelists and dramatists) within the ranks of those treacherous clerks who have sacrificed a properly humanist mission in favour of one of the modern 'political passions', in particular those organised in relation to issues such as race, class or nation (50–2). By '[placing] itself at the service of the nation or of a class' (54), this form of modern art deprives the reader of 'that self-examination to which every spectator is impelled by a representation of human beings which he feels to be true and solely preoccupied with truth' (53).

I'm not aware that O'Flaherty ever read Benda, and he certainly couldn't have engaged with his thesis in 1924. Nevertheless, the issues broached in the latter's book were central to the cultural and critical discourses of the 1920s – indeed, to modernism generally. In some senses, O'Flaherty's turn to literature after a period of 'passionate' political activity might be regarded as a rejection (or betrayal) of lay 'realism', and the embrace instead of a traditional 'clerkly' role. But this raises a question: does a contemporary author such as O'Flaherty betray (following Benda) his artistic mission by allowing the 'real' to dominate within his work; or does he betray his passionate political beliefs by focusing on abstract (or bourgeois) notions of truth and justice? We may observe this dilemma emerging in the fiction itself. Although clearly caught up in 'the real', characters such as Fr Hugh McMahon in *Thy Neighbour's Wife* (1923), and Fergus O'Connor in *The Black Soul* (1924) are (like the author) in search of some kind of accommodation between the demands of the material world with its inevitable passions, and the search for an abstract notion of truth – one that is always 'human' before and after it is anything else.[5] Interestingly, both these characters are also implicated in adulterous relationships, thus reflecting at the level of plot the author's implicit concern with questions of treachery.

As O'Flaherty's dilemma reveals, the question becomes one of perspective and emphasis: who has the right to blame whom of betrayal? From what authority does such a right derive? And how is the individual writer to process the conflicting demands of the clerk and the layman? The nineteenth-century clerks may have betrayed their traditional role but according to some contemporary figures that role was itself already treacherous vis-à-vis the seminal significance of 'the real' in human history – that category that pertained to the greatest part of human experience throughout history. One such instance of 'the real' was provided by the category of class, and one such figure was the literary critic and sometime Hungarian politician György Lukács.

Stalin's decree relating to the necessity for Socialist Realism as an adjunct to permanent revolution was still a few years away, and the tendentiousness of that system was to remain an embarrassment for left-wing writers and critics throughout his reign. But questions concerning the aesthetic principles and practices demanded by a dictatorship of the proletariat had been debated in European cultural circles since Marx and Engels, and had entered a period of intensity in the years after the October Revolution. Lukács it was who developed the case for a form of realism thoroughly and properly informed by the fundamental tenets of dialectical materialism:

> The basis for any correct cognition of reality, whether of nature or society, is the recognition of the objectivity of the external world, that is, its existence independent of human consciousness. Any apprehension of the external world is nothing more than a reflection in consciousness of the world that exists independently of consciousness. This basic fact of the relationship of consciousness to being also serves, of course, for the artistic reflection of reality. (1971: 25)

The career of Lukács is focused (with much wavering and revision) on the relations established here between reality, consciousness and art. For him, it's the realist rather than the romantic or the modernist who can best encapsulate and communicate the contradictions of capitalism. Whereas the romantic and the modernist are content to 'describe' the results of capitalist reality, the realist can effectively 'narrate' the struggles implicit within that reality. Whereas romanticism and modernism deny agency to the subject, rendering him the passive tool of natural or psychological influences beyond the will, realism locates the subject at the nexus of direct sensory and extra-sensory forces – a dialectical product of his own physical and psychological experience in relation to the variety of natural and cultural systems within which he's caught up. It was up to the realist writer to combat the 'reactionary obscurantism' of late romanticism and modernism, and to contribute to 'the inexorable uncovering of truth and reality, together with an unshakeable faith in the march of mankind and their own people towards a better future' (Lukács 1950: 19).

As the latter sentence reveals, there's an implicit moral agenda couched within Lukács's aesthetics: when they fail to depict the depredations of modern capitalism, modern writers (whether of a romantic or a modernist bent) act treacherously in relation to their characters and to the world in which they live, producing a model of reality that is 'inadequate, diluted and constrained' (1971: 147). Such assaults as have been mounted against the fundamental contradictions of bourgeois life – late nineteenth-century naturalism, for example –

> are without artistic consequence when they do not probe the *root* of the emptiness of life under *capitalism*, when they do not afford direct experience with the struggles to restore meaning to life, and when they do not investigate and seek to depict artistically such struggles with ideological understanding. (1971: 147, original emphases)

This inability or unwillingness on the part of contemporary writers to depict the struggles which permeate capitalist society represent more than just an aesthetic failure; it's a denial of the right to meaning on the part of ordinary people, an indissolubly ideological act within the cultural system that is literature. So, whereas Benda indicts the treacherous clerks who have mortgaged their work to 'realism', Lukács attacks those who have betrayed reality itself by refusing to engage with or account for its ideological constitution.

O'Flaherty was clearly engaged with all these issues from the outset of his writing career. Born and raised in one of the primal scenes of Celtic Romanticism; an Irishman fighting in the army of Ireland's traditional enemy; a communist making common (if temporary) cause with nationalists and republicans – in all these contexts the idea of betrayal (as both perpetrator and victim) was embedded within O'Flaherty's life from the outset. These issues then re-emerged in relation to his chosen career, in which simply to put pen to paper entailed all sorts of potential denials and abrogations. If he was a long way from Yeatsian romanticism on the one hand, he was not much nearer Joycean modernism on the other. Whether his actual practice in *The Informer* qualifies to be described as 'realist' remains to be seen; but it's not assuming too much to contend that the principal device deployed in this text – an act of betrayal on the part of an ostracised member of 'the organization' – reflects the author's confrontation with issues emerging from his own experience as an Irish writer in the modern world.[6]

Revolution? Which revolution?

After an unsuccessful beginning to his career as a man of letters, O'Flaherty decided that he must write about what he knew.[7] Both *Thy Neighbour's Wife* and *The Black Soul* are set on Inishmore and engage with issues that were of the first importance to him in so far as each novel features a main character attempting to reach an accommodation between the milieu into which he has been born, with its particular array of cultural and political systems, and his own desires and needs. Fr Hugh McMahon and Fergus O'Connor are thus to all intents and purposes O'Flaherty avatars; and the narratives in which they feature represent various possible routes through (and from) the author's own life. *The Informer* continues this pattern: both the stupid, treacherous brute Gypo Nolan and the intelligent, deceitful Dan Gallagher are still more versions of O'Flaherty in his various roles as pariah, fool, renegade and alienated 'black soul'. By now, however, the action has switched to another scene with which the author was intimately familiar: Dublin during the early 1920s, in particular, the treacherous landscape of Irish revolutionary politics.

That landscape comes into focus in relation to two inter-related issues, the first of which concerns the dynamics of decolonisation – in particular, the conflict that emerges between ethnic/nationalist and class elements once 'independence' has been (even partially) achieved. In what is now a standard theoretical line, Frantz Fanon argued in his book *The Wretched of the Earth* that a 'national middle class' achieves hegemony when it seizes moral and military control of the revolution at the expense of other interested factions. Fanon's description of this national middle class '[sending] out frenzied appeals for help to the former mother country' (1961: 120) recalls the provisional Free State government's use of British weaponry on 28 June 1922 when its army shelled the anti-Treaty forces that were holding Dublin's Four Courts under the leadership of Rory O'Connor. The revolutionary front splinters and cracks, Fanon continues, as '[the] national bourgeoisie steps into the shoes of the former European settlement' (122), becoming 'the transmission line between the nation and a capitalism rampant though camouflaged' (122). Nationalism, Fanon concludes, 'that magnificent song that made the people rise against their oppressors, stops short, falters and dies away on the day that independence is proclaimed'

(163). One of the inevitable 'pitfalls of national consciousness', then, is the national bourgeoisie's apparently inevitable betrayal of its former allies in the national struggle.[8]

Fanon's thesis is borne out in *The Informer* by the insights of Biddy Burke the brothel owner:

> The country is goin' to the wall. That's all there is to it. I knew they'd make a mess of it with their revolutions an' their shootin' the peelers. Not that I didn't do me bit to help the boys, God bless 'em, but 'tisn't the boys that done the fightin' that get the jobs. So it isn't. It never is, if ye ask Biddy Burke. It's them publicans an' bishops that were always top dog in this country. 'Twas that way before an' 'tis that way now, an' 'twill be that way when Biddy Burke is goin' to meet her God on the day of judgment. They were talkin' about English tyrants, but sure nobody ever saw the likes o' these tyrants with their searches an' their raids, an' every divil's wart of a farmer's son that can pull on his breeches without his mother's help runnin' around an' callin' himself a gineral.[9]

Biddy's reference to the 'farmer's son' is interesting here, as she is in fact talking to one at this very moment. Gypo is far from being a 'gineral', however; and the new Free State was far from supporting the rights of workers: on the contrary, as Biddy's pointed diatribe suggests, '[the] Free State was able to capitalize on the waging of the Civil War to simultaneously wage war against the working class' (Kostick 1996: 190).

A *revolution* ushers in an entirely new situation that has never existed before (O'Sullivan 1983: 4). The forces that dominated in Ireland in the period between 1916 and 1923 appear to have been pursuing something akin to a *rebellion* – which is to say, a programme designed to reinstate a desired situation that formerly existed (in the minds of its proponents, at least). It's important to remember that, regarded from this perspective, figures such as Liam O'Flaherty and Roddy Connolly (of whom more presently), as well as the fictional Commandant Dan Gallagher, were 'revolutionaries' in ways that even hardline republicans such as Rory O'Connor, Liam Mellows and Ernie O'Malley were not.

Biddy's speech occurs within the context of a general complaint about poor business. The second issue to consider when approaching *The Informer*, then, concerns the general economic conditions within which Irish revolutionary politics of the early 1920s were conducted. Post-war recession created a situation in Ireland

in which high unemployment, low wages, poor conditions and
lifestyle insecurity had politicised a significant proportion of the
population (Kostick 1996: 187). In particular, conditions in Dublin
remained desperate throughout the 1920s – especially in the north
inner city where much of *The Informer* is set (T. Brown 1985: 16).
It's instructive to learn that the ethno-nationalist struggle was shadowed throughout this period by a protracted class struggle in which
Irish workers were attempting to organise themselves in order to
improve their pay and conditions (Berresford Ellis 1972: 243ff.;
Kostick 1996: 179ff.). In the same week (the end of June 1922) that
Free State troops were preparing to attack the Four Courts, for
example, the provisional government was attempting to defeat a
number of uncoordinated soviets that had sprung up around the
country. One of the most important disputes concerned workers
involved in the farming industry, who, after initially going on strike
in response to worsening conditions and a proposed wage cut in
March 1922, eventually began to occupy work places and collectiv-
ise their labour. As might be expected, such actions were forcefully
resisted by the bosses in the shape of the Irish Farmers' Union; more
dishearteningly, working-class militancy was by and large either
ignored or suppressed by both sides (Free Staters and anti-Treaty
IRA) in the 'real' Civil War.[10]

Labour disputes, including those involving the Farmers' Union,
continued throughout the Civil War and into the early years of the
new state. It's one such dispute that, in O'Flaherty's story, Frankie
McPhillip and Gypo Nolan are ordered to monitor around October
1923, six months before the day on which the main action of the
novel takes place. The 'Revolutionary Organization' from which
the 'Devil's Twins' (1925: 12) are subsequently expelled is clearly
based in large part on the Communist Party of Ireland; and the
sometime leader of that organisation, Roddy Connolly – son of
executed 1916 leader James – was in many ways the model for the
character of Dan Gallagher.

O'Flaherty and Roddy Connolly had met when the former returned
to Ireland after two years of post-war globetrotting with the intention of helping to foment an Irish social revolution. In Dublin, as
remarked above, he found an impossibly complex situation. Initial
working-class support for Bolshevism had quickly reverted to the
unions and to the parliamentary Labour Party (O'Connor 2004:
2–3). Soon afterwards, the newly formed Executive Committee

of the Communist International began to take an interest in Irish affairs. The principal issue was the constantly mutating relationship with the various nationalist and republican factions who were, frankly, in a much more influential position compared with Ireland's few active communists.[11] Of this latter group, Roddy Connolly retained (until the return of Jim Larkin in 1923) the most glamorous profile. As a fifteen-year-old he had fought alongside his father in the General Post Office during Easter Week 1916. Along with O'Flaherty he usurped the leadership of the Socialist Party of Ireland in October 1921 and relaunched it as a Communist Party precariously affiliated with the Comintern.[12] In November and December 1922, he attended the Fourth World Congress in Petrograd and Moscow, where he discussed the Irish situation with Lenin. Amongst the movers and shakers of Irish politics in the early 1920s, then, he appeared to be a man to reckon with.

Connolly Junior was a charismatic if somewhat unstable figure. Part of his appeal lay in the claim to be able to deal with the different elements within contemporary revolutionary politics – a claim based in large part on his father's strategic decision (for which he had paid with his life) to throw his lot in with the nationalists in 1916. Like his father, however, Roddy Connolly found it difficult to navigate between the ideals of international socialism and the local demands of a largely bourgeois nationalist/republican revolution.[13] And like his father he naturally gravitated towards the more radical elements within the latter movement. Although the Comintern continued to advocate popular front, reformist tactics after the ratification of the Anglo-Irish Treaty on 7 January 1922, Connolly remained opposed, if rather inconsistently so. The historian Emmet O'Connor characterises Connolly's outlook as '[lurching] between fantasy and reality' (2004: 49). Although capable of incisive analyses of the day-to-day politicking between the various factions, his position on issues such as the Treaty 'swung wildly' (55); his plan to smuggle in communist hegemony on the back of a republican victory in the Civil War was a 'daft pipedream' (61); while his offer of a 'Red Guard' paramilitary unit to republican forces during the early stages of that war 'was a feeble gesture' (62).

As noted earlier, O'Flaherty was also active during the volatile period after the ratification of the Treaty in January 1922. The seizure of the Rotunda was not supported by the CPI, however, and this – allied to Connolly's inconsistent personality – coloured

O'Flaherty's depiction of Dan Gallagher, commandant of the 'revolutionary organization', in *The Informer*. It's for this reason that O'Connor refers to *The Informer*, and in particular the depiction of Gallagher, as 'the penman's revenge' (2004: 60). In any event, Connolly's star was eclipsed by the return of Big Jim – in the eyes of those who mattered (which is to say, the Comintern and the Communist Party of Great Britain) a much more attractive figure to lead Irish communism, although such, as it turned out, was not Larkin's desire in any case.

It's in the light of the foregoing (decolonisation and capitalist recession) that we can begin to approach an understanding of the bitter comment made by Jack McPhillip – Frankie's fifty-year-old father, and 'a thoroughly respectable conservative Socialist' (1925: 37) – to Dan Gallagher, the self-styled 'revolutionary Communist' (71):

> 'It's the likes o' me that's the revolutionaries, but we get no credit for it. It's the likes o' me that does the hard work, eddicatin' me fellow-men, an' at the same time strikin' an honest blow for better conditions. But men like you are criminals. Criminals, criminals, that's what yez are.' (72)

The narrator is unsympathetic towards both characters, although it's the disdain of the (quiescent) communist for labour unionism, with its faith in education and honesty and reform, that comes through most clearly here. The more interesting thing from our perspective is the vehemence of Jack's anger, directed not towards a class enemy but towards a 'natural' ally whose 'crime' is to pursue a putatively shared left-wing agenda by different means. Many people (including Roddy Connolly) ran the gamut of left-wing Irish politics over the course of their careers, with its nuanced shades of opinion and its array of paramilitary, parliamentary and theoretical tactics. The accusation of 'betrayal' was never far away during moments of transition from one strategy to another, as when Connolly himself was accused of 'treachery' in December 1921 by his own sister Nora (O'Connor 2004: 52). This illustrates once again a point made throughout this book: that one is betrayed not by enemies but by allies – friends, families, lovers. Invariably, the closer in outlook and conviction someone is to one, the greater the betrayal that is felt when those differences are accentuated.

The general revolutionary context also enables us to approach an understanding of the life and career of the novel's central character. Gypo Nolan conforms to one of the stereotypes that were prevalent in contemporary anti-revolutionary discourse, in as much as he is 'a burly ruffian type ... unmistakably of the rabble class to be found in every large town'. His opposite is the intellectual – 'young men with high foreheads and thin lips ... a moral and physical degenerate'.[14] These descriptions, culled from contemporary contributions to the British press, uncannily anticipate O'Flaherty's description of the 'ruffian' (44) Gypo Nolan and his erstwhile boss Dan Gallagher:

> The two men, unlike in their features and bodies, were exactly alike in the impassivity of their stare. Gypo's face was a solid and bulging granite rock, impregnable but lacking that intelligence that is required by strength in order to be able to conquer men. Gallagher's face was less powerful physically, but it was brimful of intelligence. The forehead was high and it seemed to surround the face. The eyes were large and wide apart. The nose was long and straight. The mouth was thin-lipped. The jaws were firm and slender and refined like a woman's jaws. (57)

If these two stereotypes represent a toxic alliance in respect of the establishment, neither are they particularly well regarded by nationalists. After the October Revolution there was a general international fear of what the Gypos of the world might do under the direction of these various Gallaghers with their high foreheads and thin lips. As *The Informer* reveals, however, the alliance between brain and brawn was always a volatile, fraught relationship, constantly operating under the sign of deceit and potential betrayal.

The novel tells us that Gypo Nolan was raised on a small farm in the Galtee Mountains region of Tipperary, and that he's thirty years of age when the action commences in March 1924. This profile allows him to be placed fairly accurately in terms of modern Irish history, in so far as he hails from one of the heartlands of militant republicanism, and is of an age to have experienced the entire revolutionary era from the Dublin lock-out of 1913 (aged nineteen), through the Easter Rising (twenty-two), the War of Independence (twenty-five to twenty-seven) and on to the recently ended Civil War (twenty-eight to twenty-nine).[15] Gypo's career has followed a somewhat unusual trajectory, however:

> [He] had once been a policeman in Dublin, but he had been dismissed owing to a suspicion at Headquarters that he was in league with the Revolutionary Organization and had given information to them relative to certain matters that had leaked out. (12)

Amongst the questions *not* posed in *The Informer* are: why is Gypo not a republican guerrilla fighting in his home county? At what stage, by what means and for what reason does he become a policeman in Dublin? Why, having been ejected from the police force, did he elect to join a communist, rather than a nationalist or republican or moderate left-wing class-based organisation? Does he maintain any coherent sense of an Irish identity at all?

It's not at all clear, in fact, that Gypo is obvious material for a modern urban communist revolutionary. He is in fact to a large extent the product of Dan Gallagher's imagination as well as the answer to some of the latter's revolutionary requirements. The novel explains how Gypo was 'turned' by Gallagher, how 'he used to sell Gallagher little titbits of information over a drink: little harmless, he thought, bits of information, about headquarters routine and the disposition of the detective-force personnel' (66).[16] Gypo is thus already a 'traitor' (vis-à-vis a prior commitment to the forces of law and order that are both bourgeois and imperial) *before* he informs on Frankie McPhillip. Before that again, he had already turned his back on the republican/nationalist values of his peasant upbringing.[17] Gypo will in time be betrayed by his sometime girlfriend, the drug-addled prostitute and former revolutionary Katie Fox. Not only is he surrounded by treachery from beginning to end; Gypo embodies the treachery of the modern subject in so far as he's betrayed by the discrepancy between his powerful body and his feeble mind, by his own inaptitude for secrecy of any kind, and by his inability to control the principal medium – language – through which the key textual category of 'information' is organised.

Language and information

Despite the comparisons with Joyce and O'Casey at the outset of his career, and despite the fact that *The Informer* won the James Tait Black Memorial Prize the year after its publication (Costello 1996: 54), O'Flaherty's reputation as an irredeemably minor writer was well established in Irish critical circles during his own lifetime. By and large it remains so into the present. His short stories, as well as some of his Gaelic writing and later fiction, were eventually welcomed in the Free State and its successors, but much of his output (including the memoirs and the early novels) remained suspect. The principal cause for this may have been what many regarded as the widespread invocation of subjects that were both salacious and seditious, but there were other reasons too.

For the literary critic Patrick F. Sheeran it comes down to the quality of his writing. He talks about O'Flaherty's 'unhappy style' (1976: 30), for example, and indicts the Dublin thrillers of the 1920s in particular for being 'frequently badly written, poorly constructed and repetitive' (259). All four, he opines, 'are heavily – and disastrously – influenced by Dostoyevsky'.[18] For a more politically orientated critic such as Joseph Cleary, on the other hand, O'Flaherty's writing is positioned as part of Irish naturalism's second phase (after Moore and early Joyce), redolent of 'a more programmatically or self-consciously anti-Revivalist edge' (2007: 140). For Cleary, *The Informer* is 'strong on oppressive atmosphere and a sense of dumb victimhood'; as with Jack London, O'Flaherty's naturalism is 'shot through with a contradictory mix of socialistic critique of the existing bourgeois capitalist order and proto-Fascistic feeling for an elemental world of primitive force altogether anterior to civilization'. Because 'Nolan is an almost animal-like creature trapped in an action beyond his very limited comprehension ... the work's diagnostic ambitions on any socio-historical level are nugatory' (144).

It should be clear by now that I'm not interested in trying to redeem *The Informer* from this generally negative context.[19] The novel's chief interest lies, rather, in what it reveals to us of a number of discursive categories and effects that were abroad and active within contemporary Irish life; and of these, the most significant from my perspective are the various competing versions of 'reality', while the most significant discursive effects are those achieved or exposed through particular uses of language.

It's interesting to consider O'Flaherty's own thoughts regarding what he intended or desired to do in this text. A series of letters to his friend and publisher Edward Garnett reveals the evolution of the novel between May and November 1924. The young Irishman refers to 'the creation of a monstrous character called "Gypo Nolan" ... a wonderful character and quite original, nobody has touched him' (Kelly 1996: 95). The novel 'would make a good German film' (95), he muses; later he reports how 'Gypo always parades before my mind with ponderous movement, scowling, shaking his tremendous head, yelling now and again. I really will weep when I kill the beautiful monstrosity' (98). Finally, in a letter of 18 September (101–2), he offers Garnett a long exposition of his methods and intentions for the book, the most striking aspect of which is a willed correspondence between style and content. O'Flaherty intended that the style of the writing should follow Gypo's changing orientation within the narrative. Thus, his initial depiction as 'a tool for evil-minded intelligence' is described in a prose that is 'brutal ... without finesse, without deviation, without any sweetness, short and curt like a police report'. As the character's vulnerability begins to emerge, however, 'the style becomes definitely sympathetic, lengthens itself out, softens, strikes a note of joy in the eternity of nature'. And when Gypo makes his bid for escape towards the end, 'the style completely changes and becomes like a wild storm, cascading, abandoned, poetic'.

This account had changed somewhat by the time O'Flaherty came to write his 1934 memoir *Shame the Devil*. He was still making expansive claims for the novel's technique, in as much as he declared it to be

> a sort of highbrow detective story and its style based on the technique of the cinema. It should have all the appearance of a realistic novel and yet the material should have hardly any connection with real life. I would treat my readers as a mob orator treats his audience and toy with their emotions, making them finally pity a character which they began by considering a monster. (1934: 189–90)

At the same time, *The Informer* is described as a kind of elaborate hoax played on a contemporary critical community ignorant to a great extent of the complex realities of Ireland's revolutionary period:

> The literary critics hailed it as a brilliant piece of work and talked pompously about having at last been given inside knowledge of the Irish revolution and the secret organizations that had brought it about. This amused me intensely, as whatever 'facts' were used in the book were taken from happenings in a Saxon town, during the sporadic Communist insurrection of about nineteen twenty-two or three. (190–1)

So, in the first instance, the author cites two influences – one generic (the detective story) and one medial (cinema). He also reiterates the claims made in the letters of 1924 that he deliberately manipulated the style of the writing in relation to the developing narrative. At the same time, the 'Irishness' of the text is now regarded as in some senses a red herring – a ruse to hoodwink the 'pompous' critical establishment.[20] The inference is that O'Flaherty was writing about 'what he knew' (as with the early novels and short stories), but 'what he knew' in this instance was international (as opposed to national) in inspiration and humanistic (as opposed to nationalistic) in scope. But how is all this borne out in the actual writing?

Let's consider the opening paragraphs:

> It was three minutes to six o'clock in the evening of the fifteenth of March 192–.
>
> Francis Joseph McPhillip ran up the concrete steps leading to the glass-panelled swing door that acted as street entrance to the Dunboy Lodging House. The House, as it was called in Dublin, among criminal and pauperized circles, was a grey concrete building of four stories. It stood on the left-hand side of a wide wind-swept asphalt lane off B— Road on the south side of the city. A maze of slum streets surrounded it. An indefinable smell of human beings living in a congested area filled the air around it. From the building itself, a smell of food and of floors being scrubbed with soap and hot water emanated.
>
> A drizzling rain was falling from a black bulging sky. Now and again a flock of hailstones, driven by a sudden gust of querulous wind, clattered down the lane, falling in little dancing groups, on the hard, perspiring asphalt. (1925: 5)

The 'realism' here is established in a number of ways. The use of exact times and dates, of proper names and of 'precise' descriptive language, suggests a species of documentary or police reportage, immediately establishing the 'criminal' milieu within which the narrative will unfold. Realism segues into naturalism (and criminality into poverty) with the allusion to various 'dirty' details (smells, for example) associated with the lower reaches of this particular society.[21]

More subtly, the reality of this milieu is insinuated by the emergence of a clear gap between the world of the narrative and the extra-textual world of the narrator – that world in and from which the writing takes place. This is a world, moreover, which the reader is invited to acknowledge and to share. In some senses, this extra-textual world is re-established with every use of the definite article – 'the' – as this seems to refer to a pre-existing world which the reader *will* know or *should* know: '*the* concrete steps leading to *the* glass-panelled swing door that acted as street entrance to *the*

Dunboy Lodging House'. But it's also there in the constant use of generalised assumptions (Dublin's criminal and pauperised circles), and the recurring invocation of a roster of familiar character types: the prostitute, the mother, the virgin, the revolutionary, etc. – all the 'types' O'Flaherty would have encountered during his career as a communist revolutionary caught up in a nationalist-republican revolution. In this way, the reader is invited to participate in a kind of anthropological conspiracy vis-à-vis the object culture; and the 'meaning' of the narrative is established as a function of the relations between these two cultures, these two realities: the one inside and the one outwith the text.

At the same time, we recall the author's claims regarding the artifice of the text, the attempt to co-ordinate style and plot, and the subsistence of an alternative reality beneath 'the appearance of a realistic novel'. This tendency is presaged in the opening paragraphs by the introduction of a discourse that is at odds with the language of documentary realism already identified. How 'wide' is the 'wide wind-swept asphalt lane'? What does a 'wind-swept' lane look like? How does one define an 'indefinable' smell? In what sense may one refer to 'a flock of hailstones'? This discourse – by turns poetic, impressionistic and figurative – is emphasised as the narrative progresses, and as Gypo's initial character 'type' – 'a tool for evil-minded intelligence' – begins to buckle under the weight of his guilt and fear.[22] Thus we observe that despite his disdain for the phrase-makers of the Celtic Twilight and for the wilful obscurantism of the modernist avant-garde, O'Flaherty the artist was not averse to using 'poetic' language to achieve specific textual effects.

O'Flaherty attempts to introduce 'highbrow' artistry into his novel by the use of certain key words and images that recur throughout the narrative: Gypo's snout-like eyebrows, for example, his distended eyes and bullish strength, his hat, and so on. One crucial word that features in the early part of the text is 'information'. Its importance has already been established by the title, but it soon begins to accrue resonance within the narrative itself. 'Information', it emerges, connotes a specific meaning within the particular milieu of the text, referring to the ways in which, as well as the moment when, someone from 'our' side imparts secret or dangerous knowledge to someone on 'their' side. O'Flaherty's slum-dwelling characters use 'information' as they would an oath or an imprecation; it leaps from their dialogue as any technical and/or taboo term would

(12, 17, 21, 22, 32, 35, 36). Given this significance, it's ironic that Gypo's failure to come up with a plan, after his act of betrayal, is described as an inability on the part of his brain to provide any 'information' (24).

As the text progresses, a complex series of binary oppositions begins to emerge: the world of the narrative and the world of the narration; documentary realism and poetic reflection;[23] the city and the country; Gypo Nolan (body) and Dan Gallagher (mind); a putative revolutionary reality and an established national reality; street language and political language; and so on. This is a situation primed for treachery: firstly, because of the nature of the binary itself, the two component elements of which are locked together in a relationship that is always potentially duplicitous; and secondly, because these various binaries comprise a fragile discursive structure in which affiliations and alliances are subject to constant architectural reorganisation. Thus, to consider just the main character, we observe that Gypo 'belongs' both to the city and to the country; the reader looks *at* him and then *with* him; he is both Gallagher's 'man' and at the same time his archetypal other; he's a different prospect sober and drunk, he's a man with and without a hat – in all these ways and more, in fact, Gypo is always already in the process of betraying himself, as every thought, every gesture and every word carries within itself the seeds of its own negation.

The treacherous condition of *The Informer* is a condition of language itself, then; but it has been exacerbated in this instance by a number of factors that we've been examining in this chapter, the first of which was O'Flaherty's wide-ranging life experience as a poverty-stricken boy growing up on a remote Irish island; a soldier fighting for his country's traditional enemy; and a communist caught up in what was gradually revealed to be a bourgeois revolution. Equally important were the times in which he was living and working – in particular, the competing ideas of what literature was, how it worked and what it was for; the competing claims of a residual Celtic Romanticism and (in the Irish context) a still-emerging avant-garde modernism; and the competing theories of how class, ethnicity and national identity relate to one another in a modern political context.

The argument of this chapter has been that these two factors combined in the author's literary imagination and informed his depiction of betrayal in *The Informer*. O'Flaherty was a walking contradiction in so many ways: peasant/intellectual; imperialist soldier/communist revolutionary; Irish/internationalist; writer/worker; family man/womanising free spirit. And then to find oneself living in a period of profound, rapid change in which the First World War, the Easter Rising and the October Revolution has swept away so many of the certainties of the old order – it's no wonder that he was drawn constantly to the subject of betrayal, or that he overtly thematised it in what remains his most famous (if not necessarily his most successful) novel.

The Informer may have been an attempt to glamorise recent Irish history, or it may represent a piece of cynical opportunism on the part of an impecunious writer. It may represent the ongoing, inherent failure of Irish naturalism, or it may encapsulate O'Flaherty's shortcomings as a writer. It remains a document of its time, however – compelling, revealing, contradictory: yet one more perspective on Ireland's complex landscape of betrayal.

5

A spy in the house of love: Elizabeth Bowen's *The Heat of the Day* (1949)

Nothing cracked my heart
until that evening
at the stony end
of the healing garden
when you turned and said,
as if remembering a secret
known long ago and long forgotten,
'I love you.'

Brendan Kennelly, The
Little Book of Judas, 151

Introduction

Even during her own lifetime Elizabeth Bowen was regarded as a writer for whom issues of interpersonal betrayal featured centrally. Her major theme was always (in the words of one of her most evocative titles) 'the death of the heart' – the annulment of an emotional attachment of some kind in the face of a betrayal of some kind. On at least two occasions, however, that concern spilled over into the political realm. *The Last September* (1929) is a 'Big House' novel focusing on the eclipse of Anglo-Ireland (the community within which she was born and bred) by nationalist revolution in the early twentieth century. Twenty years later in *The Heat of the Day* (1949), she explored the complex dynamics of interpersonal treachery and political treason against the backdrop of wartime London and Irish neutrality.[1]

Bowen's personal life was complicated, and her own status as a long-time committed adulteress no doubt influenced her conception and articulation of love as an emotion that was in some senses always endured in the shadow of betrayal. At the same time, many critics have speculated on the extent to which Bowen's aesthetic concerns were influenced by her Anglo-Irish condition: born and raised in an Ireland she professed to love deeply, she nevertheless felt a strong allegiance to Britain and British culture. This internal conflict was accentuated during the Second World War when Bowen exploited her Irish connections to make secret reports to the British government on certain issues relating to neutral Ireland.

It was out of this conflicted matrix of personal insight and political conviction that Bowen fashioned what remains probably her most effective novel. On one level *The Heat of the Day* works as a kind of wartime spy thriller: three characters – a middle-aged woman named Stella Rodney, her lover Robert Kelway and a sinister figure named Robert Harrison – are caught in a web of desire and treachery in wartime London. On another level – that which encompasses the experience of 'minor' characters such as Louie Lewis, Roderick Rodney and Nettie Morris – this story represents Bowen's fullest exploration of the fatal illusoriness of all human experience, especially that experience which we are disposed to believe will rescue us from illusion: love.

Two related aspects of the author's make-up bear strongly upon this project: firstly, her identity as an Anglo-Irish subject strung out between competing cultural and political allegiances; and secondly, an attitude towards language (partly deriving from that hyphenated condition, partly from her exposure to international modernism) as an inherently compromised means of communication. If the latter accounts in some respects for the style of the narrative, which most readers agree is opaque and highly mannered, the former invites the kind of critical perspectives afforded by a postcolonial theory which is itself organised to a large extent around the issue of 'identity' in a decolonising context such as the one to be found in Ireland during Bowen's lifetime. Particularly interesting from our perspective here is the degree to which each of these elements (style and identity) features betrayal as a key element of its discursive constitution.

Anglo-Irishness

Elizabeth Bowen was descended from an Anglo-Norman Welsh soldier who came to Ireland as part of the Cromwellian invasion in 1649. After military victory (in 1653) Lieutenant-Colonel Henry

Bowen was granted an estate called Farahy in the north-eastern corner of Co. Cork (Bowen 1942: 62). There, in the decades and centuries which followed, his heirs established a typical 'Anglo-Irish' presence, characterised by a number of recurring faculties and traits: Church of Ireland Protestantism; relative wealth compared to the great majority of their Catholic neighbours; a 'Big House' and all that such entailed in the way of sport and culture; intimate knowledge of the land in which they lived; and implicit (although often conflicted) loyalty to the land across the water.

That Elizabeth Bowen was 'Anglo-Irish' seems plain enough; but what does that mean? What does such a description entail by way of a recognisable identity, and the social, cultural and political allegiances that comprise such an identity? To ask such a question is to attempt to bear the entire weight of Irish history – or rather, of Irish *historiography*, for it's there, in the annals of its copious, conflicted interpretations, that the meaning of 'Anglo-Irishness' has been, and continues to be, made and unmade. I have no desire to make a positive intervention in such a debate, other than to remark that it was Bowen's fate to be born (in 1899) at a time of acute crisis for Anglo-Ireland when, under pressure from a variety of forces (some of which have been described in earlier chapters), it was in danger of annihilation – complete eradication from island life. To prove this would require a dedicated volume; I suspect, however, that in some senses Bowen's entire life and work may be regarded as a response to such a threat.

'Anglo-Irishness' represents a classic hyphenated colonial identity; such, indeed, is the status which has determined its function within that strand of modern Irish Studies conducted under the auspices of international postcolonial theory. Again, this is not the place to rehearse debates relating to the legitimacy or the scope of postcolonial theory for Irish history.[2] What I would say is that any hyphenated identity must be of central importance from the perspective of a discourse (treason and betrayal) organised around ideas of secret knowledge and hidden, 'unnatural' affiliations. To employ a musical conceit: the 'Anglo' is always in tension with the 'Irish', and even when that tension resonates harmonically there is always the danger that the slightest touch, the smallest discrepancy of emphasis on one side or the other will result in dissonance. Irish historiography is replete with accounts of such dissonance, and of explanations of how it occurred, who was involved and what was at stake.

The fate of settler communities is one of the most complex issues emerging from postcolonial history. In the case of Ireland, two general tendencies recur. The first sees the Anglo-Irish subject identify with the native culture – however conceived – becoming 'more Irish than the Irish', and dedicating their energies (political and/or cultural) to the severing of links with the 'parent' state. In this regard, names such as Theobald Wolfe Tone, Robert Emmet and Douglas Hyde spring to mind. The second is one in which the Anglo-Irish subject exploits their hyphenated condition in order to become a kind of mediator between its component identities, utilising their intimate knowledge and experience of each culture to 'translate', as it were, one to the other. Much of Elizabeth Bowen's work, especially her non-fictional writings, retains a smack of this latter tendency.[3]

Anglo-Irishness was above all an ambivalent condition, and this helps to account in some measure for certain recurring characteristics displayed by those writers who, for whatever reason, to whatever degree, experienced that condition: characteristics such as dislocation, alienation, insecurity, fracture – what might be described as a kind of love under erasure. The literal in-betweenness of the Anglo-Irish subject ensures that the political and cultural history of the island during the modern era has necessarily been conducted under the sign of hybridity; and this in turn registers in literary discourse as a radical *hesitation* – of emotion, of knowledge, ultimately, of the promise of representation encoded in language itself. The concept of such a *hesitation* brings us back to Bowen.[4]

Elizabeth Bowen, writes Roy Foster, 'was never quite able to place herself ... She lived ambivalently between two worlds' (1993: 102). She was in fact one of the most compelling examples afforded by literary history of a writer trying to make their home along that hyphen between the English and Irish components of their identity. In this fate, she bears comparison with that long line of hyphenated writers (in Ireland and elsewhere) who – at different times and in their different ways – attempted the same trick. Aspects of her dilemma resonate in figures such as Wilde, Yeats, Shaw, Synge, O'Casey and Beckett – in their approach to writing as well as the critical contexts within which their work has been engaged. There's no doubt, furthermore, that Bowen was aware of her conflicted condition and of how such an inheritance might bear upon her own work. This awareness may account for the recurring presence of betrayal as a central theme in all her writing, including that which bears no apparent trace of her Anglo-Irish background.

War and neutrality

'The tensions of being Anglo-Irish at a time when Britain was at war while Ireland remained neutral', argues Éibhear Walshe, 'accentuated Bowen's ambivalent attitude towards her own country' (2011: 14). By the outbreak of war in 1939, Bowen had been living in England for a number of years. She had married a veteran of the First World War named Alan Cameron, and had established herself as a successful modern writer who was acquainted with many of the important figures from the contemporary English literary scene. Her ancestral home, Bowen's Court in Cork (which she had inherited in 1930), was maintained as a kind of holiday getaway where she occasionally entertained some of her English and American friends.[5] There seems little doubt, however, that England, and increasingly London with its complex cosmopolitan culture, represented her preferred milieu. It was there, in a house on Clarence Terrace just off Regent's Park, that Bowen and her husband made their home in 1936; it was there that she got to know the personalities and the networks – intellectual, artistic, political – which may in retrospect be seen to have a bearing on *The Heat of the Day*.[6]

The outbreak of war precipitated a crisis in the already brittle relations between the newly constituted Eire and its former imperial master. The Taoiseach, Eamon de Valera, declared Irish neutrality and refused the Royal Navy use of key port facilities in the parts of the island which fell under his government's jurisdiction. Over in London Winston Churchill waxed muscular, in which attitude he was joined by the British press (Duggan 1985: 126); the former colonial state's refusal to contribute to such an obvious (in British eyes) *guerre juste* rendered it, if not officially traitorous, then certainly treacherous – morally culpable in the eyes of right-thinking people the world over (Wills 2007: 5–7). De Valera refused to budge, however, and the situation festered. Matters were complicated still further by the large numbers of Irish people who contributed in one way or another to the British war effort, and then again by the presence of US military personnel in the six northern counties after America's entry into the war in 1941. All in all, it's fair to say that

Ireland's tactical presence as both a weakness and an opportunity haunted British-Irish relations for the next six years.

Within a year of the outbreak of hostilities, Bowen was in Dublin writing secret reports for the British Ministry of Information on the situation in Ireland. Her initial brief appears to have been to gauge opinion on the possibility of an enforced British reoccupation of Eire's Atlantic ports, but she also ranged widely over the contemporary Irish political and cultural landscape, reporting on various personalities and situations, and advising as to Britain's preferred tactics with its erstwhile dominion.[7] This was a role for which she had volunteered and for which, apparently, she felt herself uniquely endowed.

Bowen was not a professional spy; given the complex legal situation pertaining to the relations between Eire and the United Kingdom at this time, neither is it likely that she could be described as a traitor. It's certainly not the case (as the Aubane Historical Society of Millstreet, North Cork, would have it) that '[she] never pretended to be anything but a staunch Britisher of Churchillian complexion'.[8] On the contrary, she could be a severe critic of some aspects of British life, especially as it pertained to Ireland; and her 'Irishness' was certainly more secure than that claimed on occasion by the likes of contemporaries such as Olivia Manning, Cyril Connolly or Lawrence Durrell (Patten 2012). Bowen did exploit her dual nationality in order to engage in covert intelligence activities on the part of a belligerent power, however, and to operate unsanctioned (she had no diplomatic credentials) within the neutral territory of a democratic state – activities for which she was well paid by the British government. If she was neither spy nor traitor, she did skirt perilously close to the role of 'informer', a practice which (as observed in the previous chapter) continues to resonate discordantly throughout Irish history.

As an Anglo-Irish woman, a professional writer and an implicit supporter of Britain's fight against what she believed to be fascist aggression, Bowen had the opportunity, the means and the motive to adopt the role she did – to exploit her hybrid status for the practical end of passing information to London. It's interesting to speculate whether, as someone with a deep and personal appreciation of the poetics of betrayal, such a role appealed to her on an aesthetic as well as a political level.

The secret reports of 'Mrs Elizabeth Cameron' did not emerge until the 1970s. One of the first figures to engage with them, the historian Robert Fisk, regarded Bowen's 'gentle, sensitive dispatches from Eire [as] still a delight to read' (1983: 355); later, Roy Foster described the author of these reports as 'an acute observer of the Irish mentality during the early 1940s' (1993: 110). Some of her pronouncements, however, seem infelicitous to say the least: for some, indeed, talk of Irish 'childishness and obtuseness … of her intense and narrow view of herself' (Walshe 2011: 52–3) smacks all too clearly of Anglo-Irish arrogance and condescension, and contributes readily to an image of that community as a permanent fifth column operating at large throughout modern Irish history.

Bowen wrote sympathetically in November 1940 about Ireland's stance of neutrality; it was, she said, the fledgling country's 'first *free* self-assertion'; even so,

> [it] is typical of her intense and narrow view of herself that she cannot see that her attitude must appear to England an affair of blindness, egotism, escapism or sheer funk. (Walshe 2011: 53, original emphasis)

Two years later, after the London Blitz (during which she served as an Air Raid Precautions (ARP) warden), Bowen's attitude had changed markedly. She found the country to be 'morally and nervously in a state of deterioration' (85):

> [T]he heroic illusion has been stripped from Irish neutrality … Its glory – as being Eire's first autonomous gesture – appears to fade … It would be too much to say that the people would feel relief if they were to be precipitated into the war. But participation in the war is not regarded with the same superstitious horror as it was two years ago. (98)

It's instructive from a historical perspective to consider that some kind of enforced Irish entry into the war might have been still on the Allied strategic agenda in July 1942. More interesting from our perspective here is the change in Bowen's attitude towards the continued recalcitrance of one side of her bifurcated identity: the condescension is still present, but it has been joined by a distinctly more judgemental attitude towards neutrality.

It was precisely out of the 'crisis of loyalties' (McCormack 1994: 18) she experienced vis-à-vis her dual identity that, as many critics have pointed out, a novel such as *The Heat of the Day* could have emerged. The main action of the plot covers a time period similar to the one in which Bowen was writing her secret wartime reports – that is, autumn 1940 to autumn 1942. And as with her own relationship with Ireland – which, conditioned by her experience of living through the Blitz, had moved from a kind of patronising sympathy to impatience, if not outright resentment – the story of Stella Rodney and Robert Kelway moves from a kind of commitment (conceived in the surreal atmosphere of the Blitz) to mistrust and indictment.[9] In both instances, moreover, the relationship is (or at least is later revealed to have been) shrouded from the outset in deceit and secrecy: Bowen's covert reports to the Ministry of Information, on the one hand, and Kelway's passing to the enemy of information derived in all likelihood from the same institution.

If Bowen may be identified with her creation Stella in so far as both women learn to mitigate an implicit allegiance, she is also linked with the traitor Robert Kelway inasmuch as each traffics in secret information and hidden agendas. There is, in other words, a fundamental correspondence between Bowen's hyphenated identity, her wartime experiences and her artistic projections. The same is true of Bowen's attitude towards love and her understanding of creative writing as a means by which to articulate that emotion.

Adultery and the condition of language

Like many of her generation, Elizabeth Bowen took a pragmatic line on questions of love and marriage. Six years older than she, Alan Cameron had returned from the First World War with a Military Cross and the desire to lead a useful life. Bowen enjoyed being the wife of a local government administrator in a series of posts, most especially in Oxford, where she responded positively to the intellectual inter-war world. In 1935 Cameron took a job at the BBC and the couple moved to London, where their Regent's Park residence became the centre of a brilliant set, and where in 1941 Bowen met and fell in love with another 'spy' in the house of British upper-class society – a Canadian diplomat named Charles Ritchie.

Ritchie was the latest in a series of affairs pursued by Bowen, each conducted with the full knowledge and apparent acquiescence of her husband. According to Judith Robertson, the Camerons' marriage was functional and friendly, with the husband maintaining an acute understanding of his role in the liaison, which was increasingly one of support and companionship (Glendenning and Robertson 2008: 5–7). But if divorce was not an option for Bowen, neither was the passionless fellowship and sexual abstinence of many twentieth-century upper-class British marriages; and although she understood and appreciated the importance of her husband's support and company, these qualities could never outweigh what was, to the female partner at least, the more important realm of love and sex.

As many critics and historians have argued, one of Bowen's affairs (with the Irish writer Sean O'Faolain) was to have a clear bearing upon the questions pertaining to her national identity (Foster 1993: 111). I would suggest that the liaison with Ritchie (which ended only with her death in 1973) had a much more fundamental impact upon both her moral and her aesthetic imagination. Already acutely sensitised to the prevalence of secrecy and betrayal in matters of the heart, the emotional logistics of conducting a long-term, inter-continental affair affected Bowen profoundly, and nowhere more so than in her sense of herself as a writer who had emerged from, and whose principal theme was always going to be, conflicted allegiance.

For thirty-two years Bowen and Ritchie pursued their affair across cities, countries and continents; the emotional intensity of that attachment is preserved in the letters they wrote to each other, and also in the diary he kept throughout his life. Reading that material, it's clear that Ritchie's understanding of what he described as 'Love's queer civil war' (Glendenning and Robertson 2008: 318) mirrored Bowen's, and that she had in some senses met her match in terms of the articulation of that emotional conflict. On 18 August 1952, he writes: 'With me love for a woman is always linked with a need to betray that love; a compulsion which I dread and desire' (182). Two years later (13 December 1954) he wonders if 'treachery' (200) could break the pattern of infidelity they have set. October 1957 finds him questioning if 'disloyalty to E' (287) is the correct way to describe an affair with another woman; and the lovers pass '[a] happy guilty day, full of betrayals' (322) in New York on 16 February 1958, he racked by the secret knowledge of yet another affair.[10]

If both parties found the exigencies of such a liaison difficult, Bowen at least must have been interested to observe that the emotional contours of pursuing and maintaining an extra-marital affair followed the twisted, ambiguous patterns of love that she explored in her creative writings.[11] Such patterns, moreover, generated a particular style, and one could do worse than 'twisted and ambiguous' when it comes to describing Bowen's characteristic approach to the written word. Even during her lifetime Bowen was known as a 'difficult' writer. This difficulty manifested itself in a variety of ways, but certainly included: an approach to syntax that often seemed counterintuitive, not to say outlandish; manipulation of tense to create uncertainty; rare word usage and neologism (especially in the deployment of adverbs and adjectives); slow pacing, with long passages of narratorial commentary; widespread use of multiple voice zones and free indirect discourse; unrealistic dialogue in which even the most minor of exchanges seems overburdened with significance; subtle, complex plotlines in which the status of 'major' and 'minor' characters remains uncertain; and so on.

Bowen developed this characteristic style over the course of her career, and she did so in order to do justice to reality itself – in particular, the reality of human relationships – which she understood to be complex, subtle and frequently paradoxical. Life, in other words, was always *other* than it appeared to be; despite our best attempts to marshal it into knowable patterns – whether those be political or cultural (as in *The Last September*, 1929) or interpersonal (as in *The Death of the Heart*, 1938) patterns – human life was always 'excessive', always unequal to the medium through which we try to describe it.

That 'excess' manifests itself in everyday life under the sign of pretence, performance, passing – ultimately, of treachery, as in this example from *The Last September*:

> Lois walked alone up the avenue, where she had danced with Gerald. She thought what a happy night that had been, and how foolish Mr Montmorency now thought them. He had seemed annoyed at her being young when he wasn't. She could not hope to explain that her youth seemed to her also rather theatrical and that she was only young in that way because people expected it. She had never refused a role. She could not forgo that intensification, that kindling of her personality at being considered very happy and reckless, even if she were not. She could not hope to assure him she was not enjoying anything he had missed, that she was now unconvinced and anxious but intended to be quite certain, by the time she was his age, that she

had once been happy. For to explain this – were explanation possible to so courteous, ironical and unfriendly a listener – would, she felt, be disloyal to herself, to Gerald, to an illusion both were called upon to maintain. (1929: 32–3)

This is a very 'Bowenesque' passage in terms of its language, its syntax, its time-space dispersion and various other formal features – what W.J. McCormack has referred to as her distinctive 'nervousness of style' (1993: 218). But it is also highly characteristic of her work in so far as it describes someone caught between competing desires (Gerald and Mr Montmorency), and who is at the same time aware, to a degree almost debilitating, of the absolute contingency of the desiring 'self'. Lois Farquahar is just one of a series of characters – including Portia Quayne (from *The Death of the Heart*), Karen Michaelis (from *The House in Paris*) and indeed Stella Rodney – through whom Bowen observes the apparently inevitable presence of illusion, and thus of treachery, in human relations. The implicit question facing Lois at the end of this passage is the one facing all Bowen's fictional avatars: how can one be 'disloyal' to an image if that image itself is always already an 'illusion' of the reality it purports to represent?

So, inasmuch as it remains centrally concerned with issues of illusion, reality and truth, there is for Bowen a sense in which the novel as a form is always already caught up with issues of loyalty and betrayal. In an essay entitled 'Notes on Writing a Novel' (1986: 35–48), originally published in 1945 – right in the throes, that is, of her work on *The Heat of the Day*[12] – she explains that '[the] novel lies, in saying that something happened that did not. It must, therefore, contain uncontradictable truth, to warrant the original lie' (35). It's the conviction and skill that the novelist brings to the *telling* of the lie that determines the novel's ability to reveal truths about the human condition. At the same time, the novelist herself is a figure who in some senses must learn to be disloyal to 'normal society' and to their own established role within that society. Bowen describes this (in an essay entitled 'Disloyalties' published in 1950) in terms deeply resonant with her recently completed novel:

[The writer] has exhausted his native air – can his imagination learn to breathe another? ... He cannot free himself from the hereditary influences without the sense of outraging, injuring and betraying them – virtually, it appears to him, he must cease to honour his father and his mother. From the moment he has perceived this, there is no choice – the matter decides itself according to whether he is or is not a valid writer ... he has not necessarily forsaken the old scenes; what has happened is that he sees them newly ... The disloyalties of the writer, evidently, are not a privilege; they are a test and a tax. They are the inverse of an ultimate loyalty – to the pursuit, the search, the range of the exploration, the hope of the 'extra dimension', wherein lies truth. (1986: 62)

It's difficult not to equate the novelist's higher calling – her willingness to (be seen to) outrage, injure and betray in pursuit 'of the "extra dimension", wherein lies truth' – with Bowen's apparent willingness to forsake the 'old scenes' of her Anglo-Irishness in the name of an 'ultimate loyalty' located elsewhere. These are necessary, noble betrayals; the novelist's validity as an artist is of a piece with Bowen's validity as an Anglo-Irish subject constrained (under pressure of war) to emphasise one element – the first – of her dual identity. And just as the novelist regards this as a *revision* (seeing newly) rather than a *denial* of the previous dispensation, so Bowen no doubt undertook her taxing clandestine activities in the name of a greater truth which would in time reinvigorate the exhausted native air of Ireland.

The Heat of the Day was dedicated to Charles Ritchie, and Bowen considered it to be a book that belonged to both of them: 'Short of there having been a child', she wrote in a letter of 17 June 1948, 'there could be no other thing that was more you and me' (Glendenning and Robertson 2008: 124). He concurred, writing (in a diary entry from 18 August 1973 – that is, after her death):

For me it is filled with echoes, reflections (as from a mirror, or a mirror-lined room). Also of premonitions, backward questionings, unanswered, and now unanswerable guesses. It is the story of our love, with a flaw in it, or did she feel a flaw in me?[13]

'*The Heat of the Day* is a novel', as Neil Corcoran writes, 'in which the panic of possibly losing identity, and of others deceiving you about their identities, operates not only as the agency of plot but as the very texture of style' (2004: 169–70). But it is also, as he goes on to say, a novel encoded with an 'autobiographical inscription: and this indelibly marks the text with an Irish signature, impresses into it an Irish watermark' (183). It's the novel, in other words, in which all the themes of Bowen's life and work are engaged: her

Anglo-Irish background; her appreciation (within the context of war) of the impossibly delicate relationship between secrecy, knowledge and allegiance; the representation of sexual desire as always locked in to the possibility of psychological betrayal; and her absolute conviction as to the centrality of treachery as a factor within all human intercourse.

The Heat of the Day

Towards the end of the novel Robert Kelway tries to explain to his lover why he turned traitor against Great Britain. The Nazis, he claims, have perceived something fundamental about the phase of history into which humankind has entered – something to do with the end of traditional notions of nationality, democracy and freedom, and the emergence of a new dispensation characterised by order, efficiency and law. The idea itself, he claims, is bigger than the Nazis – they are merely its contemporary articulation. He was confirmed in these views, he explains, by his experience as an evacuee from the disaster at Dunkirk, which led in time to a realisation of the hollowness of democracy, especially in its insufferable British variety. Behind Kelway's political and cultural antipathy lies the shade of a father who, he says, he needed to breed out of himself in order to claim 'a new heredity' (273).

Kelway's political treason is linked to his interpersonal treachery (he lies repeatedly to Stella, for example), and is echoed throughout the story by other forms of deceit and betrayal. The novel presents a world of interconnected treacheries in which each character – minor and major – is implicated in some form and to some degree. For that reason, Bowen had to concoct a plausible motivation for Kelway's treachery, for without such plausibility the entire narrative is in danger of disintegration. That motivation, as described above, is a combination of political and psychological elements: disaffection with British political hypocrisy, a conviction as to the advent of a new phase in human history and an escape from the emotional dysfunctionalism of Holme Dene – the house in which Kelway grew up.

With regard to the first of these elements, Bowen had a useful example to hand in the form of William Joyce – also known as Lord Haw-Haw – who was hanged for treason against the British Crown on 3 January 1946. Both in his broadcasts from Germany during the war and in his elaborate defence of his own beliefs during his trial, Joyce articulated what came to represent for many of his contemporaries the case for treason. Joyce was, he maintained, dedicated to a form of Britishness other than the one in whose image the current war had been fomented and waged. He was not a traitor but a patriot who, disillusioned by the outcome of the First World War, made temporary alliance with those who shared his disillusion and who seemed willing to countenance the new attitudes that new times demanded.[14]

Like many other people who had lived in Britain during the war, Bowen was much exercised in its aftermath by the idea of treason; such an interest must have been amplified by the fact that she was at the time immersed in writing a novel in which betrayal featured centrally.[15] Hers could be one of those novels in which, as Éibhear Walshe writes, 'the parallel between the narrative treachery of modernist fiction and an unstable twentieth-century concept of treason is always being tested and scrutinized'.[16] Given his high profile during the war itself, Joyce's case was exemplary; it was even more fascinating for Bowen inasmuch as there was an Irish dimension to Joyce's background that resonated to an extent with some of her own concerns relating to the relations between Ireland and England in general, but particularly during the war.[17] I shall return to this point below; in the meantime, it seems clear that Bowen borrowed some of Joyce's rhetoric, and perhaps something also of his manner and style, when it came to contriving a plausible scenario for Robert Kelway's treason.

Part of Kelway's apology, as remarked above, concerns his troubled relationship with his father. The significance of this emerges during a chapter (six) in which he and Stella visit his family home – a large three-storeyed manor outside the city. It's an unsettling place, particularly for the son, Robert, who associates it with his father's 'impotence' (119) and with the 'illusion' (121) – assiduously maintained by his mother and sister, and perpetuated by his niece and nephew – of his own heroism. Kelway's relationship with his father is characterised by a range of negative associations: embarrassment, disappointment and death. In one particularly telling passage (119), he describes how his father would insist on exchanging gazes with him, as if to offset his own symbolic emasculation by demonstrations of manly frankness. It was at such moments, Kelway explains, that he observed the 'broken spring' of his father's life. What he does not yet say – what the novel will come to reveal – is the extent to which that gaze implicates Kelway himself in a reciprocal discourse of dysfunction and emasculation which will in time express itself as a propensity to betray.

Such a propensity is signalled soon after the 'looking' passage by two separate uses of the word 'betray'. The first, describing the Kelway family's resentful attitude towards their own home, refers to 'the betrayed garden' (121). On one level, this is of a piece with Bowen's heightened attitude towards place as an index of emotional and cultural significance. In Bowen's fictional worlds, there is always (in her contemporary Anaïs Nin's memorable phrase) a spy in the house of love; at another level, however, it establishes an implicit association between the Kelways and treachery – thus, the betrayed garden is both a synecdoche and a direct portent of the betrayed country.

The second usage describes the children's awareness that their garden exercises are being observed by their uncle and his beautiful friend from London:

> Anne's and Peter's knowing the promise [that their physical exercises would be watched from the upstairs window] was being kept betrayed itself only by sterner effort, reddening foreheads, set jaws, a fixed-eyed refusal to so much as glance at their uncle's window again. (122)

The word is deployed here in the Freudian sense of the conscious self being betrayed by drives and desires of which it is largely unaware, and over which it has limited control. There's no doubt that 'betrayed' is a suggestive term in the context of the children's attitude towards a figure they admire so intensely. More interesting, perhaps, is the choice of this particular word in this particular context: in a characteristically complex sentence, Bowen introduces a word that has, as it were, seeped in from the surrounding environment – an environment characterised by emotional failure and bad faith. Betrayal, it seems, is in the air one breathes at Holme Dene – it is, as Harrison later says, 'the first place where rot could start' (131); and this is reflected in Bowen's introduction of the language of betrayal as part of the narrative discourse within which the place itself is described.

Robert speaks of needing to escape his father's influence so that he may claim 'a new heredity'; Freudianism is not mentioned, but such, it seems, was the discourse within which such an analysis could be made. In a paper entitled 'The Psychology of Quislingism' read before the British Psycho-Analytical Society on June 12 1940, Freud's long-time British champion Ernest Jones claimed:

> Treachery, by allying oneself with the conquering enemy, would seem to be an attempt sadistically to overcome the incest taboo by raping the Mother instead of loving her. Perhaps this is why it is generally regarded as the most outrageous and unnatural of crimes, since it combines disloyalty to both parents ... I would suggest that the people who are most subject to the wiles of the Nazi propaganda are those who have neither securely established their own manhood and independence of the Father nor have been able to combine the instincts of sexuality and love in their attitude towards the Mother or other women. This is the psychological position of the homosexual. (1951: 283)

Jones's paper represents a clear attempt to harness the 'disinterested' discourse of science for instrumental purposes – specifically, for the purposes of the war effort and the demonisation of dissent. At the same time, his explicit association of treason with homosexuality (which was to have a long and lively afterlife in British culture) hovers around the shadows of Bowen's narrative; while his view of the traitor as an example of the unsuccessfully negotiated Oedipal crisis chimes remarkably well with her depiction of the treacherous character of Robert Kelway, whose psychological profile does indeed come into focus in terms of a psycho-sexual crisis which was itself apparently generated by a monstrous mother and a weak, ineffectual father.[18]

In Jones's view, each parent is a symbolic representation of the country: one (the father) as an embodiment of authority and injunction, the other (mother) as an object of desire. Treason represents an attempt to play out the family romance in real terms, as the traitor metaphorically kills the father (by shifting his allegiance to another political authority) in order to possess the mother (by redefining his country in terms of his own political desires). According to such a model, treason is a form of pathology born, and apprehensible in terms of, a very particular sexual crisis which the properly trained psychoanalyst is well placed to identify.

Bowen's imagination of treachery rehearses many of the elements of this discourse. Kelway feels himself to have been 'born wounded; my father's son' (272); for a Freudian, the juxtaposition of those two descriptions cannot but evoke the fear of castration – the symbolic emasculation of the son – a fear from which treason offers the subject temporary relief. Then, after repeatedly denying the idea of the 'country' as valid political currency, Kelway invokes Stella in terms which explicitly link the realms of the political and the psycho-sexual: 'you', he says, 'have been my country' (273). In Freudian terms, this amounts to a declaration that 'you are my mother', because it seems clear that Stella is amongst other things the object onto which Robert has displaced his illicit desire. In fact, Stella, Kelway and Harrison come to form a classic Oedipal triangle, with Stella (mother) as the object of desire, Robert Harrison (father) embodying phallocentric law and Robert Kelway (son) vying with the latter in order to possess the former. Unable to resolve this narrative in psycho-sexual terms, the latter has transposed it into the realm of the political, where it manifests itself as treason.

Towards the outset of his confession, Kelway acknowledges one key element of his relationship with Stella: 'What is repulsing you', he tells her,

> is the idea of 'betrayal', I suppose, isn't it? In you the hangover from the word? Don't you understand that all language is dead currency? How they keep on playing shop with it all the same: even you do. Words, words like that, yes – what a terrific dust they can still raise in a mind, yours even: I see that. Myself, even, I have needed to immunize myself against them; I tell you I have only at last done that by saying them to myself over and over again till it became absolutely certain they mean nothing. What they once meant is gone. (268)

With his conviction as to the advent of new times, Kelway would like to believe that the established language has lost its affective charge, and that certain key words no longer possess the ability they once had to register in the real. From that established perspective, a cluster of such words might be seen to attach itself to his behaviour: treason, treachery, deceit, lies, disloyalty. All of these words, moreover, were (and were likely to remain) highly charged during the war, precisely because there was such a premium on information in the waging of that war, and because the opposing sides in the conflict had been represented in such stark contrast.

Like any conflict, in other words, language itself becomes a key arena within which the terms, indeed the very meaning, of the struggle was conducted, as various forces vied to define what various signifiers might or might not signify. ('Freedom' is probably the most obvious of these signifiers.) Kelway's abjuration of 'betrayal' represents one such manoeuvre. Both the word itself, he claims, and the meanings and responses it elicits belong to an outmoded way of life; recognise that, and the word no longer possesses the ability to raise 'a terrific dust ... in a mind' – that is, to cause the subject to respond to and engage with the world in a particular way.[19]

Elizabeth Bowen was supremely adapted to explore the importance of language for the discourse of betrayal; as pointed out in an earlier section, such was both the quintessential insight of Anglo-Irish culture as well as the principal theme of all her work. In *The Heat of the Day* the concern with language manifests itself in terms of her familiar style, with circumlocutious sentences, elliptical syntax and dense, overloaded dialogue.[20] In this way, style is a reflection of the treacherous reality it's trying to describe. This time, however, there's an added emphasis on the absolute strangeness of the signifier itself; throughout the novel words themselves are contorted into all sorts of grotesque shapes as Bowen attempts to capture the emotional and political complexity of the world in morphological as well as semantic terms. It's as if every word is in itself a potential exercise in betrayal – and so we get: 'possessorship' (100), 'unconcentratedly' (101), 'ilexy' (146), 'disembarrassed' (176), 'unindifference' (184), 'perfectness' (188), 'ghostily' (193), 'rathering' (240), 'arrestations' (269), 'disaffectedness' (271), 'blent' (285), 'biggened' (326), 'persecutedly' (327), 'glary' (328); and so on.

For reasons already mentioned, one of the most overly burdened signifiers in Bowen's imagination was 'Ireland' – a burden which had been exacerbated by the changing fortunes of war. In a 'Conversation on Traitors' broadcast by the BBC on 21 August 1952, Bowen said of the German-born Russian spy Klaus Fuchs: 'It must be exceedingly difficult for a person displaced by forces outside himself, from his own country, to form a spontaneous, genuine, heartfelt attachment, I should imagine' (Hepburn 2010: 309). Of course, Bowen's own ancestors had been 'displaced' (albeit voluntarily) from their own country after a different war, and had likewise experienced the difficulty of forming 'a spontaneous, genuine, heartfelt attachment' to their new country of residence. Once again Bowen's conception of treason and treachery reverberates with her own status as the displaced child of a displaced history.

Chapter 9 of *The Heat of the Day* finds Stella at Mount Morris, a house not unlike Bowen's Court in terms of locale and design, where she's attempting to sort out Roderick's legal affairs after his inheritance of the estate. It's a brief sojourn during which Stella ruminates on the nature of her relationship with Kelway and on the nature of love generally. The idea of Ireland, however, performs an important function in Bowen's finely calibrated drama; 'a famous evocation of wartime England', as Roy Foster puts it, 'is brought into focus by a journey to Ireland, defining the questions of patriotism and allegiance around which the story revolves' (1993: 107).

There is a sense, as Adam Piette (1995: 172) has pointed out, that Bowen has transposed her own troubled relationship with Ireland, and more particularly her espionage activities in Ireland during the opening years of the war, into the love story we find worked out in *The Heat of the Day.* The pattern of attraction and repulsion, trust and suspicion, that characterises the relations between Stella, Kelway and Harrison is in this sense an allegory of the historical relationship between Ireland, England and Anglo-Ireland – a relationship characterised by conflicted allegiance and bad faith. It's in Ireland – in Cousin Francis's Anglo-Irish library – that Stella ponders the tortuous poetics of espionage which Harrison's revelations have unleashed in her (170–8); and this is all the more fitting because it was in Ireland – in the hotels and salons of Emergency Dublin – that Bowen, a writer super-sensitised to the politics of treachery, must have contemplated her role as the salaried agent of a foreign power.

It's for this reason that Neil Corcoran regards *The Heat of the Day* as an encoded 'apologia' offering an imaginative reconciliation between 'divided traditions'.[21] Such a possibility subsists in the image – so remote and so delicate that Bowen cannot even formulate it in the text – of a union between the young Catholic serving girl named Hannah and Stella's son Roderick, the new master of Mount Morris. With such an image

> wartime Ireland ... is moved on ... from the nullness of neutrality and the tergiversation of espionage and treachery into the figuration of a potential alternative, in which Catholic nationalist Ireland will be doubled with England, married to it, rather than separated from it by the now altogether uncertain hyphen between 'Anglo' and 'Irish'. (Corcoran 2004: 196)

Coming directly after the news of the 'terrible victory' (178) at El Alamein under General Bernard Montgomery (a man with his own Anglo-Irish connections), Hannah's simple, self-sufficient Irish beauty comes to represent an alternative source of power, one that Bowen – rehearsing a typical Anglo-Irish attitude – believed herself specially endowed both to recognise and to appreciate. Haunted by the spectre of racelessness, Bowen posits a 'city that is to come' where she no longer has to smile *and* stab – a time and a place where, finally, she will be home.[22]

It's in this sense, also, that W.J. McCormack's characterisation of Bowen as a specific kind of Irish traitor – someone who betrays 'the past in the name of a possibly continuing present' (1994: 332) – comes into focus. For if Bowen did betray Ireland, she did so (like all traitors) with a view towards changing the terms of the discourse within which the charge of 'treason' could legitimately be brought.

For Stella, Ireland provides a temporary relief from the dangers of wartime London, and offers an alternative locale from which to contemplate the complications that have overtaken her life in the wake of Harrison's revelation. It's not as if Mount Morris is some kind of rural idyll, however; to regard it as such would be a typic-ally English attitude, and both Stella and her creator know better than to patronise Ireland or the Irish in such a manner. For Bowen herself, Ireland during the war functioned primarily as a kind of moral arena – a place *of* value in itself, certainly, but a place where the discourse of value could be tried and tested. In *The Heat of the Day*, Bowen poses the traitor's question: given her own conflicted identity; given the fact and the power of the Nazi abomination, and the (albeit understandable) inconvenience of Irish neutrality; given the propensity of human relations to extend into ever more com-plicated patterns; given the propensity of language to undo itself; given the inexorable presence of treachery encoded into all human endeavour – given all these things, what was Ireland worth? What did it mean?

6

Jesus or Judas?: Francis Stuart's
Black List, Section H (1971)

The last thing in this world
Anyone I know
Would dare to be
Is wholly free.

That is, of course, with the exception
Of one man.
One man alone.

See what happened to him.
                    Brendan Kennelly, *The*
            Little Book of Judas, 38

Introduction

Despite the fact that he disdained nationality as a criterion for the
understanding of literature, Francis Stuart remains an important figure in modern Irish literary history, in significant part because of the
ways in which his work focuses questions pertaining to the meaning
of literature itself and its relationship to reality.[1] Those questions
turn to a defining extent on issues of treason and betrayal, and are
most fully explored in his celebrated autobiographical novel *Black
List, Section H* (1971).

By 1940 Stuart had been producing novels and poetry from his
base in Ireland for approximately twenty years, and was well on
his way to achieving the status of minor writer for which fate and
circumstances had apparently selected him. What would become
the defining event of his life occurred when, in January 1940, he
moved to Berlin to take up a post as lecturer in English literature
at the university in that city. Once there, Stuart accepted an offer

to write material for radio broadcasts to Eire; between 1942 and 1944 he wrote and delivered over one hundred such broadcasts to his homeland.

After his eventual return (in 1957) to what had in the meantime become the Republic of Ireland, Stuart found himself to be a figure of some controversy, a status that continued to attach to him until his death in 2000. The debate which emerged in relation to his actions during the Second World War crystallised many of the issues that had attached to Ireland itself in respect of its recent revolutionary history, its status in the modern world and the role of culture – and in particular literature – in the representation of that status. Although some may not have realised it, that debate was in fact a conversation rather than an interrogation; for part of Stuart's 'defence' was always to question the moral, intellectual and aesthetic sovereignty of those who questioned his actions. Once again we encounter the *aporia* on which the concept of betrayal is invariably deployed: when value, truth and morality are themselves at issue, then *who* has the right to describe *whom* as a traitor?

This dilemma comes into sharp focus in terms of the debates which emerged in the latter part of the twentieth century regarding the status and function of literature – debates in which Stuart himself frequently partook, albeit (as was his wont) in tangential and contrary fashion. In particular the literary theory known as deconstruction seems to be especially calibrated to address the issues attending Stuart's life and work; and not only because its characteristic approach and modes of operation are directly engaged with the relationship between writing and life – *and* with the ineluctable presence of betrayal as a figure within that relationship – but also because one of the most infamous academic scandals of the modern era emerged specifically in relation to the theory of deconstruction, and concerned a case not dissimilar to Stuart's.

Berlin calling

Before moving on to such issues, however, it would be well to acquaint ourselves in outline with the pertinent facts relating to Stuart's wartime activities.

Throughout the 1930s Stuart lived with his wife Iseult (née Gonne) and their two children in the village of Laragh in Co. Wicklow, approximately twenty-five miles from Dublin. According to various subsequent accounts written by Stuart himself (including the novel under discussion), it was not a particularly happy household.[2] Once heralded by Yeats (albeit rather grudgingly) as the potential future of Irish literature (Foster 2003: 446), Stuart's reputation had stalled in the latter half of the 1930s with a series of increasingly forced novels. And while his relationship with Iseult continued to descend into resentment and guilt, Stuart observed the political evolution of the Free State with all the disappointed scorn of a former revolutionary.

Whilst on a lecture tour of various German cities in 1939, Stuart was offered a lecturing post in the *Englisches Seminar* at the University of Berlin, such position to commence in the autumn term of that year. After returning home and consulting with Iseult, he decided to accept the offer, and in January 1940, through a combination of luck and deception, Stuart managed to make his way back to Berlin.

Besides his work in the university, Stuart found plenty to occupy him in the Reich capital. Shortly after his arrival he accepted an invitation to translate German news bulletins into English, a role he continued to fulfil for a number of years. He also made the acquaintance of William Joyce – better known as 'Lord Haw-Haw' (whom we encountered earlier in relation to *The Heat of the Day*) – and wrote three scripts for him (Stuart 1984: 31) before Joyce decided to undertake the job himself. This experience evidently predisposed Stuart to make a more formal contribution; and so it was that he accepted an invitation by Dr Hans Hartmann – the head of the Irland-Redaktion (the Irish section of the German Propaganda Ministry's international radio service) – to write and deliver a short talk for broadcast to Ireland on St Patrick's Day, 1942.[3]

As mentioned in the introduction to this chapter, over the next twenty-three months Stuart went on to make more than one hundred broadcasts for Irland-Redaktion.[4] These broadcasts were, from first to last (and despite his later assertions otherwise), thoroughly political in content. Despite occasional diversions into cultural matters, Stuart found his principal themes in the perfidy of the Allies – their hypocrisy, their aggression and their double-dealing – and the commendable, although precarious neutrality of Eire. Frequently, treason itself is the topic, as when he questions the executions of Rory O'Connor and Liam Mellowes by the Free State in 1922 (Barrington 2000: 97), or when he impugns northern unionists for their continuing support of Britain (134–5).[5]

Stuart withdrew his services in February 1944 when, as he claims, he came under pressure from the regime to introduce anti-Soviet and anti-Semitic elements into his scripts.[6] Thereafter, he managed to see out the war in relative safety, before getting caught up (along with his future wife) in the general chaos of post-war Europe. Poverty-stricken sojourns as an 'apatriate' in Paris and London followed, before relocation to Ireland was made possible by Iseult's death in 1954.

It would appear that Stuart's muse, which had been in decline in the latter years of the 1930s, was energised by his experiences during the war. Three novels – *The Pillar of Cloud* (1948), *Redemption* (1949) and *The Flowering Cross* (1950) – were written and published in a creative frenzy, and remain amongst his most successful works. Each of these novels, moreover, is explicitly engaged with experiences similar to Stuart's, in so far as each features a male artist figure of questionable integrity searching for redemption amongst the ruins of post-war Europe. That energy showed no sign of abating during the 1950s, moreover, as hundreds of thousands of words continued to pour from his pen.

Stuart spent the decade after his return to Ireland, working on the book that would become *Black List, Section H*, an autobiographical novel first published in 1971 by a relatively obscure American academic press. After he thus hove back into public view, the remaining thirty years of his life were studded with controversy, culminating in the heated debates attending his election to the position of 'Saoi' (translating as 'wise person') within Aosdána, the Irish Arts Council's organisation for celebrated artists (Barrington 2000: 53–60; Tóibín 2001: 5–6). Despite this, Stuart seemed quite content in his later life to occupy a position outside the mainstream – that, after all, was where the true artist belonged – and he remained 'an awkward presence' (as President Mary Robinson said in her conferment address) in Irish literary and civic life until his death in 2000.

The preceding paragraphs (which in some ways are merely a fuller rendition of this chapter's opening two paragraphs) have been extremely difficult to write, because it's difficult (at least I find it so) to describe such sensitive activities without using potentially emotive and/or judgmental language. The facts do not 'speak for themselves': every 'fact' requires contextualisation – a narrative of some kind within which to locate the 'event'. At the same time, each text requires enunciation – a particular idiom within which the event can be described and named. This is a complicated business; and that business has been trading for nearly seventy years at this stage, during which period every aspect of Stuart's original actions, as well as his subsequent rationalisation of those actions, has been subject to intense scrutiny. The perennial question of the relationship between art and reality has formed a seminal aspect of this process; and in the following sections I wish to examine some of the instances in which such a question might be invoked in relation to *Black List, Section H*.

The autobiographical novel

Stuart referred to *Black List, Section H* as a 'memoir in fictional form' (Natterstad 1974: 84) – a description which encapsulates the troubled relationship between reality and representation which, in so far as it's an account of an artist searching for an authentic voice to describe his response to the world, is in itself the text's principal theme. Unlike the other narratives dealing with the experiences of an artist figure similar to himself, *Black List* purports to be a truthful account of Stuart's own life between 1917 and a date shortly preceding the commencement of writing. This period includes his decision to move to Germany, his experiences once there and his attempts – once defeat for the Nazi regime had become inevitable – to ensure survival for himself and his lover (and future wife), Madeleine (Gertrud) Meissner. Although this is the section of the text which has attracted the most attention, the first two-thirds are of equal importance in so far as they provide a series of contexts – personal, philosophical, artistic – within which his wartime and post-war activities come into focus.

Black List, Section H is a species of *Künstlerroman*, a kind of experimental autobiography in which the author purports to trace the evolution of his own artistic consciousness over an extended period of time (Caterson 1997; Welch 1993: 140). The text opens with the narrator describing how he has sent a letter to a Dublin newspaper in support of Irish independence, in direct contradiction to the complacent beliefs of his own (Protestant and unionist) family. The impulse for this act of betrayal, he claims,

> came directly from having just written his first poem, and, indirectly, from a kind of faith in himself and his confused instincts that the

news of the Russian Revolution that he'd heard during his last term
at an English public school, had given him. (1971: 7–8)

Directly from the outset, then, the reader encounters a motif that
will recur throughout the text: the implicit link between art, politics
and betrayal. The 'obscure urge' (17) to betray is revisited in various scenes and images throughout the early part of the narrative;
in itself it connotes a supreme dedication to the implicitly righteous values of 'honesty' and 'truth' (as if these were unproblematic
categories), and a rationalisation of the insight that 'Dishonour is
what becomes a poet' (20). This urge in encapsulated in the image
of some Irish girls who, during the War of Independence, 'had been
found one Sunday morning chained to the railings of a church in
the local town, a notice pinned to them with the word "Traitors"
scrawled on it':

> He believed that nothing short of the near despair of being utterly
> cast off from society and its principles could create the inner condi-
> tion conducive to the new insights that it was the task of the poet
> to reveal.
>   The girls tied to the railings symbolized for H the poet who is
> exposed and condemned for his refusal to endorse the closed judge-
> ments and accept the categorical divisions into right and wrong that
> prevailed. If he survived the ordeal there would flow from the depths
> of his isolation fresh imaginative streams to melt the surrounding
> freeze-up. (41)

H returns to the image of the shaven-headed girls at various points
throughout the text, at one point even writing a novel about them.[7]
The complex of suffering and guilt symbolised by the girls' condition also helps to account for H's attraction to Christian spiritual-
ism – in particular, the enduring power of Christ's agony as in some
respects an analogue of poetic inspiration. As he put it in the after-
word to *The Pillar of Cloud*: 'pain and anguish are great evolutionary forces through which mind and heart, nervous system and
psyche, mature and develop in complexity (1948: 234). To depict
the human condition authentically, the artist must experience the
most powerful of human emotions, and these are to be found not
amongst history's 'winners', but amongst those who, for whatever
reason, have been excluded from the high table.

With language and imagery such as this, Stuart attempts to establish the profile of a young, restive, quasi-artist figure, apt to betrayal
and unfazed by the consequences. It might be suggested, however,

that this is simply the method whereby Stuart insinuates a continuity of behaviour and thought between his pre-German self and the man who wrote and delivered those broadcasts from the Nazi state in the early 1940s. It might be further suggested that the entire book is by way of an extended apology for the actions which so dominated the author's profile in the latter part of his career.

What enabled Stuart to attempt such an elaborate strategic defence was precisely the nature of the *Künstlerroman* itself. For as Joyce had established with such acuity in *A Portrait of the Artist as a Young Man*, the novel of artistic evolution poses the question of artistic fidelity with special resonance, and this is because the relationship between the narrating 'I' and the narrated 'I' throws issues of truth, honesty, authenticity and representation into high relief.[8] Observed in this light, *Black List, Section H* might be regarded as an extremely delicate balancing act in which the narrator depicts the flawed – but consistently flawed – character who will in time become himself. Stuart brutally exposes his younger self, with all his failures, infidelities and errors; but he also gives us a literary character who, given his profile and his experiences up until that time, was likely to do exactly what he did between 1940 and 1944. Unlike Joyce, however, this profile is less the product of a particular cultural and political environment than an inherent, self-contained attitude defined almost entirely by its antipathy towards whatever local environment it happens to fetch up in.

In such an instance, 'honesty' may be regarded as merely another rhetorical device, one calibrated to establish a rationale for itself. 'Honesty' attempts to engage in what linguists refer to as a 'performative' rather than a 'declarative' speech act – one which justifies itself rather than depending upon some species of value imported into the discourse from outside.[9] 'Honesty' can never be discursively out-manoeuvred: it's always-already 'honest'. But the same is true of honesty's Others: duplicity and treachery. It's in the nature of the betrayer to betray, so why should we be surprised to find that he has in fact done so? It was in Stuart's nature to operate outside the consensus, so why should we be surprised when he does so in relation to perhaps the strongest consensus of the modern era: the moral condemnation of Nazi Germany?

No doubt there is 'an element of retrospective justification discernible' (Caterson 1996: 21) at various points throughout *Black List, Section H*. Written, as Clair Wills, puts it, 'with all the benefits

of hindsight' (2007: 370), the text does not offer its reader a key
to Stuart's true nature, nor is it the lens through which the author's
life and career come into focus. It is, rather, a highly rhetorical and
astute example of literary imagination in action – all the more
powerful for the scrupulous meanness of a tone which aims for
aloofness and objectivity in equal measure. *Black List* is, as most
readers will attest, a striking book; but perhaps what is most striking about it, as Brendan Barrington has pointed out, is 'the degree
to which a work of fiction has been taken as a reliable guide to the
young Stuart's state of mind and political beliefs' (2000: 6). In fact,
Stuart's achievement in this his most famous (and most successful)
book was to insist on the essential correspondence of a particular
binary (honesty/betrayal), and to present it as the paradoxical core
of his own evolution. The novel works to show that if his younger
self *did* betray anything or anybody with his wartime activities, it
was in the name of a congenital 'honesty' which was ineluctably
linked to its own 'dark' Other: betrayal.

Art, truth and betrayal

As observed in the previous chapter, questions of betrayal were
very much in the air in both Eire and the United Kingdom in the
opening months of the war. Irish neutrality was an affront to many,
and much of the time the offence was cast as a betrayal of one
sort or another – of natural allies, of self-interest, of democracy,
of civilisation itself (Wills 2007). Whilst defending the young state
against such external accusations, de Valera invoked similar rhetoric against a range of internal enemies – dissident republicans, for
example, who regarded the European war as an opportunity to pursue more local aims, such as the reintegration of the six lost northern counties into a single island polity. It was against this backdrop
of treason and betrayal that Francis Stuart set out in January 1940
to take up his post at the University of Berlin.

According to accounts produced in various media at various
points in his subsequent career, Stuart went to Berlin for any one
(or any combination) of seven principal reasons: (1) to earn money
to support his wife and children back in Ireland; (2) to escape an
increasingly stressful and dysfunctional marriage; (3) to distance
himself from those whom he believed to be mismanaging the country he loved; (4) to experience life amongst those who seemed to

subscribe to socio-political views similar to his own – anti-democratic, anti-bourgeois, anti-capitalist and anti-imperialist; (5) to
explore and expedite the possibilities of Nazi aid for the IRA, for
which organisation he had performed espionage work at various
times in the past, and to which he was still ideologically affiliated;
(6) to observe an artistic responsibility to place himself outside the
'moral Pale' (1971: 258) by affiliating with those deemed morally
questionable by his 'own' side; and (7) to observe an equally insistent artistic responsibility to place himself amongst the abject and
the defeated – as he put it in a letter written half a century after the
events, 'to see life through the pure eye of the losers' (Natterstad
1974: 26).

In relation to point 1, it may be observed that Stuart was one
of a handful of Irish nationals who fetched up in Germany during
the war when the vast bulk of overseas Irish labour actually contributed to the British war effort.[10] Eire's neutrality meant that the
issue of treason was not legally relevant for those who chose to support either Britain or Germany, but the question of tacit affiliation
remained extremely sensitive throughout the duration of the war.
For Stuart, it appears to have come down to a question of support
for an imperial power against which a recent revolution (in which
he had participated) had taken place, and which still supported
what he believed to be an illegal regime in the north-eastern part of
the island; or support for those who apparently (initially, at least)
opposed the arrogance of imperialist/capitalist hegemony and the
complacency of bourgeois culture. Given a number of factors – his
political convictions, the parlous state of Eire's wartime economy,
the stalling of his literary career and the fact that the job offer had
been made *before* the commencement of hostilities – Berlin rather
than London may have appeared the obvious choice.

Point 2 raises the issue of interpersonal strife, and the extent to
which Stuart's political imagination, such as it was, may have been
an expression of a personality which had problems with affiliation
of any kind. The composite character who emerges from the fiction
is revealed as someone who is, initially at least, extremely anxious
about his relationship with 'the wife' and his responsibility towards
his children, but who learns to conduct extra-marital affairs (of
the heart and the body) without much compunction. On the other
hand, Stuart was just one of probably many people who endured
an unsuitable marriage – 'misery and torment', as Luke Cassidy

describes it in *Victors and Vanquished* (1959: 94) – in a state in which divorce was illegal; and his later life does reveal him to be capable of strong commitment and deep loyalty. In any case, to extrapolate a psychological profile based on parallels between his private, public and literary *personae* seems unwarranted here.[11]

Points 3 and 4 locate Stuart within a fairly recognisable modernist trajectory, one characterised in general terms by an anti-democratic (betimes anti-Semitic) response to the spiritual desolation of post-First World War Europe. In this respect he bears comparison with a number of disaffected individuals who found themselves – with alacrity or with dread, with greater or lesser levels of commitment – embracing authoritarianism as a response to an apparent crisis of authority (Caterson 1996: 18–19). W.B. Yeats had certainly flirted with such an attitude in the decade or so after the founding of the Free State, but had apparently seen through the myth of fascist autocracy well before Hitler's reconstitution of himself as *Führer* (Cullingford 1981: 234–5; Foster 2007: 471–3). Others, such as Ezra Pound and William Joyce, discerned a clear, obvious and attractive line running from the Battle of the Somme through the Treaty of Versailles to the Nuremberg Rallies and *Triumph of the Will* (Fuller Torrey 1984; West 1964). An international Bolshevik revolution was imminent; the West was weak and degenerate – mortgaged to the profit-seeking will of capitalists and Jewish financiers with no understanding or appreciation of *Heimat*; the next war would be between those attempting to protect their undeserved privilege (or rather those whom they could convince to protect it for them) and to reach some accommodation with the Bolsheviks, and those possessed of the energy, the courage and, most importantly, the responsibility to sweep away the old system and start again.[12]

There seems little doubt that Stuart, like many others, was attracted to at least certain elements of this reactionary vision, precisely because it appeared to address some of the anxieties that had been accruing over the course of his own life and career. It seems equally likely that such an identification was in part responsible for his decision to relocate to Germany and to provide support both tacit and practical for the Nazi regime that was in power there. At what precise point his convictions regarding Germany's mission (or indeed Hitler's radical profile) were disabused is uncertain – very soon after arrival, according to his own fictionalised accounts. But if such was the case, then a number of questions follow: why, if he had lost faith in Hitler so early, did he continue to broadcast for Irland-Redaktion until February 1944? At what point did Berlin become an imaginary locus for failure and defeat rather than aggression and victory? And, most pressingly, at what point, if any, did he become aware of the 'Final Solution'?

Whatever the answers to such questions (and the debates have been long, convoluted and rancorous), we do know that whereas some of those who assumed a similar profile to Stuart's were subsequently found to be legally traitorous (William Joyce, John Amery and Ezra Pound, for example), Stuart's nationality rendered him legally, if not necessarily morally, innocent. In some ways, one might say, Stuart coveted all the philosophical and aesthetic glamour of treason without assuming any of the legal risks attached to it as a political act.

The principal interest of point 5 is its indication of the extent to which Stuart retained an interest in the possibility of effective paramilitary intervention, and his adherence to the old republican maxim that 'Britain's difficulty is Ireland's opportunity'.[13] Stuart made much in Berlin of his IRA connections (Barrington 2000: 32–3), and spent a good deal of time with the veteran Frank Ryan, whom the Nazis had sprung from a Spanish prison in the belief that, despite his anti-fascist convictions, he could help co-ordinate a joint Nazi–IRA mission. Stuart's republicanism had always been influenced – and, in the final analysis, overridden – by his romanticism. During the revolutionary period in the earlier part of the century he had made common cause with certain marginal strands of Irish political opinion, and had indeed acted in support of those causes; but his concept of revolution was always more orientated towards the head than the state, and in the years after 1922 he had come to regard the republican leadership as fundamentally reactionary in nature (Natterstad 1974: 28). Nevertheless, like many writers during the 'low, dishonest decade' of the 1930s, Stuart was drawn towards the glamour of the gun, at least in so far as it was wielded in unpopular, renegade causes. The idea that an IRA mission constituted the *real* reason for his move to Berlin contributes to the image of Stuart as an artist who, despite his apparent disdain for the 'real' world and 'real' politics, was willing to adapt aesthetic and spiritual concerns to practical, often dangerous, action.[14]

It's really in relation to points 6 and 7 that the controversy surrounding Stuart's German sojourn has taken hold, however.

Although different in a number of respects, these points are often conflated because each appears to be an essential expression of Stuart's refractory personality, on the one hand, and of what Terry Eagleton has described as 'his hair-raising political naivety', on the other.[15] His suspicions regarding the morality of 'belonging' led him to embrace 'otherness', however constituted; equally, his suspicions regarding the immorality of 'victory' led him to embrace the 'defeated'. These narratives did not always coincide; often, indeed, they could overlap and clash. There was no talk or thought of defeat in Berlin in January 1940 when Stuart moved to the city; on the contrary, he found himself at the heart of a triumphant, expanding empire which was gearing itself up for a millennium of power. Two years later, when that same country was spiralling towards military defeat following the Battle of Stalingrad (in February 1943), Stuart's emphasis shifted accordingly. He was no longer the witness of history, but the documenter of abjection.[16]

Some have accused Stuart of casting his entire post-1940 *oeuvre* in terms of this shift. This in turn may be regarded as part of a wider strategy to redefine, in fact to reorientate to some extent, the entire Berlin episode. Certainly, in the novels which appeared after the war (including *Black List, Section H*) the emphasis is increasingly on suffering – with learning (as the elderly Jewish character Isaak from *Victors and Vanquished* says) to 'be content to be an outcast from the camp of the victors, whoever they may be' (1959: 203). Whether this artistic rationalisation absolves Stuart from either his decision to relocate to what has subsequently been identified as a morally reprehensible state, or, once there, from his support, both tacit and practical, for that state, remains the key issue.

If his nationality absolves Stuart in terms of legal, state-orientated treason, the issue of betrayal – moral, interpersonal, artistic – informs his post-war work at every level, and runs like an artery in particular through *Black List, Section H*. The aesthetic vision through which Stuart came to express his war experiences locates him within a romantic literary tradition in which authenticity and sincerity are the watchwords – a tradition in which, paradoxically, the notion of betrayal sits very uneasily.[17] Stuart's vision was indeed deeply spiritual yet fundamentally contradictory: like Jesus, the artist becomes an avatar of redemption, but like Judas he retains his essential humanity only by turning his back on all that claims his allegiance; like Christ, the artist seeks out and makes his home amongst the lost and the guilty, for it's there, paradoxically, 'in the company of the guilty' (Stuart 1971: 274), with the excluded and bereft (such as Judas) rather than with the deserving and the well-beloved, that he belongs. Jesus' revolutionary teaching is based upon the absolute necessity of suffering, but it's Judas who best exemplifies that doctrine, for he's the one who remains unredeemed. It is as a continuous exploration and expression of this dual, conflicted identity – Jesus/Judas – that Stuart's work continues to resonate.[18]

If such an aesthetic comes into focus in relation to all 'art after Auschwitz', thus rendering Stuart an exemplary post-war writer, it's also implicated in the development of the various schools of literary criticism which likewise emerged in the shadow of the 'Final Solution'. No strand of modern criticism is more addressed to that issue than the ideas and attitudes gathered together under the title of 'deconstruction', and no intellectual was more aware of the responsibilities of the critic – both in relation to the text and in relation to the communities from which texts emerge – than Jacques Derrida.

Deconstruction and betrayal

If we say that deconstruction challenges traditional modes of intellectual engagement (such as philosophy and literary criticism) by casting doubt on the integrity of the systems whereby such discourses organise knowledge and behaviour, we immediately recognise the shadowy profile of Francis Stuart. According to Derrida, the cultural traces through which we sustain our relationship with reality are all, to a greater or lesser extent, exercises in bad faith: close analysis reveals their essential incoherence and their inability to sustain the meanings they attempt to generate. As Christopher Norris writes, deconstruction consists 'not merely in *reversing* or *subverting* some established hierarchical order, but in showing how its terms are indissociably entwined in a strictly undecidable exchange of values and priorities' (1987: 56, original emphases). Which is to say: deconstruction is not something the critic does to the text, but something that the critic reveals each and every text doing to itself.

Over the course of a long career, Derrida extended the critical force of deconstruction to a wide range of practices and experiences: writing, secrecy, friendship, hospitality, giving, forgiving, mourning, dying. Without denying the evolution of deconstruction

as a critical strategy, I would argue that a constant factor throughout its history has been the drive to expose the radical uncertainty
which underpins all human attempts to formalise, articulate or
deploy knowledge. Culture (especially language) longs for identity
and closure, whereas the actual condition of human culture (and
especially language) is paradox and contingency: the text is always
haunted by that from which it tries to distinguish itself; at the same
time, the text always betrays its own ineluctable dependence on that
from which it tries to distinguish itself.

The logic of deconstruction leads us to the possibility that
betrayal may be the very condition of culture, of civilisation and of
human experience generally. Just as the traditional notions of treason and betrayal connote a duality (us *and* the other) that informs
a singularity (us), so the idea of the text, as formulated in deconstruction, connotes a duality (that which is disavowed or silenced
or marginalised) over and against a singularity (*the* text). And just
as every text – in so far as it betrays its own internal incoherence –
represents a practical demonstration of the deconstructive method,
so every text may also be regarded as in some senses an exercise in
betrayal.

We may observe the logic of betrayal in Derrida's deconstruction of a famous biblical story in *The Gift of Death* (1991a). In
Chapter 22 of Genesis, God tests Abraham by demanding that he
sacrifice his son Isaac. Father and son proceed to the appointed
place where, just as Abraham is about to slay his son, an angel of
the Lord intervenes:

> 'Do not lay a hand on the boy,' he said. 'Do not do anything to him.
> Now I know that you fear God, because you have not withheld from
> me your son, your only son.' (Genesis 22:12)

As a reward for his obedience, Abraham is promised a blessing from
God for himself and for his heirs, and dominion over his enemies.

In his analysis of this incident, Derrida begins by pointing out
the paradox of the situation in which Abraham is placed by God's
demand:

> If I put to death or grant death to what I hate it is not a sacrifice. I
> must sacrifice what I love. I must hate and betray my own, that is to
> say offer them the gift of death by means of the sacrifice, not insofar
> as I hate them, that would be too easy, but insofar as I love them.
> I must hate them insofar as I love them. Hate wouldn't be hate if

it only hated the hateful, that would be too easy. It must hate and betray what is most lovable. Hate cannot be hate, it can only be the sacrifice of love to love. It is not a matter of hating, betraying by one's breach of trust, or offering the gift of death to what one doesn't love. (1991a: 64)

This is the quintessential Derridean *aporia*: the idea of sacrifice connotes the value of that which is to be sacrificed, and also that in the name of which the sacrifice is to be undertaken. The loved one is betrayed in the name of another love, but he has to be truly loved in order for the betrayal to be meaningful. Such a view resonates clearly with one of the principal features of betrayal emphasised throughout this study: namely, that *true* betrayal (a striking Derridean phrase, if ever there was one) connotes a complex matrix in which a range of competing desires constantly circulate – something observed clearly in Part I when considering various religious, psychoanalytical and literary discourses of betrayal.

Abraham's sacrifice of Isaac eventually emerges as a tension between two forms of duty: one, to God, and another, to his son. Abraham cannot negate one without betraying the other: if he *doesn't* love Isaac absolutely, then the sacrifice of his son to God is meaningless; if he *doesn't* sacrifice Isaac, then his love for God is imperfect, mitigated, treacherous:

> Absolute duty demands that one behave in an irresponsible manner (by means of treachery or betrayal), while still recognizing, confirming, and reaffirming the very thing one sacrifices, namely, the order of human ethics and responsibility. In a word, ethics must be sacrificed in the name of duty. It is a duty not to respect, out of duty, ethical duty. (1991a: 67)

From Derrida's perspective, God's demand that Abraham render to Him 'the gift of death' represents an exemplary form of the paradox of responsibility. Intriguingly, 'the gift of death' is an idea explored by Francis Stuart in *Victors and Vanquished*, a novel that operates in many ways as a kind of trial run for *Black List, Section H*. In the earlier novel, an Irish poet named Luke Cassidy travels to Berlin during the early months of the Second World War, ostensibly to take up a teaching post at the university, but with the ulterior motive of resuming acquaintance with a Jewish nurse whom he had met during an earlier visit.[19] Once in the city Luke develops a relationship with Myra and with her elderly father, named Isaak.

The Irishman tries to protect his Jewish friends from the increasing threat of the Nazi state, but as conditions degenerate and danger grows, Isaak recognises that his capture is imminent. Myra reports a conversation:

> 'I've been worried lately because of some strange things Papa's been saying,' she told Luke. 'The other day, I forget how we got on to the subject, he said: "I gave you the gift of life, Myrele, and it's a great gift; I'm still learning how great it is. But there's a greater one, and that's death" ... "The gift of death, as you call it, is something anyone can give," I told him. Any of those brutes of Gestapo can bestow it right and left. "Oh no, they can't," Papa said, "no more than life is given by an act of rape. No more than the gift you get from a loved one far away has to do with the delivery van that brings it to your door."' (1959: 216–17)

Soon after, Isaak is arrested and features no more in the remainder of the story. It's clear, however, that his moral presence remains the single most powerful factor in the lives of Luke and Myra; and the enigmatic 'gift of death' that he describes to his daughter before his disappearance comes to feature as the moral centre of Luke's vision. But what does it mean? What kind of distinction does Isaak draw in the conversation reported above between the violent act or weapon that 'delivers' the death and the intention informing the death?

The narrative inference is that Isaak has made a sacrifice by allowing himself to be arrested, so that Luke and Myra – who would never desert him while he lives – may escape. He makes them a gift of his own death so that their love may survive. Stuart's 'Isaak' corresponds to Derrida's 'Isaac' in so far as each represents an implicit moral value that must be sacrificed in the name of duty – duty towards God in the case of the biblical figure, duty towards love and survival in Stuart's character. Where they differ is in respect of 'the gift of death': for whereas the biblical Isaac is to be the recipient of that 'gift' (from his loving father Abraham, in the name of God), Stuart's Isaak is himself the giver (to the Nazis, in the name of Luke and Myra). Isaac survives, Isaak does not.

The story of Isaac is one of the complex morality of sacrifice, and the undecidable temporality of love and hate that such a concept embodies; the story of Isaak rehearses that morality, the difference being that the loved one to be sacrificed in this instance is the self. Abraham found himself in an impossible position, caught between duty and responsibility, and bound to betray one or the other no matter what he did; Isaak 'betrayed' himself by voluntarily giving up his own life so that his loved ones could escape and survive.

Throughout the latter part of his career, Stuart was drawn to the kind of power that he imagined in relation to Isaak's gift. That power derived from the old Jew's abject condition, and from his status as absolute Other trapped within a historical regime that demonised and persecuted Otherness to the extreme.[20] If such regimes provide an acutely sensitive testing ground for aesthetic theories such as Stuart's, they serve a similar function for critical-philosophical theories such as Derrida's; each, in some sense, found their major themes in the moral issues raised by Nazism. Nowhere have those issues been addressed more spectacularly during the modern era than in the controversies attending the work of the critic Paul de Man.[21]

Paul de Man and collaboration

Paul de Man moved to the United States after the Second World War in order to undertake doctoral research at Harvard University. Thereafter he taught at a number of prestigious institutions in America and Europe, before taking a chair as Sterling Professor of the Humanities at Yale University. In later years de Man became one of the leading figures in what was known in academic circles as the 'Yale School'. A close personal friend of Jacques Derrida, he advocated and practised a form of literary criticism which accorded in certain fundamental aspects with Derridean deconstruction. This profile proved both influential and controversial in the highly competitive world of American academia, where certain forms of ideological criticism – strongly opposed to what was widely regarded as the 'nihilism' of deconstruction – retained a potent presence.

After his death from cancer in 1983, information regarding de Man's wartime activities in his native Belgium began to emerge.[22] It seems that after the German military victory over Belgium in May 1940 (just as Francis Stuart was settling into life in Berlin), the young de Man accepted a position as literary columnist for an important Brussels newspaper, *Le Soir*, which had come under the editorial influence of the occupying Nazi power. Over the course of the next year (December 1940 to November 1941) de Man wrote 170 pieces for *Le Soir*, for which activities he was identified by various contemporary resistance initiatives as a 'collaborator'. One article, entitled 'Jews in Contemporary Literature' (published 4 March 1941), attracted special attention for what many regarded as its explicit anti-Semitic content.

The story was major news in the United States and Europe, and a wide-ranging, bitter controversy soon developed. One crucial aspect of this controversy concerned the establishment and interpretation of the evidence pertaining to de Man's activities. What were the personal and political circumstances in which he had undertaken and made his contributions? What did he actually write? Were there mitigating circumstances or activities – at the time or subsequently – which belied the appearance of collaboration?

But what, returning to a question posed earlier in relation to Stuart, does one do with facts? Like literary texts, one interprets them; and this 'fact' allowed for the activation of another element to the controversy – one linked to de Man's profile as a professional and highly influential interpreter of texts. Of special interest for our concerns here is the extent to which de Man's intellectual profile became implicated in the controversy, and in particular how his association with Derrida and deconstruction was adduced as evidence within his public media trial. The 'De Man Case' came to feature as a battle within a much longer war, the stakes of which were nothing less than the soul of humanity itself.

Derrida himself waded into the controversy in muscular (if characteristically obtuse) fashion, arguing in detail and at length that while de Man's contributions to *Le Soir* were certainly culpable, the terms within which any indictment could be made were themselves compromised:

> To judge, to condemn the work or the man on the basis of what was a brief episode, to call for closing, that is to say, at least figuratively, for censuring or burning his books is to reproduce the exterminating gesture against which one accuses de Man of not having armed himself sooner with the necessary vigilance. (1988: 651)

For Derrida, de Man's discourse was enigmatic, conflicted, disjointed, but never less than fully responsible. A deconstructionist *avant la lettre*, 'all [his] propositions carry within themselves a counterproposition: sometimes virtual, sometimes very explicit, always readable' (135). To read de Man's war-time journalism retrospectively, from the perspective of the victors, was to miss (or to misconstrue) the contingency of his response to the apparent certainty of continued German hegemony.

The historian Jon Wiener, however, was particularly offended at what he regarded to be Derrida's implication of a 'rhetorical connection between criticism of de Man and extermination of the Jews' (1989: 798). For those whose emphasis tended towards the 'evidence' rather than *interpretation* of the evidence, Wiener's characterisation of Derrida's defence remained the last word:

> The conclusion one is left with is that what de Man did – collaborate with the Nazi occupiers of Belgium – should be understood and forgiven, but what de Man's critics have done – commit 'reading mistakes' … should be condemned as unforgivable. (803)

Wiener's argument was lambasted in turn by another high-profile American critic, J. Hillis Miller, who described Wiener's intervention as 'one of the most misinformed, distorted, and irresponsible of all the journalistic essays I have seen on this subject' (1989: 334). Hillis Miller identified the antipathy against deconstruction in American academia as the chief motivating factor in the attacks on de Man:

> The violence is a reaction to the genuine threat posed by de Man's work and by that of the so-called deconstructionists generally to a powerful tradition of ideological assumptions about literature, about history, and about the relation of literature to human life. Fear of this power in 'deconstruction' and in contemporary theory generally, in all its diversity, accounts better than any other explanation for the unreasoning hostility, the abandoning of the canons of journalistic and academic responsibility, in articles like yours and the many other subsequent attacks on de Man, on 'deconstruction', and on critical theory as such. (342)

All this represented a very public washing of academia's dirty linen, giving the lie to the image of salubrious, edifying cultural pursuits underpinned by disinterested research. In some ways, this was exactly the point: literary criticism was – and always had been, despite claims to the contrary – thoroughly political, thoroughly enmeshed in the history of its own making. This represented a classic Derridean paradox, in so far as the case against de Man was being conducted on political grounds, in large part by those who opposed the notion of criticism as a political practice: what was being disavowed on the one hand was being recouped and revalidated on the other.

Those looking for evidence of de Man's aptitude for betrayal could find it amongst his extensive critical writings – an aptitude which, it could be further claimed, constituted the basis for his resonance with Derridean deconstruction. In 'Criticism and Crisis', the opening essay to his seminal *Blindness and Insight* (1983), for example, de Man argued:

> In the act of anthropological intersubjective interpretation, a fundamental discrepancy always prevents the observer from coinciding fully with the consciousness he is observing. The same discrepancy exists in everyday language, in the impossibility of making the actual expression coincide with what has to be expressed, of making the actual sign coincide with what it signifies. It is the distinctive privilege of language to be able to *hide meaning behind a misleading sign, as when we hide rage or hatred behind a smile.* But it is the distinctive curse of all language, as soon as any kind of interpersonal relation is involved, that it is forced to act this way. The simplest of wishes cannot express itself without hiding behind a screen of language that constitutes a world of intricate intersubjective relationships, all of them potentially inauthentic. (11, emphasis added)

All this talk of a lack of coincidence between sign and signified, of meaning hiding behind a misleading sign, of the discrepancy between appearance and reality, of the subject hiding behind a screen of language, and of the fundamental inauthenticity of expression – all this was grist to the prosecution's mill. In these terms, the deconstructionist is reminiscent of what Margret Boveri described as the traitor's 'controlled schizophrenia' (1956: 57). There was a direct connection, in other words, between de Man's behaviour and his critical method: the philosophical scepticism of the latter was of a piece with the political duplicities of the former. And how, or why, should anyone afford the benefit of the doubt to someone who insisted on the absolute centrality of betrayal to human experience?

Clearly, the cases of Paul de Man and Francis Stuart differ in a number of respects: the former was a young critic at the outset of his career, a member of a defeated, occupied nation; the latter was a mature writer who, despite living in, and working for, Nazi Germany, remained officially neutral throughout the war. The one subsequently disavowed any connection with a force that history has confirmed as morally repugnant, the other remained more evasive, his preferred tactic, whenever the issue was raised, being to question the grounds upon which such a question could be posed. The one longed for, and eventually achieved, institutional recognition; the other, cherishing his renegade status, disdained all institutions as categorically corrupt.

Despite this, I would argue that the profiles of the two men resonate on a number of levels, the most obvious of which is the extent to
which each becomes a kind of arena wherein a series of fundamental
questions relating to history and human experience may be posed.
These questions encompass issues of culture, language, desire, truth,
power, authenticity; ultimately, they address the question of meaning itself – what it means 'to mean', and who has the right to define
that verb. It's in the critical and political activities surrounding their
work, as much as in the work itself, that the 'meaning' of each career continues to be contested. The extremely troubled spectre of
collaboration continues to haunt each figure, and is likely to continue to do so, for it's in the nature of such a concept, with its over-
tones of conspiracy and duplicity, to endure.

Conclusion

Even if one rejects Brendan Barrington's thesis that Stuart's profile
is a self-generated fiction – one that masks a more interventionist
and proactive, and thus potentially culpable, history – the profile
which has come to dominate is in itself compromised in a number
of ways. Stuart's reputation in the latter part of his life was that of
the great nay-sayer, a holy fool and romantic outcast, a recalcitrant
artist who calmly but deliberately sets himself at odds with the prevailing consensus – as he writes in *Black List, Section H*: 'the only
side to take was always the one considered most unpardonable
by the circle in which he found himself' (206). Stuart is the traitor who disavows the concept of treason, even as he embraces the
experiences – such as guilt, shame and abjection – that have been
traditionally attached to such a concept. There has been speculation as to an apparently pathological compulsion 'to betray and
be seen to betray' (Tóibín 2001: 6), and a deep desire, born of
background and breeding, for stigmatisation.[23] The image that has
emerged from his post-war work is summed up by the historian
J.J. Lee in his Foreword to David O'Donoghue's account of Irland-
Redaktion:

> [Stuart's] politics seem to have had little to do with Nazism itself,
> and much more with a type of tormented personality searching for
> some unattainable ideal of a humankind purged of the contamin-
> ating influence of materialistic liberalism through purification by
> suffering. (1998: x)

For some, this is the profile of a true artist, one who refused to com-
promise – or to betray – his art (Natterstad 1974: 85; also Murphy
2004: 266). Such art is 'minor' in so far as it exposes the claims
to universality implicit in mainstream dissenting literature (such
as that of the 'major' writer James Joyce) – as Richard T. Murphy
puts it: 'H's messianic pursuit of the authenticity only degradation
and guilt can guarantee drives him on a crusade to tear down all
conventions, including ultimately those of the *Bildungsroman* form
itself' (2004: 262).

For others, there remains something deeply disturbing about a
man who used history's greatest conflagration as little more than a
backdrop against which to play out the drama of his own artistic
life – as Terry Eagleton has written: 'There is a fine line between
solidarity with the suffering, and a daredevil bohemianism which is
allured by "extreme" conditions regardless of their moral content'
(1998: 245).

Along with the narcissistic and solipsistic tendencies, the Christ-
complex and the almost complete lack of humour throughout the
entire *oeuvre*, there strikes me as something fundamentally adolescent about Stuart's work. In *Black List, Section H*, the narrator's
personality is (as observed above) initially established in terms of
a blow against his family; his activities throughout the remainder
of the book – including his German adventure – may be regarded
as nothing more than an elaboration of this compulsion to annoy
the significant authority figures in his life, whether they manifest in
the form of family, state, society, moral consensus or aesthetic doctrine. Adolescent also is the insistence on the moral precedence of
absolute sincerity in art, when the artist should be the first one to
acknowledge that all art is necessarily partial – the willed product
of a calculating imagination rather than a spontaneous response to
existential phenomena.[24]

Stuart remains a compelling figure less for his writing than for
his personification of a fundamental crisis which underpins human
experience: the temptation to betray versus the desire for truth. The
agency of the traitor is opposed to the anxiety of the truth-seeker;
at the same time, they are ineluctably linked inasmuch as each is
determined by our experience as language-using subjects. Despite
his deficiencies *qua* writer, Stuart's embodiment of this crisis renders
him in some senses *the* emblematic Irish writer of the later twentieth century.

7

'Cangled both to treachery': Eugene McCabe's *Death and Nightingales* (1992)

And now they intend
To set up The Hot Pursuit Of Judas Zone
For ten miles on either side of the border

Dividing me from my redeemer; but the bond
Between that man and me will go on and on
Despite church, state, stories of betrayal and murder.
                                                Brendan Kennelly, *The*
                                        Little Book of Judas, 61

Introduction

A range of circumstances contrived to position Northern Ireland at the centre of Irish political history in the latter part of the twentieth century; those same circumstances ensured that the issue of betrayal would feature time and again as a crucial trope in discursive engagements with that part of the island.

Eugene McCabe's first (and to date only) novel represents one such engagement. Set on a farm on the shore of Lower Lough Erne in Co. Fermanagh in May 1883, *Death and Nightingales* is a story in which political betrayal is shadowed and to an extent mirrored by interpersonal treachery. This is a novel in which characters betray themselves and one another throughout; at the same time, each character is aware, to a greater or lesser extent, of inhabiting a political landscape in which the idea of betrayal – both historical and contemporary – features powerfully. One of the things Eugene McCabe looks to explore in this book (as indeed in all his writing) is the relationship between these two levels of experience.[1]

In relating such a story, the author engages with a range of literary traditions – some of which are explicitly focused on the local context (which is to say, the roots and the dynamics of conflict in the north-east of Ireland), some of which have their bases in other, more wide-ranging traditions. The most obvious indication of the latter is the title's reference to the tradition of romantic poetry encapsulated in John Keats's 'Ode to a Nightingale' (1819); but other texts and other traditions proliferate throughout the text, and in the central section of this chapter I wish to describe points of intersection between some of these influences and an indigenous tradition of Northern Irish fiction. I want to suggest that it's in relation to the tradition of gothic, and in particular that tradition's heavy reliance on images of treachery, that such a relationship comes into focus in this instance.

Death and Nightingales is a historical novel in which the writer turns to the past in an attempt to understand the present. Like any such text the analytical emphasis tends to oscillate between two contexts or moments: the one in which it's set – in this case the 1880s, the period of the Land War and the rise to political prominence of Charles Stewart Parnell; and the one in which it's written – the late 1980s and early 1990s, a particularly bleak period of the 'Troubles' preceding the Provisional IRA ceasefire of 1994. In the first and final parts of this chapter I shall consider the political dimensions of these two moments, focusing in particular on three defining events: the Phoenix Park murders of 6 May 1882, the Maamtrasna murders of 17/18 August 1882 and the Enniskillen 'Poppy Day' bombing of 8 November 1987. While the first features explicitly within McCabe's novel, the latter, I shall argue, represents the determining moral context within which the text was conceived and written – in particular, for the images of betrayal and tragedy invoked throughout the novel.

Land wars

Death and Nightingales is set in May 1883 on a medium-sized estate named Clonoula near Lower Lough Erne in Co. Fermanagh.[2] The estate is owned by a Protestant named Billy Winters, whose ancestors took possession of the land in 1610 from the Gaelic Maguire family through the legal process known as 'escheatment'. In a secret service report quoted at length in the text, Billy is described as a

> Petty landlord. Church of Ireland. Old-fashioned Butt-type Unionist. Not a member of the Land League. Parnell stayed with him Feb. '83. Prone to drinking bouts. Fluent Irish. Attends Catholic funerals.

Station masses at the house. Widower. Employees and tenants half
R.C., half Protestant. Only daughter R.C. Well got with Catholic and
dissenting clergy. (99)

Twenty-five years prior to the commencement of the narrative,
Billy (which is of course a heavily freighted name in the context of
Irish history) married a Catholic woman named Catherine Maguire
(descended, she believes, from the local pre-Plantation aristocracy),
only to discover after the wedding that she is already pregnant.
Despite his continued love for her, Billy is deeply aggrieved; their
subsequent relationship is fraught with bitter resentment, some of
it sectarian and violent in nature. Billy feels he has been a fool twice
over – once for marrying outside his tribe, and once again for taking a cuckoo into his nest. Eleven years later, Catherine – pregnant
with Billy's child – is killed in an accident with a rogue bull which
is part of her dowry. After time spent in Italy, her daughter Beth
(who is nominally a Catholic) returns to live at Clonoula, where
she endures an uncomfortable relationship with her 'father'. Billy
resents her presence as a constant reminder of Catherine's deception – she is a 'living portrait of treachery' (42); at the same time he
feels attracted to her precisely because she is her 'mother's daughter'
(174).

As the narrative commences, Beth is planning her elopement with
Liam Ward, one of the estate's Catholic tenants. Liam has also spent
time abroad – in England and in the United States; we also discover
that he has been involved in some way with the Invincibles – the
splinter Fenian group responsible for the brutal murders of two
important colonial administrators in Dublin's Phoenix Park on 6
May 1882. We learn further that Liam has absconded with funds
belonging to the organisation and is being hunted by both his
former colleagues and by the state's secret police. Beth discerns a
hint of 'mongrel treachery' (75) in him, but is attracted nonetheless.
Having become Beth's lover, and having learned from her of a gold
hoard kept by Billy Winters in the safe at Clonoula, Liam persuades
her to steal the money and elope with him to America.

On the night of their departure, Beth goes to meet her lover
with the gold but is intercepted by a local beggar named Dummy
McGonnell, who warns her that Liam and another of Billy's tenants – Blinky Blessing – are planning to murder her with a spiked
hammer, with the intention, she presumes, of burying her and steal-
ing the gold. Beth is badly beaten by Billy when he comes upon her

returning his treasure. Desirous of revenge on her deceitful lover, she goes to Ward's house, where she reveals that she is pregnant with his baby. Liam offers to row her to an island in the lake where she can wait while they decide what to do; instead, knowing that he cannot swim, she sinks the boat and swims to safety on Corvey Island, an ancestral holding of her mother's family. There she is found by Billy, who suggests that they marry and leave. The novel ends ambiguously, as Beth replies to Billy's inquiry as to whether she is sick: 'Unto death, Mr Winters ... unto death' (231).

McCabe first encountered the story upon which his celebrated novel is based from a farming friend in Monaghan. In an interview, he said:

> I was more than fascinated by details, by the gross betrayal at the heart of this unlikely tale. Clearly betrayal, and its devastating effect, is the major theme in the novel.[3]

As he makes clear, this story of violence and interpersonal betrayal is set against a wider socio-political situation characterised by pervasive levels of violence.[4] Two incidents from 1882 encapsulate this situation: the Phoenix Park murders in May, and the Maamtrasna murders in August. The first, as mentioned above, is explicitly invoked in *Death and Nightingales*, and it speaks to the emphasis which the struggle for Irish independence had taken at this point in history, and also to the pervasive atmosphere of treachery which accompanied that struggle.

The launching of the Land League by Michael Davitt in 1879 marked the point at which the movements towards political independence and a modernised system of land use coalesced, at least temporarily. The 'New Departure' of June 1879 represented a tactical alliance between physical-force separatists and constitutional reformers – the first embodied in the Irish Republican Brotherhood and the Fenians, the second in the Irish Parliamentary Party led by the charismatic landlord turned politician Charles Stewart Parnell. 'For the first time since the 1790s', as one historian writes, 'large sections of the Irish people were drawn into a campaign which had revolutionary aims, was well organised and vigorously led, and which involved every county in the land' (Campbell 1991: 282). Soon, calls for the Three Fs – fixity of tenure, free sale and fair rents – would echo from platforms across the island, as well as up and down the corridors of Westminster.

It was in his role of chairman of the Land League that Parnell travelled the country encouraging Irish people of different religious and political persuasions to acknowledge, and thereafter to resist, the evils of landlordism. The first Land League meeting held in Ulster was at Belcoo, Co. Fermanagh, in December 1879. Parnell himself launched the formal opening of the campaign in Ulster at Belleek in the same county in November 1880 (Campbell 1991: 283). Although the Land War was effectively over by the winter of 1882, it's presumably after one of these meetings – in February 1883, according to the fictional secret service report included in the novel (99) – that he is a guest of the Winters family at Clonoula.

Agrarian agitation registered strongly amongst the Protestant tenant class in Ulster; '[in] no county in Ulster', moreover, 'did the Irish National Land League have a greater impact on landlord–tenant relations that in Fermanagh'.[5] Although the Orange Order maintained a strong presence throughout the county, so also did memories of the Great Famine, in which many poor Protestant tenant farmers and labourers had suffered alongside their fellow Catholics (Crawford 2004). The 1870s was a poor agricultural decade (Thompson 2004: 288) – not on the disastrous scale of the 1840s, but enough to alarm many, including those amongst the dissenting community, who had always endured a less favourable relationship with the state compared with their orthodox kin, and who had a tradition (most fully articulated in the rebellion of 1798) of active resistance. Parnell himself was a Protestant, as were some of the principal figures associated with the league, such as the Ulsterman Joseph Gillis Biggar. Within months of Parnell's claim (at Belleek in November 1880) that 'the land movement is not a sectarian movement' (quoted in Campbell 1991: 288), 'every part of Fermanagh had been penetrated by the movement, and both Catholic and Protestant farmers were flocking to its meetings' (Thompson 2004: 287). By the beginning of 1881 the land issue was at the top of the political agenda in the county, with Dublin Castle working on information that significant numbers of Protestants – including some Orangemen – had joined the Land League.

This was the context within which the Invincibles emerged – a loose affiliation of Fenians and fellow travellers from the Dublin area whose currency was violence, and who, in opposition to the spirit of the New Departure, took it upon themselves to undertake a memorable blow for Irish independence. The ferocity of the attack upon the new Chief Secretary, Lord Frederick Cavendish, and Thomas Henry Burke, head of the Irish Civil Service, as they strolled through Phoenix Park on the evening of 6 May 1882 shocked even republican hardliners. In truth, the murders represented an exacerbation of contemporary violence rather than something completely untoward or unexpected; it was the transposition of that violence into an urban milieu, and the relative social and political status of the victims, that caused alarm. But if the deed itself revealed the extent to which violence was (and had always been) embedded within the colonial relationship, the fallout was a clear demonstration of the ways in which a context of inequality, secrecy and discontent functioned as a breeding ground for treachery.

The Invincibles case threw up a spectacular instance of Irish betrayal in the form of James Carey, a prominent Fenian of long standing and one of the founding members of the group, who had fallen under suspicion because of his access to surgical instruments (of the kind believed to have been used in the slaying) in Dublin's School of Medicine.[6] Under prolonged pressure from the chief investigating officer, John Mallon, Carey agreed to inform on his colleagues, and on 17 February 1883 testified in a public court as to the planning and execution of the crime. It was on the basis of his evidence that five men were hanged during May and June of that year. The first to die – Joe Brady – went to the scaffold on 14 May, ten days after the death by drowning of his fictional fellow conspirator Liam Ward.[7]

Amongst other things, Carey's treachery threatened to undermine the non-sectarian profile of the Land League so assiduously developed over the previous three years. Ulster Protestant support for the League had already been undermined by Prime Minister Gladstone's Land Bill of August 1881, which seemed to address many of the grievances which had stimulated that support in the first instance (Thompson 2004: 298). There was in fact enough peripheral Land League activity surrounding the Invincibles to arouse suspicion – in particular, the suspicion that land agitation was merely a front behind which stalked what was to many in Ulster the ghastly spectre of Home Rule.[8] Protestant support for the Three Fs could only extend so far: when push came to shove, it seemed, religion would always replace class as the determining factor in the North's political climate.

Despite a degree of confusion surrounding the extent of his information and his motivation for testifying, Carey was vilified far and wide. As an editorial in the *Freeman's Journal* of 19 April 1883 put it:

> It is impossible for human power to add one hideous feature to the foul thing he is. He sinks into an abyss of infamy, in comparison to which the pit into which the other conspirators are buried in a pinnacle. (quoted in Molony 2006: 207)

Whatever his own understanding of the role he played in the perpetration of the outrage and its subsequent exposure, 'traitor' was the word echoing in Carey's ears as he set sail for South Africa with his family in July 1883.[9] On the 29th, on board a ship named the *Melrose* twelve miles off Cape Town, Carey was shot dead by an Irish-American named Patrick O'Donnell. There was rejoicing in Ireland at the demise of a much-hated figure; bonfires were lit and effigies were burnt. The fact that O'Donnell (who was hanged for the deed in London's Newgate prison on 17 December 1883) was not a Fenian agent, and that the murder was opportunistic rather than calculated, did not dissuade contemporary opinion as to the long arm of the Irish secret societies. The message – that treachery would be met with vengeance – seemed clear enough: and it's a message that the fictional character Liam Ward understands well.

The Invincibles conspiracy spread far and wide throughout contemporary Irish society, and Carey was only the most prominent and most damaging of a series of informers who were willing to turn Queen's evidence when the chips were down.[10] Dublin Castle ran its own sophisticated system of spies and informants, many of whom were implicated in the case to some degree. It's not unlikely that a figure such as Liam Ward – with his intelligence, his international experience and his resentment at what fate and circumstances had vouchsafed him – should be involved in such a movement, nor that, in the context of violence and treachery within which such a movement emerged, he should be willing to extort money from that organisation. Neither is it at all unlikely that, having been discovered and threatened by his former comrades, he should look to exploit the opportunity provided him by Beth Winters' infatuation, or Billy Winters' gold.

As Superintendent Mallon was hunting the Invincibles through the streets of Dublin, another shocking case came along to rock

Irish (and British) society: the murder (on 17/18 August 1882) of five people, members of the Joyce family – husband, wife and three children – at their home in an isolated townland named Maamtrasna in Connemara. The motive for the attack remains shrouded in the complexities of local agrarian politics; certainly, issues of betrayal were prominent, although given the number, the kind and the highly fluid nature of local affiliations, as well as the fact that most of those originally involved spoke Gaelic, the issue of who betrayed whom remains elusive (Waldron 1992).

Violence was an undeniable fact of agrarian life in Ireland, and had been at least since the late seventeenth century. Violence and secrecy represented traditional forms of resistance to an unsatisfactory condition which was itself subject to different emphases in different contexts – religion, nationality, land ownership and, as occurred in the Maamtrasna case, family. The number of violent incidents had been on the rise throughout Ireland since the advent of the Land War in 1879, especially in the western counties of Mayo and Galway. Rents were being withheld, landlords and their collaborators were being boycotted, attempted coercion was being met with violence: the west was a powder keg of atavistic resentment and entrenched prejudice. A number of high-profile cases (the murders of Lords Leitrim and Mountmorres, and the infamous Boycott situation) seemed to confirm British opinion regarding 'natural' Irish proclivities towards rebellion and violence.

The Maamtrasna murders were initially processed in these terms, with *The Times* editorialising two days after the events:

> No ingenuity can exaggerate the brutal ferocity of a crime which spared neither the grey hairs of an aged woman nor the innocent child of 12 years who slept beside her. It is an outburst of unredeemed and inexplicable savagery before which one stands appalled, and oppressed with a painful sense of the failure of our vaunted civilisation.[11]

Soon, however, the case became political: the image of Irish-speaking peasants at the mercy of anglophone justice fed nationalist rhetoric regarding the failed marriage of two civilisations, while the conviction and botched execution (on 15 December 1882) of one man in particular – the patriarch Myles Joyce, widely believed throughout Ireland to be innocent – was an acute embarrassment to English liberal opinion, eventually (on 17 July 1885) becoming the subject of a debate in the House of Commons.[12]

The Maamtrasna case broke when the English novelist Anthony Trollope was in Ireland researching material for his latest (and, as it turned out, last and unfinished) novel *The Landleaguers*.[13] In the context of a story dedicated to exposing the basic soundness of the landlord system and the irrationality of its opponents, the horror of the incident was a gift, and the ageing, reactionary Trollope made the most of it. *The Landleaguers* details the trials and tribulations of a boycotted estate on the shores of Lough Corrib in Co. Galway, and the breakdown of law and order in the context of the Land War. The perpetrators of the Maamtrasna outrage (although it's not explicitly identified) are sarcastically described as members of an aspiring 'aristocracy' looking to replace the incumbent class: in reality they are ruffians and miscreants, bereft of humanity or honesty. 'Think of the country we are living in now!' says the heroic enforcer Captain Yorke Clayton to Frank, the eldest son of the Big House:

> 'Think of your father's condition, and of the injury which has been done to him and to your sisters, and to yourself. If that could be prevented and atoned for, and set right by the hanging in one row of ten such miscreants as those, would it not be a noble deed done?' (Trollope 1883: 397)

Interestingly, Trollope invokes the discourse of betrayal in his description of the Maamtrasna murderers:

> And thus they came together, dreading each other, hating each other at last; each aware that he was about to put his very life within the other's power, and each trying to think, as far as thoughts would come to his dim mind, that to him might come some possibility of escape by betraying his comrades. (396)

Conspiracy is a toxic brew, the narrative implies, composed of hatred, ignorance and certain betrayal. This, for Trollope, is Ireland's tragedy – that the context of conflict engineered by a few ensures the inevitability of betrayal as an issue for the many. In such a case it became necessary to differentiate between different kinds of betrayal; it's interesting in this regard to observe the manner in which the English novelist configures the contemporary Irish land crisis in terms of a discourse of betrayal – or more precisely, in terms of a discourse of duty which determines the way in which information is ordered in this society. The apostate Flory is 'a traitor to [his] father' (108) because he has converted to Catholicism, and because he refuses to divulge the name of the tenant who has sabotaged his father's land; Terry Carroll is considered a 'traitor' (264) by his own people (that is, the Catholic tenant class) because he offers to give evidence against his own brother, the suspected saboteur. Each character pays for the act of betrayal with his life. Whereas the first description is clearly 'correct' within the moral economy of the story, the second – focalised from the perspective of the agitators – is 'incorrect', because Terry Carroll's information is orientated towards the restoration of the established order. If Flory is a 'bad' traitor, Terry is a 'good' one, and the novel offers the reader a position from which to identify and position themselves in relation to these values.

Literary contexts

Eugene McCabe has spent the greater part of his life running a farm in Co. Monaghan (traditionally part of the province of Ulster), near the border with Co. Fermanagh in Northern Ireland. He is what another Monaghan writer-farmer, Patrick Kavanagh, described as a 'parochial' (as opposed to a 'provincial') writer, in so far as his imagination is founded on a thorough knowledge of the ways in which humans inhabit a particular local landscape – in this case, one that is historically and geographically contested.[14] At the same time, McCabe is a highly allusive writer, alert to the intertextual ties that link his stories to a range of other stories and other perspectives. For any writer during the 'Troubles' to tell any story about the conflict was to engage with a discourse freighted with a range of formal and conceptual concerns: *how* the story may be told, *where* and *when* it may be set, *how* the reality of sectarian conflict may be imagined and resolved, and so on.

One obvious strategy deployed in *Death and Nightingales* is the introduction of a historical perspective: the story is set in 1883, over a century before it was written. This distances the text from a strand of fiction (including some of McCabe's own[15]) which attempts to describe the 'Troubles' in terms of an overwhelmingly urgent present – a present that, because of its constant state of potential eruption, appears to demand attention (artistic as well as political). Instead, McCabe parachutes the reader into a historical setting in which sectarianism is already well established, which is itself undergoing a profound crisis (the Land War of the early 1880s

and the advance of Home Rule politics) and in which violence has
re-emerged as a significant presence within the community. The
similarities with the 1980s are clear, and it's in this sense that a
character such as Liam Ward bears comparison with the 'gangsters and guerrillas' of the typical late twentieth-century 'Troubles
thriller' (Magee 2001; Smyth 1998: 113–43). By introducing the
element of historical perspective, however, McCabe defamiliarises
those discourses and obliges the reader to engage with their contin-
gent, material nature. There's nothing natural or inevitable about
conflict: things are the way they are, the text implies, because of
specific decisions and developments in the past. For McCabe to
write a historical novel about Ulster at this stage in the history of
the 'Troubles' was to insist upon the possibility of 'change' and 'perspective' as significant forces within the discursive economy of contemporary Northern Ireland.

I've already mentioned *The Landleaguers* as a text with which
McCabe's novel is, if only implicitly, in conversation; but there are
a range of other literary presences discernible throughout the text.
The opening scene, for example, sees the character of Beth Winters
coming to the aid of a cow suffering from 'bloat': in the absence
of her 'father' Billy (he's abed recovering from the previous night's
drunkenness) and the other male farm hands, she saves the animal
by driving a 'cannula – a hollow pointed instrument with a clear-
ing plunger' (3) – into its stomach, thereby allowing the trapped
gas to escape. This scene operates on a number of levels. For one
thing, it establishes the novel's deployment of a complex system of
animal symbolism, appropriate to the author's penchant for agricultural settings (Pelaschiar 1998: 84). For another, it foreshadows
the aborted murder scene towards the end of the novel, in which
Beth herself is intended to be a dumb, helpless animal subject to
the penetrative violence of Liam Ward and Blinky Blessing. Rather
less obviously, perhaps, the scene also recalls a similar one from a
famous English novel published a few years before the period in
which the action of *Death and Nightingales* takes place. In Thomas
Hardy's *Far from the Madding Crowd* (1874), Bathsheba Everdene,
another woman of independent mind and complicated social standing, comes to the rescue of a herd of bloated cattle – although in
this case she is obliged to rely on the expertise of the impoverished
shepherd Gabriel Oak. Hardy is not mentioned in McCabe's novel;
given Beth's expansive literary imagination, however, and her sense

of herself as a farming woman (like Bathsheba) subject to the attention of a range of potential lovers, it's not an inappropriate reference.

Back across the sea, meanwhile, Irish writers had been attempting to engage with various national 'troubles' (as opposed to 'Troubles') for at least two centuries before the publication of McCabe's novel. Approaching the period in question, writers such as Samuel Lover and Charles Lever dealt – in various forms, to various ends – with Irish matters. The latter's *Lord Kilgobbin* (1872) tackled the issue of Ireland's political status head-on; it's no surprise, therefore, to find that treason and betrayal feature strongly in the plot. The following year, the Fenian Charles Kickham turned his attention to the rotten land system in his novel *Knocknagow, or the Homes of Tipperary* (1879). At the heart of Kickham's episodic text is the fundamental betrayal of traditional Irish culture by an array of hostile alien forces, of which landlordism is the most potent. Amongst other things, *Knocknagow* underscores the growing importance of the land question during the 1870s, before it exploded onto the national stage with the foundation of the National Land League in October 1879.

Probably the most influential Irish writer of the period was William Carleton, whose work *Traits and Stories of the Irish Peasantry* (1843–4) is invoked on three separate occasions in *Death and Nightingales* (53, 107, 110). Like her 'father', Beth Winters is well-read – she has Jane Austen, Emily Brontë and Charles Dickens on her bookshelf; but it's Carleton who makes the strongest impression:

> The story 'Wild Goose Lodge' [sic] she had read last night, a story based on fact and so disturbing she lay awake for hours trying to exorcise it from her mind. (107)

In 'Wildgoose Lodge' members of the agrarian secret society known as the Ribbonmen take revenge on people identified as 'thraitors' and 'informers' (Carleton 1843–4: 353, 360) by burning them alive in a house. One particularly gruesome description has a mother and infant skewered on a bayonet and thrust back into the flames (360–1). Carleton was a notoriously ambiguous figure – one who strained hard for the perspective of an outsider with insider knowledge. His function in McCabe's novel is to contribute to the atmosphere of violence and secrecy which gradually overtakes the story, and to invoke the inevitability of divided loyalties in the context of a society (such as was found in south Ulster in the 1880s) so fundamentally split along religious and political lines.

Two books which Beth might have had on her shelf, but which remain unmentioned in the text, are *The Ribbon Informer: A Tale of Lough Erne* (1874) and *Tully Castle: A Tale of the Irish Rebellion* (1877) – both by Fermanagh writer Peter Magennis, The novels are melodramatic tales of local life, although as may be observed even from their titles, the focus is each case is on conflict and the inevitable betrayals that ensue. *The Ribbon Informer* is based on a local legend concerning the murder of a local Ribbonman named Dominic Noon, whose tortured and battered body was dumped in a cave (subsequently named after him) near the tiny hamlet of Boho close to the southern shore of Lower Lough Erne. Noon apparently disguised his treacherous activities behind a flamboyant exterior – thinking, perhaps, that none would suspect someone who drew attention to himself; the strategy backfired, however, and he was subject to the field justice of the local 'boys', for whom, then as subsequently, 'touting' was categorically unforgivable. Although absent from McCabe's intertextual weave, the grotesquery of Noon's career and the violence of his demise serve to locate rural Fermanagh within the wider network of nineteenth-century Irish conflict, from the secret agrarian societies at the beginning of the century to the highly politicised land campaigns towards the end.[16]

Another writer associated with the county is Shan Bullock (1865–1935) – in the words of one literary historian, 'the most prominent writer produced by nineteenth-century Fermanagh … [and] also one of the most undeservedly forgotten figures of Irish literature' (Maume 2004: 459). Growing up on the Crom Castle estate owned by the earls of Erne, Bullock came from the same Ulster-Scots background as the fictional Billy Winters – one uneasily integrated into the landscape, and sensitive always to its own precarious inheritance, yet not without the capacity for empathising with its Catholic neighbours (Hill 2004: 405). With texts such as *By Thrasna River* (1895) and *The Loughsiders* (1924) he produced sophisticated fictional treatments of Fermanagh life.[17] Written with all the affection and sentimentalism of the emigrant, Bullock's Fermanagh is a place locked in to the agricultural cycle, where God's inscrutable will provides the first cause and the final explanation for every development. Although the Jebb family (in *The Loughsiders*) 'had been there or thereabouts since before King William's time, good Protestants and loyalists all of them' (1924: 43), there's a strong sense of cultural removal from 'the great English law' (78) across the sea. The widespread poverty depicted in Bullock's fiction afflicts both Catholics and Protestants, in which sense it nods to the cross-sectarian element of Land League politics. At the same time, the assault upon landlordism was to a significant degree an assault upon Protestant hegemony and the implicit link with Britain. The echoes of this ambivalence – of a strong, shared bond with the landscape which is to some extent belied by a barely suppressed history of sectarian conflict – are discernible throughout *Death and Nightingales*.[18]

Inasmuch as his entire imaginative output is focused on a particular geographical region, McCabe probably qualifies to be described as a 'regional' writer. And in so far as such is the case, an important literary influence must be *December Bride*, Sam Hanna Bell's powerful novel of life amongst a Presbyterian farming community on the Ards Peninsula at the beginning of the twentieth century. Beth Winters recalls Sarah Gomartin (the central female protagonist of Bell's novel) inasmuch as each actively resists the life of domestic servitude for which both biology and recent economic history has selected her.[19] One such practice is the control of one's own sexuality: whereas Sarah takes both Echlin brothers as lovers, Beth resists the drunken advances of her 'father', but readily enters into sexual relations (as did her mother before her) with a desirable male. Pregnancy ensues in each case, and in each case the legal and moral status of the child registers as a point of crisis for the local community. If such instances of independent female sexuality are scandalous for the Protestant Sarah, they are positively seditious for the Catholic Beth – for in Victorian Ireland, as Tom Inglis writes:

> Sexual love is about self-denial and surrender to one's spouse. Anything outside the pure intentions of married sexual love is a threat to the natural order of things and can lead to social and moral disease and decay. (1998: 25)

The experiences of Sarah, Beth and Catherine give the lie to the image of nineteenth-century Ireland as some kind of asexual era in which women and men consistently disciplined themselves according to the precepts of various ideologies or institutions. On the contrary, Ireland was typical of the period in so far as it was home to a wide range of secret sexual activities and practices. With secrecy comes betrayal, however, and Bell's novel reveals the extent to which the politics of interpersonal relationships emerge from, and at the same time reflect, the politics of community identity: in each novel, treacherous interpersonal relationships resonate in terms of a community that functions within a context of perceived political treachery. This is a lesson that McCabe clearly learned well with the composition of *Death and Nightingales*.

McCabe's title is a clear indication of the text's engagement with nineteenth-century gothic literature. The English poet John Keats, whose famous 'Ode to a Nightingale' is invoked by Beth (39), encapsulates certain aspects of that tradition: an enigmatic, romantic hero haunted by the prospect of an early death. Keats's profile contrasts strongly with that of the popular Irish singer-songwriter Percy French; although he is a personal friend of Billy Winters, Beth dismisses his work as 'wretched doggerel ... unfunny and all of it spiced with a painful sentimentality' (38). The introduction of French as a character within the novel (and others, such as Parnell and James Donnelly, Catholic bishop of Clogher) is one of the ways in which McCabe establishes the realism of this world. At the same time, the Keats/French opposition represents one of the moral and cultural continua along which the text functions: the benign sentimentality of the latter is gradually overtaken by the deathly seriousness of the former, and this is a lesson not just for the Winters family but for the wider community within which they live.

Although she may not realise it, Beth is drawn to Keats because she is in some senses playing the female role within the classic gothic narrative. Behind her stands a long line of vulnerable gothic heroines, beginning with Isabella and Matilda in Horace Walpole's *The Castle of Otranto* (1765), and developed in characters such as Emily from Ann Radcliffe's *The Mysteries of Udolpho* (1794) and Elizabeth from Mary Shelley's *Frankenstein* (1818).[20] This strand of gothic is particularly associated with central and southern Europe, and like many of these heroines – like, indeed, her poetic champion John Keats, who died there – Beth has experience of that part of the world, having lived in Naples for an unspecified period of time after her mother's death, before returning to live on the family farm at Clonoula.[21]

A particular strain of Irish gothic emerged in texts such as *The Collegians* (1829) by Gerald Griffin, reworked as a hugely popular stage play entitled *The Colleen Bawn* (1860) by Dion Boucicault.

The trend was continued by writers such as Joseph Sheridan Le Fanu, whose novel *Uncle Silas* (1864) depicts a heroine threatened with grisly death:

> Imagine a hammer, one end of which had been beaten out into a longish tapering spike, with a handle something longer than usual ... Suddenly but softly he laid ... his left hand over her face, and nearly at the same instant there came a scrunching blow; an unnatural shriek, beginning small and swelling for two or three seconds into a yell such as are imagined in haunted houses, accompanied by a convulsive sound, as of the motion of running, and the arms drumming on the bed; and then another blow – and with a horrid gasp he recoiled a step or two, and stood perfectly still ... Then once more he steps to the side of the bed, and I heard another of those horrid blows – and silence – and another – and more silence – and the diabolical surgery was ended. (1864: 436)

If this description foreshadows the death awaiting Beth in McCabe's novel, it also uncannily anticipates the Phoenix Park murders, the 'diabolical surgery' of which was expedited in part by the use of surgical knives. In Eily O'Connor and Maud Ruthyn (as, indeed, with the heroines of *Otranto*, *Udolpho* and *Frankenstein*) we observe attractive women whose apparently rational, socially sanctioned desires are undermined by the gradual emergence of an irrational, nightmarish world characterised by guilt, secrecy, violence and a past that refuses to lie quietly. In the case of the Irish heroines in particular, this pattern is linked with a wider social situation in which the category of 'desire' is implicitly linked with sensitive political issues concerning land, property and historical identity. This is the tradition which McCabe so skilfully weaves into his own narrative.

The text wherein so many of these echoes and influences are most fully concentrated is Bram Stoker's *Dracula* (1897). Here again we encounter the anxieties of Victorian female sexuality underpinning an allegory of blood and land; here again we find an attractive female character subject to the penetrative, phallic violence of a team of men:

> Arthur took the stake and the hammer, and when once his mind was set on action his hands never trembled nor even quivered. Van Helsing opened his missal and began to read, and Quincey and I followed as well as we could. Arthur placed the point over the heart,

and as I looked I could see its dint in the white flesh. Then he struck with all his might.

The Thing in the coffin writhed; and a hideous, blood-curdling screech came from the opened red lips. The body shook and quivered and twisted in wild contortions; the sharp white teeth champed together till the lips were cut and the mouth was smeared with a crimson foam. But Arthur never faltered. He looked like a figure of Thor as his untrembling arm rose and fell, driving deeper and deeper the mercy-bearing stake, whilst the blood from the pierced heart welled and spurted up around it. His face was set, and high duty seemed to shine through it; the sight of it gave us courage, so that our voices seemed to ring through the little vault. (251)

The sexual imagery of this scene is difficult to deny: the writhing, the colours, the screaming – all is redolent of Victorian anxieties relating to uncontrolled female sexuality. At the same time, the narrative rehearses deeper anxieties relating to the economy of desire and the discourses of legitimacy at large within society. 'The Thing' was always lying dormant within Lucy Westenra, waiting to betray her; it's up to the legitimate social forces (which is to say: men) to police that relationship and to execute the necessary sanctions should legitimacy be threatened in any way. The stake and hammer with which Arthur kills 'the Thing' and frees Lucy presage the 'masonry hammer with a long steel-pointed edge on one side' (McCabe 1992: 186–7) with which Liam Ward and Blinky Blessing plan to murder Beth Winters. If such an act represents an assault upon her independent sexuality, it's also an attack on the form of social legitimacy with which she (against her will, as it happens) is associated.

Through a combination of luck and determination, Beth manages to avoid the fate that overtakes at least some of her gothic forebears. Nevertheless, *Death and Nightingales* adopts the basic structure of the gothic narrative in order to dramatise the apparently inescapable cycle of betrayal within which pre-ceasefire Northern Ireland appeared to be locked.[22] Liam betrays Beth, who in turn betrays her false lover to his death; Beth also betrays Billy, who has been betrayed by Catherine Maguire, his wife and Beth's mother. If McCabe's novel performs a useful task in revealing the ways in which contemporary conflict is prefigured in the past, at the same time it carries within itself the basic question of the gothic narrative: how and when will the cycle of betrayal end?

'Enniskillen'

Death and Nightingales was written in the aftermath of one of the decisive actions of the 'Troubles': the detonation of a forty-pound bomb in the centre of Enniskillen on Sunday 8 November 1987. The explosion caused the immediate deaths of eleven people and the injuring of many more who had assembled before a memorial commemorating those from the area who had died during the two world wars. As with the events in Maamtrasna and the Phoenix Park a century earlier, the result was widespread revulsion and 'almost universal condemnation from all shades of the political spectrum' (Dawson 2007: 288). The name itself assumed metonymic status; depending on the circumstances, 'Enniskillen' could mean atrocity, horror, tragedy, intransigence, hatred and a host of other negative connotations. For a period, indeed, 'Enniskillen' came to symbolise the 'Troubles' more than the mean streets of Belfast, or the estates of Derry, or even the badlands of south Armagh. The Provisional IRA issued an immediate apology, but it soon became clear that 'Enniskillen' represented a turning point in national and international attitudes – an act that certainly encouraged, if not directly precipitated, a series of secret political negotiations which led in turn to the IRA's declaration of a ceasefire (temporary, as it turned out) on 31 August 1994.

Death and Nightingales was written in the period between 'Enniskillen' and the first ceasefire, and it's my impression that this fact influences the *kind* of novel that McCabe wrote, and the *kind* of resolution – or non-resolution, as it happens – that he tried to imagine.[23] It's a *traumatic* novel, in terms of its content, certainly, but also the wider psycho-social context within which it was conceived and written. The trauma of such a devastating event in a major population centre so close to his own home turned McCabe to previous crises in Northern Irish history to search for parallels and understanding.[24] To understand this in our turn, we have to consider the dominant modes of 'Troubles' writing up to that time, and to develop an awareness of the extremely sensitive ways in which cultural discourses (such as fiction) mediate political realities.

After the Hunger Strike of 1981, strenuous diplomatic efforts were made throughout the remainder of the decade to try to redefine the public nature of the relationship between the Republic, Northern Ireland and Great Britain. Although Garret Fitzgerald's

New Ireland Forum was an imaginative initiative exploring the possibility of new perspectives and new languages, for many it was easily dismissible as an academic talking-shop which lacked purchase in the context of Northern Irish *realpolitik* (Foster 2007: 127). On the diplomatic front, the Anglo-Irish Agreement (15 November 1985) enraged both republicans and loyalists with its formal acceptance of shared British/Irish responsibility for the fate of Northern Ireland. The emergence, in the shape of David Trimble, of a viable liberal unionist leader was an apparent incentive to moderate optimism, especially when compared with the image of unionist-loyalist intransigence regularly rehearsed by Democratic Unionist leader Ian Paisley (Foster 2007: 133).

Despite this, by the time of 'Enniskillen' the situation in Northern Ireland was as entrenched as it had been at any time over the previous twenty years. For many people, 'Northern Ireland' had become a perverse, problem-orientated concept – lacking attraction, or even interest, for either of the societies (southern Irish or British) in whose ostensible name and idealised image the struggle continued.[25] In his book *Paddy and Mr Punch* (published in 1993, the year after *Death and Nightingales*) the historian Roy Foster attempted to stress 'connections' (as in the subtitle of his book) rather than discontinuities in Irish and English history. He undertook this mission as an explicit rejoinder to a historiographical tradition (encapsulated in the work of F.L.S. Lyons) focused on 'an anarchy that sprang from the collision within a small and intimate island of seemingly irreconcilable cultures, unable to live together or to live apart, caught inextricably in the web of their tragic history' (Foster 1993: 22). In the face of such a perspective, Foster's book represented an invitation to all the relevant stake-holders to exercise a 'cautious ambition' (39) with regard to island history – to search for and emphasise those exchanges and trends and personalities which resisted the intractable 'tragic' fate.

Caught up in the trauma of 'Enniskillen', however, Eugene McCabe appears not to have heeded that invitation. It was a difficult request, after all. In a collection entitled *Northern Ireland and the Politics of Reconciliation* (also published in 1993), a group of scholars (including Foster) and diplomats come together to challenge the concept of 'Ulsterization' – a word which, although defying 'rigorous definition ... is meant to convey the idea of an intractable intercommunity conflict' (Keogh and Haltzel 1993: 1). Despite a desire to appear upbeat, the findings of the majority of the contributions are unpromising, if not downright pessimistic. Regarded from a range of wider historical and geographical perspectives, the message is, things might not be quite as bad as they seem – in any event, it's more helpful to believe so than to succumb to the hopelessness of a rising death toll and continued lack of popular support for initiatives such as the Anglo-Irish Agreement. As one American contributor (Donald L. Horowitz) put it, Ulster remains 'something of a deviant case in Western terms' (174) – a perfect storm of entrenched identities, civic and institutional prejudice and inauspicious history; but that's no reason to give up on it, or to pander to an unhelpful myth of fatal atavism The Introduction echoes Foster's point in *Paddy and Mr Punch* by insisting that it's up to those who know better – academics, politicians, religious leaders – to give a good example by refuting sectarian analyses, by opening up new lines of inquiry, and by supporting the democratic system and encouraging moderation whenever possible.

As it happens, a series of secret negotiations had been in process for a number of years before the book's publication which were to result in the 'game-changing' initiative – a unilateral ceasefire – that neither the editors nor the contributors could envisage.[26] In the meantime, in the realm of cultural/critical discourse, the prevailing talk was of revisionism, postcolonialism and the validity of historical 'grand narratives' such as nationalism or unionism.[27] Scholars were troubled: it may be commendable to search for new perspectives with which to re-envisage the ongoing tragedy of Northern Ireland, but must that be at the expense of the perspectives which still defined many people's outlook on the world? Or was it not the case that we all constantly – individually and socially – redefine the traces of the past in order to remake the present we desire? The first three volumes of *The Field Day Anthology of Irish Writing* appeared in 1991, and crystallised many of these debates, but the project's canonical ambitions alienated those who felt marginalised from the narrative thus envisaged, as well as those who questioned its working terms, and indeed its overall conception (Thompson 2006).

Amidst all this debate, the 'problem' of Northern Ireland remained constant, and two related ideas persisted: betrayal and tragedy. The first, as we have observed and as is widely recognised, was embedded in 'Troubles' culture at a constitutive level. Three 'sides' (Ireland, Ulster, Britain) and multiple complicating factors (class, gender, religion, education, etc.): history, it seemed, had bequeathed to Northern Ireland a socio-political dispensation primed for betrayal. With so many potential relationships available, and so many possible affiliations available for emphasis, it's no wonder that a recurring trope of the 'Troubles' narrative became the protagonist's encounter with an act of betrayal, or that such narratives typically work towards the discovery of the secret behind the façade, the reality behind the appearance, the truth behind the pretence.

This is a pattern we see repeated in *Death and Nightingales* – a story in which simplistic models of Northern Irish affiliation are repudiated in favour of a highly complicated and thoroughly enmeshed social history. The novel's central act of betrayal – that of Beth Winters by Liam Ward – operates on a number of levels, and with reference to a number of discourses: gender (woman by man); religion (Catholic by Catholic); class (petty landlord by tenant); temperamental (emotional by material); and so on. It is presaged by a wide range of other betrayals throughout the text; and all this activity is in some sense the product of a history and a society in which betrayal remains both a constant danger and a constant opportunity. Indeed, it's of such dangers and such opportunities that the novel as a narrative form is constituted.

The other term widely invoked in relation to the 'Troubles' is 'tragedy'. This concept has a long tradition in relation to the history of Ulster, and, as Joseph Cleary has suggested, '[several] different kinds of "tragic" narrative have been adapted to the Northern Irish situation. Genres such as revenge tragedy, romantic tragedy, domestic tragedy and versions of classical Greek tragedy have all shaped the imagination of the conflict'. As he goes on to point out:

> [T]he meaning ascribed to 'the family' – which tends to provide the social basis for nearly all modes of tragic narrative – can vary significantly … The family, in short, is a critical site of meaning in nearly all modes of tragedy, but its function differs from one mode to another.
>
> During the course of the 'Troubles', the Northern Irish conflict was viewed mainly within standard variations of romantic and domestic tragedy. (2007: 234)

Cleary refines his point by arguing that 'tragedy' in Northern Irish culture has by and large operated to underpin a liberal unionist perspective, inasmuch as 'the internal divisions opened up within Protestant identity tend to be cathected as the true source or motor

of tragic suffering, and the standpoint of the victims of state sectarianism is steered, wittingly or not, into the background' (259).
What he appears to mean by this is that dominant conceptions of
Northern Irish 'tragedy' implicitly work to privilege a Protestant/
unionist perspective – albeit a liberal one – in which the death of
the old order is invariably engaged on an interpersonal and psycho-
social level rather than a political or materialist one. (As already
observed, it was their inability or unwillingness to embrace such
a 'tragic' fate that led Protestant – and sometimes Orange – supporters of the Land League to disavow such a connection after the
Acts of 1881 and 1882.) Such a manoeuvre ignores the historically privileged relation of one particular perspective (the Protestant/
unionist) with the state. The traditional 'victims of state sectarianism' – which is to say, the Catholic/nationalist community – may
experience a range of negative emotions, such as grief and loss and
despair; but the 'tragedy' is properly that of a unionism which will
have to come to terms with the loss of its once privileged relationship with the state.

Again, *Death and Nightingales* seems to adapt itself to this profile in at least some of its aspects: despite allusions to contemporary politics (such as Parnell) and the public realm (Percy French,
James Donnelly), it is in essence a domestic novel structured around
two failed romantic relationships – the second of which (Beth and
Liam) echoes the first (Billy and Catherine) in its emotional contours
and its physical enactment. ('Liam' is the Irish form of 'William' –
Billy's proper name.) We note, however, that three of these individuals are Catholic, and that the fourth – the liberal, educated Billy
Winters – has already stepped 'across the divide' by entering into an
exogamous marriage. The 'tragedy' represented by these treacherous
relationships, in other words, does not work to adumbrate a liberal
Protestant/unionist perspective: it is, rather, of a more fundamental
kind – one which, while not entirely drained of a political dimension, manages to implicate each and every subject in a discourse of
betrayal which itself appears to be encoded into human experience at
a constitutive level. The Land War, community sectarianism, family
secrets – these are merely the means by which betrayal is articulated
in time and space: in reality, the possibility that things are not as they
appear, or that things might have been other than they currently are,
means that we are all always already betrayed, fooled again and
again by a mode of existence that refuses to answer our desires.

Such an analysis means also that we are all always in danger of adopting the personae and performing the roles of 'Beth' and 'Liam' in relation to the 'Billys' and 'Catherines' that have preceded us. This is an interpretation that must have resonated particularly strongly in the years between 'Enniskillen' and the first ceasefire of 1994, when McCabe was writing his novel, and when the situation in Northern Ireland appeared to have ground to a moral and political halt. The circumstances then in place determined the versions of betrayal and tragedy invoked by McCabe, or at least strongly influenced the versions to which (as his work before that period reveals) he was predisposed. Betrayal is elemental, instinctual, hard-wired into the human brain at the same level as the 'fight or flight' response; tragedy is similar – the product not of a particular sectarian history but of history in general. *Death and Nightingales* testifies to a contemporary conviction regarding the incursion of gothic aesthetics into everyday life in Northern Ireland – in short, the propensity of the past to inhere in the present, and of the present to repeat the betrayals of the past.

Conclusion

Early in the novel Billy and his Catholic employee Mickey Dolphin walk across the farm towards the quarry, where they encounter the Dummy McGonnell sleeping on the edge of a bog. Looking at the surrounding bog-holes, Mickey takes a funny turn which he refuses to explain to his boss; it's left to the Dummy to describe – using the same methods (gestures and images) he will use later to warn Beth – how in his youth a drunken Mickey had been responsible for the death of his young daughter by drowning in a well. This tragic story leads Billy to brood on his own experience, and on the condition of people in general: as he looks across 'his' land he thinks of 'treacherous wombs and treacherous wells and how everyone, less or more, had some shameful and painful secret to conceal' (49). The archetypal imagery of wombs and wells implicates everyone in a form of primordial treachery – none more than the person who claims the insight. Part of Billy's culpability lies in the fact that he's unable or unwilling to acknowledge the extent to which his own condition – his own identity – is the result of treacherous acts perpetrated in the past in his name. Billy was *already* implicated in a discourse of treachery before Catherine Maguire came to him with another man's baby in her womb. He perpetuates the cycle by revisiting Catherine's betrayal upon her daughter, who in turn betrays her treacherous lover.

In the closing lines of the novel Billy describes himself and Beth as 'cangled both to treachery' – a fitting description (in its use of a Scots-Ulster word) for their relationship, and for the wider political relationship they symbolise. Betrayal, it emerges, is a fluid, complicated proposition, psychologically and practically; and this gives the lie to the image of an immutable sectarian stand-off between easily discernible blocs or staunch, implacable identities. Besides its inherent aesthetic qualities (and it is amongst other things a wonderfully structured novel) the principal achievements of *Death and Nightingales* are its insistence on the constitutive complexity of the conflict in Northern Ireland, and its testament to the haunting presence of treachery in the dark hours before some kind of dawn.

8

'A family – a whole fucking country – drowning in shame': Anne Enright's *The Gathering* (2007)

> Herod's way of coping with children?
> 'Knife the little fuckers, one by one.'
> Brendan Kennelly, *The
> Little Book of Judas*, 33

Introduction

The final case study in this account brings us to Anne Enright's Man Booker Prize-winning novel focused on the sexual abuse of a child (or perhaps children – the narrator, as we'll see, is unsure) in modern Ireland, and the traumas that ensue from such events. Enright already had a reputation as an accomplished writer on the subject of contemporary Irish sexual mores when she decided to tackle a subject that, for a variety of reasons, had been catapulted to the forefront of Irish public discourse in the decades on either side of the millennium. At the heart of this discourse was the concept of betrayal – which is to say, the abuse of power and the exploitation of trust. This betrayal, moreover, subsists not just on the level of the individual: *The Gathering*, rather, indicts an entire nation – Ireland, however it may be defined – for the systematic, ongoing betrayal of its people, and in particular those members of society most at risk from the abuse of trust and power: children.

The Gathering is narrated by a middle-class, middle-aged woman named Veronica who lives in modern-day Dublin with her husband and two daughters. At the outset of the story we learn that Veronica's younger brother Liam has died in England, and that she has retrieved his body so that it may be waked and buried in his native Dublin. Forgotten tensions and resentments emerge as various surviving family members 'gather' in their mother's house in order to prepare for Liam's funeral. The real motor of the narrative, however, is Veronica's conviction that '[the] seeds of my brother's death were sown many years ago' (2007: 13); in short, Veronica is convinced that Liam was sexually abused as an eight- or nine-year-old child by a family acquaintance, and that she herself witnessed one such act. It's this event, she contends, which determined the future shape and tenor of Liam's disappointing life and (probable) suicide; it's the witnessing of this event, and her failure to act on it, which, as we observe over the course of the narrative, is threatening to drain Veronica's own life of any happiness.

In the absence of hard evidence, Veronica is forced to speculate on the background to this traumatic event; in order to understand what has happened to her and her brother, that is, she has to try to understand the experiences and motivations of the other people involved and the context within which the event itself took place. In imagining the protracted relations between their maternal grandmother Ada and her two suitors, Charlie Spillane and Lamb Nugent, moreover, Veronica cannot help but imagine an alternative history of the country in which she and her family were born and raised – a history determined not (or not just) by the issue of national identity but by an alternative discourse of sexual desire. Given the political, social and cultural contexts, the image of the Irish boy betrayed by someone in a position of trust resonates throughout twentieth-century Irish history, and demands that anyone and everyone claiming an affiliation with that national signifier assume one or more subject roles somewhere within the discourse – as victim, perpetrator, witness, acknowledger or, perhaps most challengingly, forgiver.

Beyond belief

The Celtic Tiger was a phenomenon that few people born in Ireland in the half century or so after the 'Emergency' could have anticipated. A series of factors – amongst which were increased foreign investment, attractive corporation tax rates, light state regulation and a mobile, educated work force hungry for the 'success' that had eluded (or been denied) their parents and grandparents – coalesced within a favorable international climate to bring about a 'miracle' which saw the Republic achieve unprecedented levels of economic success. And with that success came social and cultural change: so rapid and so marked was the economic turn, indeed, that no one seemed quite to know what the consequences would be for established discourses of national identity. Of course, traditional notions of Ireland and Irishness did not disappear overnight; even in the eye of the storm, however, it was possible to observe those notions becoming subject to a general instrumental rationality that was at large throughout Irish society in the twenty or so years running up to the crash of 2008 (McWilliams 2008).

The Celtic Tiger era was also the era of 'Tribunal Ireland' as the state, under pressure from various elements within the public sphere, attempted to assert a measure of control over the prevailing hysterical materialism and the growing evidence of blatant inequality throughout Irish society (Kirby 2002). One of those elements was the *Irish Times* journalist Fintan O'Toole, who remained a vociferous critic of some of the practices, as well as the general informing ideology, of the country's new economic times. Looking back after the crash, O'Toole wrote:

> What became ever more apparent as the years went on and the revelations from the tribunals continued to unfold was that the ideal of the republic hadn't just slipped away in a process of economic and social change or been stolen from us by perfidious Albion. It had been deliberately and cynically betrayed from within. (2010: 32–3)

Such misgivings were exacerbated by the crash itself and the ensuing revelations of the extent to which the economic miracle had been enabled – and then disabled – by staggering levels of greed, stupidity and corruption (Allen 2009; Kirby 2010). As the banking community was condemned, as governments fell and the country suffered the ignominy of a European Union-sponsored bail-out, the euphoria of the Celtic Tiger was replaced by disbelief and anger. The country itself seemed traumatised by the depth and the speed of its fall: and at large throughout the country there was, as O'Toole wrote, 'a rage fuelled by a deep sense of betrayal' (2010: 131).

This economic betrayal was shadowed by another – arguably much more fundamental – instance of treachery. For many people, the slow death of Irish Catholicism has been a bitter, harrowing process to observe; for others, the decline of a fundamentally flawed institution's unwarranted role in modern Irish life was already long overdue by the time it began to come under serious pressure during the 1990s. Whatever the perspective, however, it has been the form

and the detail of the Church's precipitous downfall that has shaken
the nation to its core.

Catholicism was embedded in Irish life well before the Treaty of
1922, and with it came that institution's peculiar take on human
sexuality as a secretive, implicitly sinful and essentially problematic
discourse.[1] The position of the twenty-six counties (in its various
embodiments) as a *de facto* Catholic state was legally ratified in
the Constitution drawn up in 1937 by Eamon de Valera which, in
Article 44, stated that: 'The State recognises the special position of
the Holy Catholic Apostolic and Roman Church as the guardian
of the Faith professed by the great majority of its citizens' (quoted
in O'Day and Stevenson 1992: 196). As the century wore on, the
Republic of Ireland remained to all intents and purposes a Catholic
country, and the Church continued to play an extremely powerful
role in all aspects of national life, including the imagination and
regulation of sexual desire.[2]

And yet, for adherents to an institution founded on a range of
benign ideals (love, empathy, forgiveness, etc.), the reputation of
Catholic religious in Ireland throughout the twentieth century was
never particularly healthy. Anecdotal instances of bullying, intolerance – and indeed cruelty and corruption – were common enough
in society at large; there was also an accumulating body of literary
material – memoir, fiction, as well as other genres – which testified
to the less than salubrious standing of certain aspects of Catholic
Ireland. Indeed, the existence of religious corruption and exploitation had been an open secret of Irish life for a long time. Individual
cases that occasionally came to light might be explained away as
instances of the odd 'bad egg' to be found in any basket; with the
emergence of a number of high-profile cases during the 1980s and
1990s, however, the extent of clerical turpitude – and the extent
of the Church's attempts to keep that condition secret – began to
emerge.[3]

The result has been a fully-fledged national (indeed international)
scandal in which some of the core precepts of Irish identity have been
thoroughly undermined. What began to emerge, in fact, was a widespread realisation that the Industrial Schools and the Magdalene
Laundries had been running a system of physical and psychological
terror that operated outside the official parameters of the state;
that there existed what amounted to a network of sexual abuse –
much of it paedophile in orientation – amongst Catholic religious

throughout the state;[4] and that the Church hierarchy was to some extent aware of these facts, but – as an 'autonomous' organisation operating more or less independently within the state – was reluctant (on occasion to a criminal degree) to submit itself or its agents to official state sanction.

The Irish state itself has also been heavily criticised for its systematic collusion in the betrayal of the most vulnerable members of its society. The Proclamation of 1916 famously promised to cherish 'all the children of the nation equally', but this was a promise that subsequent generations – those charged with the task of running an impoverished post-colonial state – found difficult to honour. 'Throughout the first two-thirds of the twentieth century', writes Moira J. Maguire in the introduction to her book *Precarious Childhood in Post-Independence Ireland,*

> lawmakers presented a façade of caring and compassion while their social policies repeatedly ignored the needs and best interests of the neediest of Irish children – those who were illegitimate, poor, neglected, and abused ... All of this served to mask the gap between the idealized Ireland of republican fantasy, and the reality of everyday life for Ireland's poor and marginalized children. (2009: 2)

Amongst other things, Maguire notes 'the gap between Catholic rhetoric that insisted on abundant fertility, and economic and social conditions that made abundant fertility a foolish aspiration', and the state's assertion of 'its constitutional right to care for these "excess" children in whatever way it saw fit' (2, 3). The damning conclusions are

> that far from protecting and upholding the family, Irish social policy had the effect of destroying family life when it did not conform to middle-class norms and expectations, or when it threatened the nationalist ideal of simple, content if poor, morally pure Irish society ... [and that] some aspects of Catholic social teaching made women's lives extremely difficult and contributed to the misery of countless thousands of poor and working-class children, who lived a precarious existence on the margins of survival. (4, 7)

The political journalist Bruce Arnold goes even further in his analysis of what he calls 'the Irish Gulag' (2009), describing how successive twentieth-century administrations sanctioned a system that was cruel and unusual when measured against the avowed aims of the state itself; how time and again a blind eye was turned towards the psychological and physical devastation wreaked by Catholic religious in institutions throughout the land; and how, once the truth did began to emerge during the 1990s, it was manipulated by elements within the state so as to avert attention from its own role in what was by any standards an execrable history. The subtitle of Arnold's book – *How the State Betrayed its Innocent Children* – leaves little to the imagination.

It's interesting to note that this process of disintegration over-lapped significantly with the life of the Celtic Tiger, raising the issue of some form of causal relationship between the two phenomena. Certainly, the exposure of the Church's failures in its pastoral and spiritual mission has contributed to its steady erasure from Irish life; but it may be that this has only sped up what was happening in any case. It may be that Catholicism (like the Irish language) has become a victim of Irish pragmatism, and that once economic success and cultural empowerment became a part of the Irish experience, a practice traditionally associated with failure and sub-ordination would be delicately jettisoned.

Besides the expanding number of official reports and investigative journalism, some of the most damning indictments of the Catholic Church in Ireland have appeared in the form of testimony – tele-visual or written accounts in which the 'survivor' describes the pro-cess of abuse and the means by which it was escaped or endured. Paddy Doyle's *The God Squad* (1988) sounded an early warning of what would emerge, once the need to testify finally outweighed the stigma of abuse. Doyle's description of the various brutal regimes he endured alerted many Irish people to the cruelty that was endemic throughout the Irish child-care system; in particular, the account of his sexual assault at the hands of a nun (1988: 55) helped to estab-lish the idea of abuse perpetrated by religious as a primary feature of that system.

Doyle's memoir is a direct precursor of a book such as Colm O'Gorman's *Beyond Belief* (2009). This account of the author's extended abuse at the hands of a paedophile priest in rural Co. Wexford in the early 1980s is a typical example in many respects, the most telling of which being the fact that 'betrayal' constitutes the single most important emotion informing the narrative. In the first instance, the act itself represents a gross betrayal of trust – a betrayal, that is, of the child by the adult, and of the communi-cant by the priest. 'It is perhaps hard for the reader who has not experienced abuse in childhood to imagine fully the impact of this level of betrayal', writes one commentator; '[the] horror is too painful to permeate fully into consciousness' (Walker 1992: 62). Nevertheless, it was just such a 'horrendous' betrayal of trust that the Catholic Primate of All-Ireland, Archbishop Sean Brady, would acknowledge after the publication of the government report into clerical abuse in the Diocese of Ferns (Arnold 2009: 295).

In *Beyond Belief*, the adult narrator also describes how his younger self felt betrayed by his own body's response to the priest's sexual activities, and how these feelings exacerbated the guilt and confusion which weighed so heavily after the event, and which in turn (he believes) contributed in large part to his subsequent social and sexual dysfunction (2009: 49). Research has in fact revealed that this is a common response on the part of the abused – one that, when manipulated by a skilful abuser, can in itself form part of the pattern of exploitation (Briere 1992; Walker 1992).

After the betrayal of the act itself, there was the betrayal of the attempted cover-up by those who enjoyed elevated social positions based on their apparent moral standing within society – those who, for example, ordained Sean Fortune as a Catholic priest even after complaints of paedophile abuse had been made against him (O'Gorman 2009: 224). This, for many people, represents the most distressing aspect of the entire abuse scandal: that one act of (sexual) betrayal may be compounded by another that is psychological and intellectual in nature, one that is so evidently underpinned by a discourse of institutional power. This may account for the fact that much of the official response to the ongoing abuse scandals tends to focus not so much on primary acts of betrayal but rather on the processes whereby such acts were time and again 'contained' within the institution itself.[5]

Finally, there is the constant possibility of the betrayal of the youthful victim by the adult survivor. O'Gorman is presented with a number of opportunities, and plenty of reasons, to desist from his quest to testify. The 'truth of my experience' (177), he avers, was brutal abuse: any attempt to mitigate that truth, to deny it or attempt to outmanoeuvre it in any way, represents a 'betrayal' of self which would leave him permanently in thrall to the asymmetrical power relation encoded in the initial act (priest/communicant, adult/child, active/passive, abuser/abused). Paradoxically, it's only by retaining the memory and the identity that is indelibly attached to that act that the subject can survive. What O'Gorman suggests, in fact, is that 'survivor' and 'victim' are, and should remain, two sides of the same coin – one unthinkable without the other.

O'Gorman's book communicates a sense of the confused response – incorporating disbelief, anger, grief, guilt and a range of other negative emotions – on the part of the generation whose fate it was (and continues to be) to face up to the extent of Irish clerical abuse. That the latter emerged alongside an equally damning narrative of economic abuse – itself characterised by repeated acts of gross betrayal – made for a highly traumatic national experience on either side of the millennium. Such was the situation facing Anne Enright when she came, in her novel *The Gathering*, to imagine the act of abuse as in some senses the determining condition of modern Irish identity.

Freud, betrayal and 'traumaculture'

Before turning to consider Enright's work, however, it's important to acknowledge two related debates that bear on a consideration of her most successful novel. Firstly, there's the fact that the recent, very public engagement with issues of child abuse in Ireland also resonates in relation to a narrative of betrayal that is both wider in scope and more fundamental in its potential impact. This narrative in fact takes us to the heart of (and once there threatens to undo) one of the most influential modern accounts of human experience: psychoanalysis. And secondly, such issues also bear upon some of the recurring concerns of modern Irish cultural criticism – a discourse whose emergence has in large part overlapped with both the Celtic Tiger and the abuse scandals. This is a particularly important consideration in respect of cultural criticism's imagination of an Irish subject who is both the agent and the product of a particular form of memory.

Turning to psychoanalysis, in April 1896 the young Sigmund Freud read a paper entitled 'The Aetiology of Hysteria' before the Society for Psychiatry and Neurology in Vienna, in which he proposed

> that at the bottom of every case of hysteria there are *one or more occurrences of premature sexual experience*, occurrences which belong to the earliest years of childhood but which can be reproduced through the work of psycho-analysis in spite of the intervening

decades ... Our view then is that infantile sexual experiences are the
fundamental precondition for hysteria, are, as it were, the *dispos-*
ition for it and that it is they which create the hysterical symptoms,
but that they do not do so immediately, but remain without effect
to begin with and only exercise a pathogenic action later, when they
have been aroused after puberty in the form of unconscious memories. (1896: 271, 277, original emphases)

The burden of Freud's paper is that premature sexual experience
is endemic within the species; that the repressed trauma of such
experiences creates a wide range of hysterical symptoms within the
subject; and that the proper task of psychoanalysis should be the
retrieval, identification and alleviation of those repressed memories.
This thesis became known in subsequent commentary as 'seduction
theory'.[6]

'The Aetiology of Hysteria' constitutes an alternative point of
departure for the entire psychoanalytical project, but one that Freud
himself was to abrogate in quick time. Instead, he came up with the
theory of the drives and the concepts of spontaneous childhood
sexuality and repression, the structure of the unconscious and the
analytical primacy of dreams; and it was on these bases – rather
than on the seduction theory of 1896 – that classical psychoanalysis
was to raise its house.

Freud's turn away from the implications of seduction theory has
been regarded as a betrayal on a number of levels. In his book *The*
Assault on Truth: Freud's Suppression of the Seduction Theory
(1984), Jeffrey Masson claimed that Freud withdrew from the radical potential of his initial thesis under pressure from nineteenth-century sexual and social mores, and that he (and his closest followers,
including Freud's own daughter) colluded with the systematic suppression of materials relating to his youthful claims:

In Freud's later theories and in psychoanalytical theory after Freud
... [the] implication is that the 'seduced' child is also the seducer, and
has brought on the sexual act by his or her behavior. However, in
the early paper, there is no doubt as to what Freud meant by sexual
seduction: a real sexual act forced on a young child who in no way
desires it or encourages it. A seduction, in this context, is an act of
cruelty and violence which wounds the child in every aspect of her
(or his, though Freud makes it clear that usually it is a young girl
who is the victim) being. Her body is not ready for the adult act of
intercourse ... nor are the child's emotions prepared either for the

immediate impact of the sexual passion of the adult or for the later
inevitable feelings of guilt, anxiety, and fear. (1984: 5)

The radical Swiss psychoanalyst Alice Miller is even more damning in her identification of Freud's 'betrayal', which, she claims, is
symptomatic of a history that is constitutive of 'civilization' itself.
In her book *Thou Shalt Not Be Aware: Society's Betrayal of the
Child* (1981), Miller wrote:

> [Freud] shrank from the reality that was being revealed to him,
> instead allying himself from that time on with the patriarchal society
> of which he was a member ... He founded the psychoanalytic school,
> which likes to think of itself as revolutionary but in fact remains
> committed to the old ideas of casting blame on the helpless child
> and defending the powerful parents. When a patient who has been
> sexually abused as a child enters analysis, she will be told that it is
> her fantasies and desires that she is relating, because in reality she
> dreamed as a child of seducing her own father. Thus, with the aid
> of the invention of the concept of 'infantile sexuality,' which was
> a figment of Freud's imagination, the absurd childhood situation
> is repeated: the patient is dissuaded from recognizing the truth the
> same way the child was once dissuaded from recognizing her percep-
> tions. (1981: 324)

For Miller, abuse constitutes a recurring pattern, as those who
become victims in childhood revisit the trauma upon succeeding
generations.[7] Inculcated with the precepts of drive theory, repression and infantile sexuality, however, classical psychoanalysis (she
argues) simply cannot countenance the truth of endemic childhood
abuse; it thus colludes with a patriarchal society constituted on the
open secret that is the systematic abuse of children by older people
in positions of trust and power, including parents. According to
Masson and Miller, in fact, the Freudian school of psychoanalysis
represents a form of second-order betrayal, one specifically developed and organised to deny a first-order act of betrayal – that of
the child by the adult.

The concepts of childhood hypostasised in the ongoing debates
around 'seduction theory' are far from straightforward: the image
of 'natural' innocence encoded in the one camp remains in some
respects as problematic as the theory of 'natural' drives underpinning the other.[8] What may be said is that amongst other things,
such debates encompass issues of power, memory, repression and
return – all terms, uncoincidentally, which resonate powerfully in

modern Irish cultural criticism. In many influential accounts, as Conor Carville suggests, Irish history (including contemporary history) is a story of the abuse of the powerless by the powerful, of traumatic acts and repressed memories and of forms of analysis (cultural criticism, for example) which collude in one form or another with the initial act of abuse. At the same time, the Irish subject (including the contemporary subject) is frequently figured as the traumatised product of that history.[9]

Carville has considered the extent to which the discourse of contemporary Irish cultural criticism is in fact organised to a defining extent around the concept of trauma, and the various ways in which that discourse has smuggled a particular model of psychoanalysis into its constitutive language. 'Traumaculture', as Carville describes it, is linked to wider developments in global culture, but performs particular functions in relation to a society and a subject that are (or at least are widely perceived to be) the essential products of a violent, fragmented history. That history – embodied in the ineluctable 'fact' of the Famine – has been undeniably traumatic; in itself, however, the discourse of trauma tends to incorporate a particular notion of the subject and how the subject processes traumatic memories. In the case of modern Ireland, Carville argues, trauma has come to function 'as the wound around which a culture and an identity coalesces' (2012: 29).

For Carville, the normalisation of the traumatic subject as part of a supposedly radical or dissenting Irish cultural criticism has been an unhelpful, and ultimately untenable, development. In the traditional view, 'trauma' is precisely that which shatters the subject; but to premise a model of (Irish) identity on this shattered subject is deeply paradoxical. At the same time, such a definition assumes the existence of a non-shattered, pre-traumatised subject who might, under certain circumstances, be retrieved and their repletion restored. There is also the concern that trauma encourages the analyst/critic to fixate on the idea of a disrupted temporality – on the relations, that is, between past and present – to the detriment of other interpretive axes. 'Trauma', Carville argues, 'becomes the ground on which an identity is constructed: the excluded past event – as absence – is posited and becomes a fixed point' (34); and such a model implicates contemporary Irish Studies in the 'perpetuation of conventional notions of Irish identity' (51).

Richard Haslam develops a similar line in his essay 'A Race Bashed in the Face: Imagining Ireland as a Damaged Child'. Pointing out that infantilisation (along with feminisation) represented a recurring strategy in colonial relations between Ireland and Britain, Haslam argues that a particular age conceit has likewise been central to Irish postcolonial culture (including its critical culture), and that the image of the nation as a traumatised child continues to influence (often unconsciously or in a highly metaphorical register) analyses of Irish history and Irish identity into the present. As with Carville's notion of 'traumaculture' (with which it shares a number of concerns), however, such a model is fraught with difficulties and inconsistencies.

In the first place, the infantilisation of Irish identity operates by ways of an unwarranted correspondence between the individual and the nation; but to speak about repression or neurosis on a communal or even a national level is to drain the analytical gesture of any meaningful force. In this view, the image of a 'childish' nation – abused or not – is a fantasy of nineteenth-century racism, allied to all kinds of aggressive/exploitative programmes (such as imperialism and colonialism), and something which the postcolonial critic would probably do well to avoid.

Secondly, infantilisation as a model leads cultural agents (creators and/or critics) to fetishise the category of memory; this in itself leads to endless, irresolvable debates about the function of the past in relation to the present, such as those that obtained in Ireland during the so-called 'revisionism wars' of the 1990s. Haslam suggests that the debates surrounding Irish revisionism echoed in some respects a contemporaneous stand-off that was exercising the psychoanalytical community – that between 'Recovered Memory Therapy' and 'False Memory Syndrome'. The first looks to stimulate repressed memories of what is widely referred to in modern psychology as 'betrayal trauma' (Freyd 1996), while the second formalises concerns about the unreliability of memory and the influence of such stimulation – both issues, as we'll see, which exercise the narrator of *The Gathering*. In the meantime, we note that despite their different emphases, the abused child, the damaged adult and the historical act of abuse remain the foci of these accounts; but this in itself, as Haslam argues, is not an unproblematic model.

This latter point is linked to a third – namely: that the damaged child of modern Irish culture has by and large been made in the image of the child that Freud postulated as part of his 'seduction theory' – vulnerable, abused, betrayed – and not the child that Freud subsequently imagined as the source of various sexual drives which must be repressed in order for 'normal' development to occur. Of course, as a mechanism for understanding psychological dysfunction, the former is just as problematic as the latter; but this has not impeded the vogue for imagining Ireland as a damaged child struggling to retrieve (with the aid of the sympathetic cultural analyst), and then to cope with, the memory of some foundational act of abuse.

All in all, the infantilisation of Irish culture has not been a helpful development, Haslam claims, for such a 'distorting and reductive' model fails 'to do justice to the complexities, conflicts, and catastrophes that have contributed to the formation of the lives of multifarious Irish peoples, past and present'. One thing such a development has achieved, however, is the fostering of a certain *style* in Irish cultural – and especially literary – discourse:

> [A]s Benedict Anderson notes, communities 'are to be distinguished, not by their falsity/genuineness, but by the style in which they are imagined'. It also modulates particular *narrative forms*: as Luke Gibbons notes, memory involves 'not just a matter of retention or recollection but of finding the narrative forms that will do justice to this troubled inheritance [Irish history] without sanitising it, but also without succumbing to it'. (1999: original emphasis)

The emphasis on style and narrative form links to Carville's description of the emergence of Irish 'pathography' – a term adapted from psychology to describe 'the many memoirs that appeared during the [1990s] … exploring the significance of childhood ordeal in the formation of adult identity' (2012: 24). Besides well-known examples such as Frank McCourt's *Angela's Ashes* (1996) and Nuala O'Faolain's *Are You Somebody?* (1996), Carville cites Anne Enright's *The Gathering*, the novel that is the focus of this chapter.[10] Before considering that text, however, I want to turn briefly to Enright's other writings in order to understand the formal and conceptual concerns that paved the way for her award-winning 'pathography'.

Enright and betrayal

Heidi Hansson suggests that Enright's profile as 'an Irish writer' has been adversely affected by a discrepancy that exists between her formal and conceptual concerns, and a literary critical discourse which tends to be preoccupied 'with issues of national identity and the state of Irish society' (2009: 216). As it turns out, Enright's writing is all about such things, albeit in ways that, initially at least, seemed resistant to established critical approaches. Hansson characterises Enright as a 'postmodernist' writer who eschews received discourses of narrative progress or character coherence in favour of dissonance and fragmentation; she is at the same time a 'post-nationalist' writer in a society undergoing changes to all its constitutive discourses of identity. In each case, of course, Enright emerges as heiress to a long tradition of writing (including the likes of Lawrence Sterne, James Joyce, Flann O'Brien and Samuel Beckett) characterised by a kind of comic scepticism towards the pretensions of any form of identitarian narrative – especially those operating in the service of some or other preferred political dispensation.

The greater part of Enright's writing (creative and otherwise) focuses on the emotional and psychological minefield that is the Irish family. Each of her books, moreover, tends to incorporate identifiable 'pathographical' elements – dysfunctional families, creaking relationships, the repressed past erupting with greater or lesser violence into the present, and so on. At one level all this makes for good reading: traumatic things happening to ordinary people provides a kind of narrative experience that's unavailable in other forms of writing. At another level, however, Enright's continued focus on various forms of modern family-orientated trauma renders her in some senses the emblematic Irish writer of the period, for it's there in her novels and short stories that we encounter again and again the traumatised subject of contemporary Irish pathography.

A recurring characteristic of Enright's discourse is a nervous, ironic style in which painful experience is rendered obliquely, tangentially, as if to confront such experiences directly might bring the whole narrative edifice crashing down. Such a style is apparent from the outset of her career, as in this example from the title story of her debut collection *The Portable Virgin*:

> I knew that when Ben made love to her, the thought that she might break pushed him harder. I, by comparison, am like an old sofa, welcoming, familiar, well-designed.
>
> This is the usual betrayal story, as you have already guessed – the word 'sofa' gave it away. The word 'sofa' opened up rooms full of sleeping children and old wedding photographs, ironic glances at

crystal wine-glasses, BBC mini-series where Judi Dench plays the deserted furniture and has a little sad fun. (1991: 81)

Here in essence is the typical Enright milieu: a middle-class Dublin home, a tired marriage on the edge of disintegration, ironic popular cultural references and the cheap thrill of illicit sex. Here also is a narrator whose own trauma is conveyed by means of a recognisable writing style that, in Susan Cahill's words, 'is fragmentary, episodic, and postmodern in its emphasis on parody, intertextuality, and narrative incoherence' (2011: 97). And here, finally, is the self-conscious invocation of 'the usual betrayal story' that lies at the heart of modern Irish pathography – that moment when the subject becomes aware of another narrative, some secret affiliation of which they were previously unaware, impinging upon what had until that time passed for reality.

These conceptual and stylistic concerns are carried forward to Enright's debut novel, *The Wig My Father Wore* (1995). Families and lovers again feature centrally, albeit in the fantastic context of an affair between the narrator – a thirty-something television producer named Grace – and an angel called Stephen. This outlandish premise is the narrative analogue of a formal discourse characterised by fragmentation and incoherence – *meaning*, the text reveals, is always a function of the discursive contexts within which it's invoked; *meaning* is always getting ready to move elsewhere and *mean* otherwise. Grace is confronted by crises of various kinds: at home, at work, in her own mind and body – but Enright is reluctant to name these as crises, preferring instead to *evoke* moods and impressions rather than to *invoke* actual states and conditions.

Grace's relationship with her father is in some senses the key to her behaviour. There is no sense of an abusive dimension to that relationship – on the contrary, despite the dementia from which he's suffering her father remains an essentially positive presence in Grace's life, especially compared with her controlling, judgemental mother. It seems apparent, however, that it's out of a matrix of memories of her father and his currently addled condition – each of which is encapsulated in the image of his wig – that she conjures Stephen. And it seems equally apparent that in this her debut novel Enright was searching for an effective method to explore the realities of modern Irish identity in all its contradictory, fragmented nature.

Enright continued to explore this theme in *What Are You Like?* (2000) – a novel, as Cahill says, 'palpable with a sense of absence' (2011: 114). Once again we encounter a range of modern Irish subjects who are all damaged to an extent and in various ways – the twins separated at birth; the orphan who suspects that her conception may 'have started in a priest's fumblings, or an old uncle pulling down his fly' (136); the remarried widower; the second wife; the dead mother. Once again we are offered images of people struggling to fit in with the modern world and struggling likewise to account for the various mismatches they embody; and once again, crucially, we observe the child as a problematic presence in Irish life – trailing various kinds of traumatic experience (death, separation, guilt) in its wake. As with her other writings, we also observe Enright's attempts to develop a style equal to the challenge of telling such a story. *What Are You Like?* is a fragmented, multi-perspective story which struggles, like its various protagonists, to find either a moral or a corporeal centre from which to understand the ways of the world. Despite the upbeat ending it remains what might be described as a neurotic narrative, and this is an apt condition in respect of the society and the characters it tries to encompass.

Enright returned to the issue of children in modern Ireland in *Making Babies: Stumbling into Motherhood* (2004), which began as a series of light journalistic observations on pregnancy and motherhood but grew into a more substantial meditation on the role and representation of the Irish family. This book underpinned its author's profile as an apparently comic writer who was nonetheless exercised by profoundly serious matters. In *The Pleasure of Eliza Lynch* (2002), Enright captured an exotic Irish voice from a dark corner of history, while in the nineteen short stories comprising *Taking Pictures* (2008) she undertook an ambitious delineation of the modern Irish woman in her varied role as daughter, sister, wife, mother and lover.

In *The Forgotten Waltz* (2011) Enright wrote what is perhaps the most compelling account of adultery in Ireland since *Ulysses*. The novel is particularly interesting because of the way it parallels two forms of betrayal: one – illicit desire – as old, apparently, as the species; another – the Celtic Tiger – the extent of which was slowly becoming apparent as the novel itself appeared. Gina Moynihan's betrayal of her husband is of a piece with her lover Seán Vallely's interest in what he describes as 'The Culture of Money' (32), for in such a context, everything – including desire – has its price: 'You think it's about sex', Gina muses, 'and then you remember the money' (153). There's a brief allusion to the economic crash (in the form of a crisis in the housing market, p. 185), but it's the more fundamental sense of a country still profoundly dissatisfied with its own image that the novel communicates.

Enright is a writer, then, who is focused to a formative extent on the ongoing crisis of the modern Irish subject, especially as that subject has itself emerged from the salient discourses of sexual desire and family experience. She's a writer, moreover, who is alert to the importance of style in the delineation of those discourses, and to the ways in which the culture of everyday life – bodily gesture, facial expression, linguistic comment, and so on – is imbued with resonances beyond the apparent or the immediate. Put another way, Enright is a writer sensitised to Irish betrayal in its many forms and manifestations; as such, she was well placed to engage with a particular form of betrayal whose slow emergence so severely demoralised modern Irish society, and which, alongside the revelations accompanying the economic crash, so traumatised Irish identity in the opening decades of the new millennium.

The Gathering

The abusive event described in *The Gathering* adheres to a recognisable profile: a child is seduced by an adult acquaintance into an inappropriate sexual exchange, and suffers a range of damaging psychological consequences that will blight his adult behaviour.[11] In her book *Surviving Secrets: The Experience of Abuse for the Child, the Adult and the Helper*, Moira Walker provides a good description of what might have been Liam Hegarty's experience:

> Children who have been abused do not have high expectations of others ... It is essential to recognize and acknowledge that abuse of a child leads to huge developmental damage which has ongoing implications. The effects do not simply disappear or evaporate as the child reaches adulthood ... [The] ripples from abuse spread far and wide into the adult's world, the adult's experience and the adult's relationships. (1992: 1)

Enright's task as an imaginative writer is to conceive of an appropriate discourse within which to relate such a story – a textual event in which form and content map onto each other in a way

capable of doing justice to such sensitive material. This was a task
for which her previous experience – as the chronicler of an unstable
post-national Irish identity, and in particular of the alienated Irish
body – had well prepared her.[12] The principal device she employs
is that of a character who is herself struggling to find a means to
accommodate *three* roles or personae within her own life: those of
narrator, witness and victim. Amongst other things, *The Gathering*
is an exploration of how these three roles, although clearly diver-
gent in some senses, relate to one another in the context of a society
that is itself historically primed for the trauma of betrayal.

The impetus for the story, as Veronica tells us in the opening
lines, is her 'need to bear witness to an uncertain event' (2007: 1).
This need generates a narrative in which some kind of order may
be imposed on the apparently random series of events which, she
believes, led to her brother's death. Various problems are already
signalled in the original formulation, however, not least of which is
the fact that 'bearing witness' is not a straightforward or easy task –
on the contrary, it describes a complex, difficult set of positions and
relations, each of which generates its own traumatic resonances.[13]
At the same time, the 'event' itself is described as 'uncertain', and
this raises the issue of the notoriously unreliable resources – such
as memory and language – that are required in order to be able to
hear and comprehend such resonances. Of the experience of abuse
victims, Walker writes:

> [T]heir abuse was so horrifying that even at the time it was obliter-
> ated from consciousness or was confused and interwoven with an
> adult's version of events, or an adult's denial. Others could not recall
> clearly or accurately: their trauma was such that details became
> blurred and different incidents were confused. Inability to describe
> abuse clearly and concisely does not mean it did not happen, only
> that recollections are fragmented and cannot be presented as a neat,
> precise and sequential account. (1992: 96)

It's precisely the absence of 'a neat, precise and sequential account'
that accounts for the 'fragmented' nature of Veronica's narrative.
After all, *The Gathering* tells what is in some senses a very simple story: a child is abused by an adult – and this is the 'event'
alluded to above. In other ways, however, it's a very complex story,
each and every element of which – people, times, places – is locked
into a wide array of personal, political and institutional experiences. Taken together, these experiences constitute what is in effect

'Irish life' in the twentieth century; and in order to understand the 'event' – and her own relationship to it – Veronica must engage with the 'Irish life' within which it occurred and which, in some senses, generated it.

This need accounts in part for the specific tripartite time structure of the novel. One time frame is based in 'the present' – the weeks after Liam's death leading up to his funeral – and it's here that we observe Veronica's recognition of a half-forgotten childhood event as the probable cause of her brother's death and the possibility of her own victim status. Here also we witness the narrator slowly buckling under the weight of the guilt she feels for not understanding or acting sooner.

A second time frame concerns Veronica's childhood in Dublin in the late 1960s, and the series of familial and social contexts within which the 'event' was enabled to occur. This will be a familiar milieu to Enright's readers; herself a child of the 1960s, much of Enright's writing (indeed, many examples of the pathographic genre described earlier) invokes that decade as the crucible within which old and new versions of Irish identity mingled and clashed. Although the Catholic Church maintained its 'stern authority over the faithful' (Tobin 1984: 38), elements were abroad throughout society – in economics, in politics, in cultural attitudes towards the world beyond Ireland – which offered the possibility of a new perspective.[14] The 1960s witnessed an encounter between those (such as her maternal grandmother Ada) who came to maturity during the formative years of the nation-state, and those (such as Veronica and her siblings) who would go on to experience a very different form of Irishness on either side of the millennium, including the heady materialism of the Celtic Tiger.

One such encounter was that which occurred between Lamb Nugent and Liam Hegarty. Veronica cannot remember the precise role played by the former in her childhood – only that as an adult occasionally encountered in the home of her grandmother he would have been regarded as an authority figure to whom deference and politeness were due. It was this socially sanctioned position (as well as the opportunity presented by the appearance of three underprotected children) that Nugent abused so blatantly. The result, for Liam, is shattering and life-long: 'already hurt and utterly betrayed', he 'is left struggling to make sense of the senseless' (Walker 1992: 95). The adult world has turned from a place of at least nominal protection to one of pain and danger: without trust in others, without faith in his own worth, Liam turns towards the future as a deeply damaged individual.

The third time frame is the one in which Veronica speculates on the 'origin' of the story which culminates in her brother's suicide – Dublin in the 1920s, and the first meeting and early relations between Ada, Lamb and Charlie. Comprising bits of family gossip, a few letters and other documents as well as her own observations and memories, this element likewise stands as an attempt to comprehend the 'event', although this time largely from the perspective of the perpetrator. Nugent's evil, as imagined by Veronica, is exemplary; and yet there's more to it – another dimension which implicates the wider context from which such a figure emerged and in which he was enabled to act as he did:

> I know he could be the explanation for all of our lives, and I know something more frightening still – that we did not have to be damaged by him in order to be damaged. It was the air he breathed that did for us. It was the way we were obliged to breathe his second-hand air. (224)

Lamb Nugent's abuse of Liam Hegarty is in this sense a betrayal of Ireland's future (the 2000s) by a present (the 1960s) that is itself the product of a traumatic, treacherous past (the 1920s). It's also as much a social as an interpersonal act – an act of betrayal, that is to say, which resonates outwards from the 'event' itself into a wide range of cultural and historical contexts. And it's this sense of betrayal as a kind of social disease, contractable in the air itself, which informs Veronica vision of 'a family – a whole fucking country – drowning in shame' (168).

All these issues weigh on Veronica in her role as narrator – in the light of which it's no wonder that she comes across as a troubled and difficult character. She nurses a series of thorny, semi-resentful relationships with her mother and siblings, for example, while also appearing increasingly estranged from Tom, her 'high-maintenance' (36) husband. It's only with the realisation that she is herself struggling with more than just the death of her brother that Veronica's behaviour comes into focus, both for herself and for the reader.

After all, Veronica is attempting to understand and describe events in which she herself partook; she is thus both inside and outside the narrative. Her role as narrative 'witness' is an echo of

her role as 'witness' to the event. Each role is, moreover, highly traumatic – the one for its observation of, and proximity to, the original
event; the second for its uncertainty over its own ability to recall or
to communicate that event. At the same time, each also activates
painful and disabling discourses of guilt and betrayal – the first
in relation to the witness's ability to intervene, or perhaps relief
at their evasion of the abusive act (if she did indeed evade it); the
second in relation to the witness's decision to reveal the occurrence
of the event itself, as well as issues relating to the timing and manner of such a revelation.

All in all, *The Gathering* is the traumatic rendering of a traumatic
event. Liam is the 'victim' in so far as he is the one upon whom the
abusive act was perpetrated, and whose life is most blighted as a
consequence. Yet Veronica's narrative reveals that she, and the rest
of the family, are also victims in some senses – all paying in some
fashion or other, to some degree or other, for the depredations of
Lamb Nugent. The novel's brilliance as a narrative lies in its insistence on the multitudinous factors feeding into and out of any single
abusive act or encounter. Its challenge lies in the delineation of contemporary Ireland as a damaged society – one in which the trauma
of betrayal is, to use the text's own image, present in the very air
itself.

In such a context, the question presents itself: where, when and
most importantly *how* can a process of healing commence? What
palliative resources may be brought to bear upon the destructive
emotions – such as pain, guilt, anger and fear – which invariably
emerge in such a context? One answer lies in the future, in the form
of Liam's young son Rowan, who appears at his father's funeral.
Veronica feels immensely attracted to the child, not only because
he is a living reminder of her dead brother but also (and more
importantly) because, representing as he does a form of positive,
protective love, he offers the damaged generation the possibility of
redemption – a chance to mitigate those complex negative emotions
in favour of one shockingly simple emotion whose name is love.
It's in the name of that emotion that Veronica contemplates having
another baby at the end of the novel – another chance to confirm
the redemptive power of love in the face of the destructive power
of abuse.

Another response to that destructive power lies in analysis, understanding, insight, perspective – in short, in narrative – and this is the

response that Veronica pursues in the account of her brother's life and death. If 'love' represents the embrace of a powerful simplicity – the great everlasting 'Yea' which we proclaim in the face of the 'No' of sexual abuse – narrative is a more complex, less secure form of relief. This is because narrative retains, in the constitutive properties of language, character and story, the remnants of all the other narratives of which it is composed. This is why even within her own narrative Veronica can find no guaranteed position from which to understand the 'event' she has witnessed, nor indeed to finish the account she has undertaken; 'I have been falling into my own life, for months', she writes in the closing paragraph, '[and] I am about to hit it now' (261).

Enright's text is exemplary in terms of the issues that have exercised us throughout this book – that is, the novelist as the chronicler of betrayal in modern Irish life. Confronted by a society in which betrayal (in its multitudinous forms) is rife – part of the air we breathe – Veronica represents the subject who, like the novelist, is both inside the action, witness to the treacherous event and infected by all its negative energies, while at the same time attempting to find a position beyond the event *from* which, and a means *with* which, to understand and describe it. The abused child, likewise, stands as the archetypal figure for a society in which past, present and future are entered in a seemingly unbreakable cycle of betrayal and guilt. In the light of this, Veronica's response – an acknowledgement of the power of love, and a willingness to enter yet again the foul rag and bone shop of the heart – may represent the best option for a society still, after nearly a century of 'independence', in search of its own soul.

Afterwards

We need a strategic plan.

And yes, of course, I'll do everything I can
To look after the money.

I'm your man.

Let the myths begin.

> Brendan Kennelly, *The*
> *Little Book of Judas*, 224

The idea for this book came to me early in 2008 while I was examining a doctoral thesis on the fiction of Raymond Williams, when the candidate described how one of Williams's characters was betrayed by his enemy. 'That isn't right', I thought to myself; 'you're not betrayed by your *enemies* – they act as they *ought* to act. You're betrayed by your *friends* – by those you believe to be "on your side", but who are in fact not.'

Intrigued by this simple insight, I incorporated a chapter on Thomas Moore and betrayal in the book I was preparing for publication at that time (Smyth 2009: 15–31). By late summer, with that MS submitted, and feeling there was more mileage in the idea of betrayal, I prepared a proposal for the current monograph. As I began to sound out various publishers for their interest in such a project, the banking crisis broke. With everyone so shocked at the speed with which, as well as the degree to which, things disintegrated, 'betrayal' became the catch-cry throughout the Irish media and the public sphere.

Soon after, the Murphy and Ryan reports confirmed people's worst fears regarding the scandal that had been rumbling in Irish society since the 1990s: in the words of the latter document, clerical abuse in Ireland during the twentieth century had been 'systemic, pervasive, chronic, excessive, arbitrary, endemic' (Bunting 2009). It was, as President Mary McAleese said on 21 May 2009, 'an atrocious betrayal of love' (RTÉ 1989). Such language (as I've pointed out in both the Introduction and the final chapter of this book) continues to be used in relation to this scandal down to the present day. Combined with the economic discourse mentioned in the previous paragraph, it has made for an extremely damaging period in Irish life – one characterised by a kind of toxic introspection in which the moral, political and emotional failings of the modern nation have been played out before the rest of the world.

The months and the years passed, and the anger grew. What had initially presented itself to me as an interesting intellectual problem had suddenly assumed a dreadful timeliness, as an extended series of issues began to emerge in relation to Irish history, Irish identity and betrayal. One crucial element of all this, I soon realised, concerned language – the unique tool that humans use to try to describe what they believe or feel has happened, or what they want to happen. Language is, amongst other things, a conduit between memory and desire – hence its fundamental importance to all aspects of human experience. The significance of language intensifies during times of crisis, when people feel their sense of reality to be under threat. Words become powerful weapons; narrative – the collection of words into complex organised groupings – becomes the terrain over which bitter battles for meaning are fought.

As a cultural historian I have been centrally concerned with language throughout my career, and particularly with that form of the written word wherein the nation contemplates itself at length: the novel. At both a conceptual and a formal level, I have found the novel to be predicated on the possibility (indeed, the inevitability) of betrayal: of secret desire, alternative motivation, ambivalent significance, insecure borders – of things, ultimately, not being as they seem. I have discussed the reasons for this at length in the main body of my book. But now, afterwards, it strikes me as suggestive that I happened to commence a study of betrayal and/in Irish fiction just at the time when the nation itself was about to enter a period of intense soul-searching during which the spectre of betrayal loomed so large.

I'm not claiming any prescience here. I am suggesting, however, that it might be interesting to contemplate the possibility of some process of synchronicity or entrainment in relation to the various cultural, critical, political and economic trajectories that have been operating throughout modern Irish history. A century after 1916, the waves from that revolutionary act are breaking upon the shores of reality at more or less the same time. It may be, in other words, that the critical theory emerged at the right time to answer the needs of the economic and cultural crises because all were developing within the same basic historical structure – one set in train by the events of a century earlier.

However that may be, the question is, as always: what next? I don't know if Ireland is beginning to emerge from the trauma of the crash and the mortifying revelations that emerged during the opening decade of the new millennium. I don't know how long the processes of grieving, blaming and obsessive scab-picking need to run before some new dispensation kicks in. It seems clear, however, that the morning after despair is as fraught with doubt and suspicion as the morning after optimism. We hear the angry, traumatised voices around us; we observe the bewildered, betrayed faces: how much good will and energy and imagination will it require to fix something so badly broken? Or should we just grasp the opportunity to rip up the old story and start again?

To adapt my virtual partner throughout this book: let the myths begin (again).

Notes

Introduction: betrayal and the Irish novel

1 The *OED* defines 'treason' as 'the action of betraying: betrayal of the trust undertaken by or reposed in any one: breach of faith, treacherous action, treachery' (Simpson and Weiner 1989 XVIII: 458). The same source defines 'betray' as 'to give up to, or place in the power of, an enemy, by treachery or disloyalty ... To be or prove false to (a trust or him who trusts one) ... To cheat, disappoint ... To disclose or reveal with breach of faith (a secret, or that which should be kept secret)' (II: 150). Synonyms (widely dispersed throughout this volume) include cheating, deceit, deception, duplicity, infidelity, perfidy, pretence, seeming, sedition, sham, subversion, treachery and unfaithfulness.

2 Gerald of Wales (1982: 106–7). One interesting aspect of the description here is the author's portrayal of treachery as an implicitly doubled discourse – encapsulated in the series of rhetorical oppositions with which the quotation ends.

3 The relationship between play and betrayal is one of many fascinating issues that I have no room to engage seriously in this book.

1 A short history of betrayal

1 Besides this fundamental usage, Freud also deploys the word 'betrayal' in the sense of 'self-betrayal' in various places throughout his work, as in this characterisation of Thanatos, the death drive, from *Civilization and its Discontents*: '[We] can only suspect it, as it were, as something in the background behind Eros, and it escapes detection unless its presence is betrayed by its being alloyed with Eros' (1930: 81).

2 Freud's model of the family romance is of course highly contentious, and for various (methodological and biographical) reasons; see Chapter 8 of this study, on Anne Enright's *The Gathering*.

3 See the Introduction, in which these issues are broached in terms of evolutionary psychology.

4 I wonder also if there is not something inherently treacherous about the Freudian concept of 'the Uncanny', which has had such a successful career in a wide range of critical schools and disciplines since its first articulation in 1919. Quoting a definition of the *unheimlich* as 'everything ... that ought to have remained secret and hidden but has come to light' (1919: 345), Freud goes on to theorise the uncanny with reference to the double, repetition and the eruption of the familiar from within the apparently unfamiliar. Each of these elements resonates in terms of betrayal – as with, for example, the agent who looks like a friend (the double), the agent who acts like a friend (repetition) and the existence of the Other (the unfamiliar) within the Same (the familiar).

5 For other potentially positive perspectives on treason and betrayal see West (1964) and Petriglieri (2005).

6 The ensuing 'betrayal trauma' would be similar to that experienced by many Irish victims of the Catholic Church's systematic contravention of its avowed pastoral mission. On the controversy surrounding 'seduction theory' see Chapter 8.

7 On the possible connections between the Jesus/Judas and Othello/Iago relationships see Gubar 2009: 181, 234–5, 267.

2 Déirdre and the sons of Usnach: a case study in Irish betrayal

1 For the sake of convenience I follow Douglas Hyde's spellings (1899: 302) throughout this chapter, except when referring to specific quotations.

2 Breatnach 1994: 99. It's interesting to note that the *Book of Leinster* was compiled under the patronage of Diarmait mac Murchada (Dermot Mac Murrough), a name redolent of betrayal in Irish history.

3 Both Rolleston (in his 1897 text for Michele Esposito's *Deirdre* cantata) and Squire (1905: 190) explicitly likened Déirdre to Helen.

4 See www.exclassics.com/ossian/oss24.htm. A version by John Woodrow – *Carthon, the Death of Cuchulain, and Darthula* – was published in Edinburgh and London in 1769.

5 For Ferguson's complex bibliography see www.ricorso.net/rx/az-data/authors/f/Ferguson_S/life.htm#Hibernights. See also Leerssen 1996: 72.

6 In a clear echo of Judas's fate, Squire notes that 'Buinne was tempted and fell; but the land given him turned barren that very night in indignation at being owned by such a traitor' (1905: 197).

7 For a classic modern exploration of the dynamics between 'one woman and two men' see Harold Pinter's *Betrayal* (1978).

8 Del Collo was not the first to conflate the O'Grady cousins, Hayes and James, nor will she be the last.

9 Not unnaturally, different critics have discerned different associations in *Deirdre*, depending upon where and how they place their emphases. In his study of Yeats, for example, Richard Ellmann argued that 'Naisi is not John MacBride, nor King Conchubar Yeats, but Naisi is the qualities in Yeats which MacBride's success made Yeats realize he had suppressed, as Conchubar is the qualities which MacBride made Yeats realize he had overly exalted' (1949: 170). In his essay 'Yeats and the Mask of Deirdre', on the other hand, Maneck H. Daruwala (2001) argues for the implicit identification of Conchubar with MacBride.

10 Casement's speech from the dock after his conviction for High Treason is a classic of Irish revolutionary rhetoric, but also of the rather less familiar way in which the concept of treason itself is interrogated.

11 The first draft of the play is dated 5 September 1907.

12 One is reminded of E.M. Forster's famous dictum: 'If I had to choose between betraying my country and betraying my friend I hope I should have the guts to betray my country' (1951: 78).

13 On the role and representation of music in contemporary aesthetic debates see Smyth (2008).

3 'Trust Not Appearances'

1 The precise date is uncertain. Brenda Maddox places it after September 1913, when Prezioso was still in friendly contact with the Joyce household; Richard Ellmann seems to have it at least one, possibly two years earlier.

2 Joyce's attitudes towards marriage and interpersonal betrayal were naturally enough influenced by prevailing discourses of gender, sex and sexuality, which, as described in Foucault (1976), Giddens (1992) and Inglis (1998), was characterised by its 'hidden' ubiquity and (in an Irish context) the Catholic Church's insistent idealisation of the patriarchal family.

3 In a speech in Cincinnati on 18 April 1891, Parnell's mother, Delia, condemned those who had 'betrayed Parnell with a kiss' (Foster 1976: 237).

4 Tanner considered Joyce (along with D.H. Lawrence) to represent the end of a bourgeois 'contractual' aesthetic, which includes not only the marriage contract which is at the heart of the nineteenth-century novel, but the implicit contract that obtains between writer and reader. For a more wide-ranging consideration of the novel of adultery see Armstrong (1976).

5 Tanner writes: 'One of the basic problems about marriage is that its security depends upon repetition … and that repetition and habit diminish the feelings, particularly the erotic intensity, upon which the marriage was

founded. Hence, and only apparently paradoxically, marriage can breed the need for "irregularité", "des explosions capriceuses," "désordre et l'infraction"' (375). It was the acceptance of the relationship between security and 'irregularité' that led the young Stephen Dedalus to disdain the marriage vow. See *Stephen Hero* (1944: 206).

6 In fact, the pattern may be much older: 'Adultery as a phenomenon is in evidence in literature from the earliest times, as in Homer (and indeed we might suggest that it is the unstable triangularity of adultery, rather than the static symmetry of marriage, that is the generative form of Western literature as we know it)' (Tanner 1979: 12). It was of course the Homeric parallels that Joyce exploited so brilliantly in *Ulysses*.

7 In an interesting chapter in his book *Terror and Irish Modernism* (2009), Jim Hansen considers the extent to which *Ulysses* may be approached from a gothic perspective.

8 Foster writes: 'The Divorce and Matrimonial Causes Act of 1857 ... had not been extended to Ireland, nor was it protested much that this was wrong. Between 1857 and 1910, there were only thirty-nine divorces granted to Irish residents, no doubt because anyone there seeking a divorce had to submit a private bill to parliament and because the costs involved in doing so exceeded £500 in 1910' (2008: 63). On Joyce's use of British divorce-court journalism, especially in 'Eumaeus', see Leckie (2003).

9 Joyce attended Beleveedere College between 1893 and 1898. There's no precise date attached to this essay, although Ellmann (1959: 36–7) seems to suggest that it probably predates 1897, when Joyce won the first of two consecutive prizes for best English composition in the national Intermediate Examinations.

10 The concept of 'the traitor's eye' has resonances in contemporary discourses focused on sincerity and revelation, such as those advanced by Oscar Wilde (Ellmann 1969: 290–434) and Sigmund Freud (1900).

11 'In creating Gretta, Joyce made a version of his own wife and then dramatized his own life-long obsession with sexual unfaithfulness, which would emerge in letters, in his play *Exiles* and in his novel *Ulysses*. It was as important as his obsession with Ireland, or with Dublin' (Tóibín 2012: 4).

12 The relatively recent loss of the Gaelic language and the highly politicised nature of language in a decolonising society may be influential factors here.

13 Another play, entitled *A Brilliant Career*, written in 1900 and apparently even more anxiously under the influence of Ibsen, was destroyed by the author in 1905 (Ellmann 1959: 80).

14 All these possibilities are invoked in Conor McPherson's introduction (1918: x). See R. Brown (1985: 18–19) for an analysis of the extent to which *Exiles* may be regarded as a response to the cuckold theme established in *Madame Bovary*.

15 One of these students became an object of Joycean sexual fantasy, as described in the prose fragment entitled *Giacomo Joyce*, first published in 1959. In his introduction and notes to that text, Richard Ellmann has explored the links with Joyce's more established works.

16 This incident would be revisited in *Ulysses* when an inebriated Stephen Dedalus is threatened by two British soldiers outside a brothel in Nighttown. As his companion Lynch withdraws Stephen says: '*Exit Judas. Et laqueo se suspendit*' (1922: 557). The Latin translates as: 'Judas left. And went and hanged himself.' The comparison took on a disturbing resonance when in 1926 Vincent Cosgrave committed suicide, not by hanging, but by throwing himself from London Bridge.

17 Joyce was suspicious and possessive from an early point in the relationship. In a letter from late July 1904, he wrote: 'Where will you be on Saturday night, Sunday night, Monday night, that I can't see you?' (Ellmann 1966: 44).

18 In the first he wrote: 'I cannot call you any dear name because tonight I have learnt that the only being I believed in was not loyal to me.' In the second: 'If I could forget my books and my children and forget that the girl I loved was false to me and remember her only as I saw her with the eyes of my boyish love I would go out of life content' (Ellmann 1966: 232–3).

19 Freud 1905a: 223. It is the anxiety relating to paternity and illegitimacy that, as we saw in Chapter 1, Shakespeare dramatises in *The Winter's Tale*. Paternal uncertainty is a 'truism' which DNA testing has rendered obsolete.

20 Maddox 1988: 127. In his memoir of his brother's early life in Dublin, Stanislaus Joyce also avers that Byrne was 'correct' and that Cosgrave lied (1958: 212), although he offers no evidence either way.

21 See the letters from Joyce to Nora on 26 August (Ellmann 1966: 48), 12 September (52), and 29 September (57), 1904. Ellmann suggests that Cosgrave was 'humiliated' (1959: 160) when he failed to lure Barnacle away from Joyce. In a letter to Nora on 3 December 1909 (Ellmann 1975: 182), however, Joyce seems to accept that Cosgrave and Nora enjoyed some level of non-penetrative sexual relations.

22 'By the time that Joyce was writing *Ulysses*', Barbara Leckie writes, 'the representation of adultery no longer carried the same transgressive charge that had marked its reception throughout the nineteenth century, but it nevertheless remained inflected by this history' (2003: 729).

23 The setting is highly significant. As sociologist Tom Inglis writes: 'The ritual sublimation of desire through drinking was also a means of males bonding and developing and maintaining their emotional independence from women, even in marriage. The pub became a sanctuary for men, a place where they could displace their sexual frustration through a repetitive, compulsive pattern of drinking' (1998: 320).

24 See Lady Gregory's *Dervorgilla* (1907) in *Selected Plays* (1962: 107–27).

25 Joyce 1922: 308. Boylan is already associated with treachery, as earlier in the chapter the citizen refers to him as the 'traitor's son' on account of his father selling horses to the British Army during the Boer War (305).

26 Peter Berresford Ellis writes: 'In the area of [modern] women's rights, much of the long struggle is only to regain what was once enjoyed by Celtic women fifteen hundred years ago … they could divorce and, if they were deserted, molested or maltreated, they had the right to claim considerable damages' (1995: 15, 18). See also Wood and O'Shea (1997).

27 Richard Brown writes: 'Matrimonial anomalies, in his reading interests and worked into the detail of the books, provided Joyce with a means of sustaining his sense of the inadequacy of conventional marriage. To take such delight in anomaly, though, Joyce needed to have an especially accurate sense of the law itself, and of his interest therein much evidence remains'; and further: 'Marriage law was a strongly present interest in the composition of *Ulysses* from the first idea of a story about a Dublin cuckold, which occurred to Joyce in 1906' (1985: 40–1, 43–4).

28 Lloyd 1993: 105. Harold Bloom writes 'Stephen's purpose is to dissolve the authority of fatherhood itself' (1994: 416).

29 Making a related point, Barbara Leckie discusses how Bloom's attempt to describe a 'simple case of adultery' in 'Eumaeus' 'is repeatedly frustrated, and the fantasy of the transparent window through which one sees the "awful truth" of adultery is exploded' (2003: 736).

30 Lawson writes: 'Adultery can be a relationship where one or the other partner does gain real power, and it seems to me that it has, unlike marriage, often afforded women power. Women have been able to begin and end relationships, to refuse and reject advances, to set the pace of involvement, to gain material advantage, to achieve status, to travel, to expand the boundaries of their lives, and to know the extent of their powers of attraction. They have been able, on occasion, to exercise control over their marriages through their adulterous liaison' (1988: 31).

4 The landscape of betrayal

1 See Costello 1996: 47–59, and Sheeran 1976: 78–91. Besides the autobiographical material present in his fiction, a series of memoirs (1930, 1931, 1934) provides a colourful though unreliable guide to O'Flaherty's intellectual and artistic development.

2 As late as June 1923 the Irish Republican Brotherhood – yesterday's man in so many ways – was still advocating 'death for any wilful betrayal of matters vital to the organisation's objects' (Ó Broin, 1976,

216–17). Brian Hanley claims that most IRA intelligence activity in the years immediately after the Civil War was focused on infiltration and informers. He makes the point that in any 'organization in which the poorer sections of the urban and rural population were over represented financial incentives could make supplying information seem attractive (2002: 48).

3 Nowhere was this more apparent than in relation to the fall-out from the Anglo-Irish Treaty itself. Anti-Treaty republicans such as Ernie O'Malley were 'angry [when he] thought of the men who had betrayed us' (1978: 42), yet he himself was widely regarded (along with his fellow recusants) as a traitor. See Ó Broin 1976: 212.

4 Cleary 2007: 144. Peter Costello writes that 'Joyce represented the cerebral and intellectual, everything that O'Flaherty did not want to be' (1996: 47–8). A reference to *Ulysses* in *The Assassin* (1928: 106) points to at least some level of familiarity with Joyce's work. Costello also points out (51) that during the period when he was writing *The Informer*, O'Flaherty was also involved (along with Francis Stuart) in producing a radical literary journal entitled *To-Morrow*, which, notwithstanding its anti-Yeats stance, recruited the recently conferred Nobel laureate to write an editorial and contribute a poem to its first and only number in September 1924. See also Sheeran 1976: 84–6.

5 Fr Hugh contributes to 'revolutionary papers in Dublin … seditious papers plotting treason against his Britannic Majesty, and advocating an Irish Republic' (1923: 16).

6 Betrayal also permeates *The Assassin* (1928), O'Flaherty's fictionalized account of the murder of Kevin O'Higgins, and a text that is even more engaged with the bitter fall-out from the Civil War and the failed republican revolution.

7 In *Shame the Devil* O'Flaherty wrote: 'While I was walking down Praed Street [in London] I suddenly realized that if I must write, I must be the spokesman of that life; for I loved it, and one can only write inspired by love. So I rushed back to the house, sat down to the typewriter and began to write about Aran' (1934: 38).

8 Peter Hart writes: 'organized labour never contemplated an overthrow of the state, except insofar as it supported Sinn Féin in doing so … The revolution did not produce an institutional upheaval either … Much of the civil service remained intact, along with its previous ideals and methods. A new political system was introduced, but its differences from the British model were matters of detail rather than principle' (2003: 21, 22).

9 O'Flaherty 1925: 107. It's in passages such as this that *The Informer* most closely approximates, in language and in ethos, O'Casey's contemporaneous Dublin trilogy. Joseph Cleary argues that O'Flaherty's

novel 'owes much to *Shadow of a Gunman*, but eschews the comedy of O'Casey for a more conventionally grim naturalism' (2007: 144).

10 As Conor Kostick (1996), writes: 'The anti-Treaty forces were united by bold words and ideals but were without the slightest concern for class politics' (182); at the same time, '[the] Provisional Government was determined to quell the ambitions of Irish workers' (186).

11 Despite periodic attempts to liaise, as Peter Hart points out, '[the] republican movement itself had no serious social agenda, and was not class-based. Its activists and membership was drawn from a wide variety of backgrounds, forming a cross-class coalition of groups, in which organized labour had little power. Nor did the new Free State – whose establishment was backed by the Labour Party – offer any adjustment to property or labour relations' (2003: 21).

12 Emmet O'Connor writes that the new CPI 'was formally recognised as an affiliate by the ECCI presidium on 13 January 1922' (2004: 51).

13 The tensions within the IRA between nationalism, republicanism and socialism (as well as personality clashes involving Connolly) were to lead to a split in the organisation during the 1930s (English 1994: 217ff.).

14 The quotations from *The Times* are reproduced in Hart 2003: 131.

15 See the chapter in Hart (2003: 110–38) on 'The Social Structure of the Irish Republican Army'.

16 'The waters cleave and the life of the informer, and their kith and kin, diverges from the tribe. There is no language for, no possibility of, "turning back". In Ireland the same term has only one other usage – to describe the social betraying of turning one's religion and adhering to the other, Catholic or Protestant, faith' (Toolis 1995: 194).

17 Although Kostick points out that Tipperary was one of the centres of soviet activity in 1922, the county is usually regarded (along with Cork) as one of the most militant republican areas in the country.

18 Sheeran (1976: 259). The reference to Dostoyevsky will develop in significance when we come to examine the work of O'Flaherty's friend Francis Stuart.

19 O'Flaherty is rather more sympathetically treated in Hand (2011: 172–77); and his status would certainly be worth exploring in the light of David Lloyd's work on nationalism and minor literature (1987).

20 Some of those 'literary critics' were still falling into O'Flaherty's trap nearly seventy years later, as when Rachael Sealy Lynch mistakenly refers to Gallagher as 'the repellant yet fascinating leader of the Irish Republican Brotherhood' (1993: 260), and insists on 'patriotism' and 'Nationalism' (261) as the significant political discourses against which his character should be judged.

21 Joseph Cleary's description of naturalism as comprising 'certain recurrent features – documentary strategies; the anatomy of discrete

(generally lower-class) milieux; entropic plots of stasis or decline; particular dispositions of character, narrator and reader' (2007: 123), seems appropriate here.

22 In *The Assassin*, the character McDara notes how 'informers present themselves before the rulers of their organization and demand that they be killed before they kill themselves, seeking escape from the cries of their wounded consciences in death' (1928: 245). The informer's death drive recalls the rigours of the Freudian unconscious, and bears upon Gypo's inability to come up with a plausible alibi, as well as his powerful compulsion to confess to Gallagher.

23 By the final chapter the 'poetic' discourse is almost entirely dominant. The final image of a forgiven Gypo collapsing into the shape of a cross echoes the Christian symbolism with which Joyce ends 'The Dead'.

5 A spy in the house of love

1 The publication of Bowen's extensive contributions to the BBC over of period of thirty-two years (Hepburn 2010) has helped to alter the perception of her as a figure who shied away from public or political engagement in order to focus predominantly on private matters.

2 For an overview of the debates relating to Ireland and postcolonial theory see Cleary 2007: 14–46.

3 Éibhear Walshe writes: 'An important strand within her writing career was her need to promote a greater political and cultural understanding between Ireland and Britain from the late-1920s to the late-1960s' (2011: 2–3).

4 Bowen suffered from a stammer throughout her life – an appropriate affliction for a writer for whom 'saying' anything at all was fraught with difficulty.

5 On 4 January 1955 Bowen wrote to Charles Ritchie: 'I think Ireland's rather a place for pleasure. I mean, the real kind – slightly dashing, more than a bit ramshackle, but totally without *calcul* and unsnobbish' (in Glendenning and Robertson 2008: 202, original emphasis).

6 W.J. McCormack writes: 'Bowen had been on the margin of political discussion through her friendship with Maurice Bowra who in turn had befriended Guy Burgess and Donald MacLean. What was later called "the climate of treason" was familiar to Bowen long before the war began' (1993: 212).

7 Walshe 2011: 52–61, 77–99. Maud Ellmann (2004: 151) speculates that one of Bowen's interviewees – the right-wing Fine Gael politician James Dillon, about whom she wrote both in 1940 and 1942 – may have served in some respects as the model for Robert Kelway. Dillon remained ignorant of Bowen's true interests, and was deeply offended

when Robert Fisk (1983: 366) revealed them during an interview for his book *In Time of War*.

8 Lane and Clifford 2009: 7. The question of Bowen's wartime status (spy, traitor, double agent, etc.) and of her wider relationship with Ireland is discussed at length in this volume, where amongst other things it's claimed that '[she] was intoxicated by her Englishness and made little pretence of being Irish until it became expedient for her to do so for espionage purposes during the War' (176).

9 Bowen's impressions of London during the Blitz are justly celebrated as some of the most evocative: see her article 'London, 1940' (1950: 217–20), which is an edited version of a longer censored piece reproduced as 'Britain in Autumn' (Hepburn 2008: 48–55).

10 In a letter of 26 March 1950 Bowen describes a visit to St Elizabeth's psychiatric hospital near Washington, DC, home at that time to the high-profile collaborationist Ezra Pound (in Glendenning and Robertson 2008: 164). It's remarkable, given the status and interests of the two, that she makes no mention of him. See Chapter 6 of this study, on Francis Stuart.

11 Bowen had already broached some of these issues in a short story entitled 'Summer Night' (1941, reproduced 1999: 583–608), in which a woman drives through the Irish night away from the dangers of Britain at war towards her adulterous lover.

12 According to Foster, Bowen began writing *The Heat of the Day* in 1944, 'sending chapters out of London for safekeeping' (1993: 112–13).

13 Glendenning and Robertson 2008: 473. Glendenning also writes: 'The love affair between Stella and Robert mirrors that between EB and CR. Regent's Park and its rose gardens are among the settings, and the edgy, heightened emotional atmosphere of their wartime London is immortalised' (124).

14 On Joyce's background and trial see Rebecca West's *The New Meaning of Treason* (1964: 1–122).

15 Hermione Lee points out that, given her experience and the circles in which she moved, 'Elizabeth Bowen would have been in a good position to write a detailed and convincing spy story ... traitors came from the heart of the British establishment. Many of the upper-class English intellectuals who were close friends of Bowen (or of Charles Ritchie) – Maurice Bowra, Isaiah Berlin, Cyril Connolly, Miriam Rothschild – were well acquainted also with Burgess and Maclean' (1981: 176). See n. 6 above.

16 Walshe 2006: 102. It was as the author of a high-profile novel on wartime treason that Bowen was invited to participate in a 'Conversation on Traitors', broadcast by the BBC on 21 August 1952. A main reference point in the conversation is Sir Roger Casement; the transcript is included in Hepburn 2010: 304–22.

17 Joyce was not, as is commonly believed, Irish; although he spent his youth in Galway, he was in fact born in New York of naturalised American parents. It was confusion relating to his national identity (partly engineered by himself) that led to his conviction and execution (Martland 2003).

18 Bowen's own father suffered a nervous breakdown when she was a child. Her subsequent connection of this event with her own lifelong stammer (1975: 12) raises the issue of a connection between voice and identity. For Bowen, as Allan Hepburn writes, 'Writing is a way of not stuttering; to write is to achieve fluency, free of the treacheries implicit in the spoken voice' (2010: 8). On the contrary, the 'fluency' of Bowen's literary discourse is disputed throughout this chapter.

19 It's interesting that Kelway's method for obviating the power of words such as 'treason' consists in repetition – 'saying them to myself over and over again till it became absolutely certain they mean nothing'. But repetition is itself profoundly implicated in the politics of treason – including the absolutely fundamental form of repetition that is encoded into the signifier/signified relationship.

20 Hermione Lee criticises what she regards as the novel's 'syntactical mannerisms' and its over use of 'double negatives, inversions, the breaking-up of natural sentence order [and] passive constructions' (1981: 165).

21 Corcoran 2004: 190–1. Éibhear Walshe makes a similar point; in Mount Morris, he argues, Stella 'experiences a sense of uncomplicated, liberating allegiance to the allied cause … This is of a piece with much of Bowen's wartime sense of Anglo-Ireland as a loyal, stable place and the Anglo-Irish home becomes symbolically implicated with eventual Allied victory. Stella comes to see this Irish Big House as an oasis of feudal certainty and this certainty is contrasted unfavourably with the suffocating, traitorous suburban villas of the English Home Counties' (2011: 18).

22 'For here we do not have an enduring city, but we are looking for the city that is to come' (Hebrews 13:14 (New International Version)). Bowen made specific reference to these famous words and images in 'Conversation on Traitors' (Hepburn 2010: 318).

6 Jesus or Judas?

1 In an interview published in 1981, Stuart said: 'National literature is to my mind a meaningless term. Literature can't be national. Literature is individual. Nationality has nothing to do with it' (Sheehan 1981: 408).

2 Besides *Black List, Section H*, the fullest fictional account of the marriage can be found in *Victors and Vanquished* (1959). For more biographical

information see Natterstad (1974), Foster (2003), Elborn (1990), Kiely (2007), O'Donoghue (1998) and Wills (2007).

3 Barrington (2000: 201–4) makes a strong case for Stuart's authorship of a broadcast dated 9 February 1942.

4 The impact of Stuart's broadcasts was limited in a number of respects, including the number of wireless sets in the country, and the Irish government's aggressive censorship practices (Ó Drisceoil 2000).

5 Stuart's imagination of treason was already exercised by his composition in 1940 of a short study of Roger Casement, the principal themes of which are the imminent victory of Casement's chosen allies, and the treachery of those who had executed him on a charge of treason. The authorship of some portions of this text remains at issue; see Elborn 1990: 137.

6 See O'Donoghue (1998: 137–8) and Stuart (1984: 40). Stuart's broadcasts are notable for the absence of anti-Semitic sentiments, in which case they contrast strongly with those of Joyce (Martland 2003: 48–50) and Pound (Fuller Torrey 1984: 157). The question of Stuart's attitude towards Jews, and the extent to which it may have informed his work (including his wartime broadcasts), is considered at length in Barrington (2000).

7 Stuart 1971: 179. The image of shaven-headed female collaborators turns up also in *Victors and Vanquished* (1959: 14), contributing to the idea of the earlier novel as in some senses a test run for *Black List, Section H*.

8 S.J. Caterson draws out the biographical and literary parallels between the two authors, writing that '[in] the guise of his persona H, Stuart is Stephen Dedalus's dark companion' (1997: 87).

9 On the difference between performative and declarative speech acts see Austin (1962). For a poststructuralist response, see Derrida's celebrated essay on the 'declaration of independence' as a genre (1986).

10 See Wills 2007: *passim*. According to David O'Donoghue (1998), Stuart was one of only three Irish people (the others being Susan Hilton and John O'Reilly) who worked directly for Irland-Redaktion.

11 The view that Stuart's behaviour was psychologically conditioned is articulated most forcefully by Colm Tóibín, when he writes: 'And all this, his novel *Black List, Section H* makes clear, had nothing to do with politics, with anti-Semitism, or fascism, or Nazism, but arose from something darkly and deeply rooted in his psyche – the need to betray and be seen to betray. It arose from something else too – a passionate belief that every organised structure, and that includes liberal democracy, is rotten' (1997). *Pace* this analysis, what *Black List, Section H* 'makes clear' – or what in fact it strenuously conceals – is precisely the issue.

12 See Griffin (2010). William Joyce and Ezra Pound certainly appeared to believe that they were working for a cause opposed to plutocracy, and in support of the proletariat.

13 A genuine fear of a German-backed IRA assault upon the state was abroad in Eire (and in certain British circles) throughout the war. On the complex politics of neutrality and sovereignty see Ó Drisceoil (2000) and Wills (2007).

14 Stuart was not called upon to return to Ireland himself, but he did give his address to an agent named Hermann Goertz, who, after parachuting into Co. Meath in May 1940, made his way to Laragh in Co. Wicklow, where he was fed and clothed by Iseult Stuart. She subsequently arranged contact for him with the IRA; see Fisk (1983: 301ff.) and Wills (2007: 156).

15 Eagleton (1998: 244). The issue of Stuart's political imagination has formed an important part of the general question relating to his culpability. O'Donoghue remarks that 'The essential quality of Stuart's broadcasts seems to be his naïvety' (1998: ix); Anthony Cronin likewise regarded him as 'an innocent abroad' (1997), while Robert Fisk referred to him as 'a political innocent' (1983: 329). Barrington (2000), however, disputes this image of political naivety.

16 Both Barrington (2000: 43–5) and O'Donoghue (1998: 105–13) remark the importance of Stuart's broadcasts during Germany's agonisingly slow defeat at Stalingrad.

17 The profile of the romantic novelist described by Henri Peyne is very suggestive: 'A graver loss ... was that of humor, and of the ability to see others, and oneself, relatively and mockingly. The narrator, who is the author's Doppelganger, must begin by taking himself seriously and by eliminating most of the outside world and the network of social relations which would normally hem him in, in order to probe into his own self in aloneness ... [This style of fiction] took it for granted that a higher capacity for suffering is the hall mark of superior individuals and is rewarded by the intellectual pleasure of watching oneself suffer' (1963: 199–200). On Stuart's susceptibility to 'the neo-romantic reactionary aesthetics of fascism' see Caterson 1996: 18.

18 See the Borges story 'Three Versions of Judas' (2000: 125–30), mentioned in Chapter 1. In later years Stuart wrote: '[My] philosophy ... derives, I think, above all from the Gospels, if from the Gospels interpreted in a personal manner. It is an instinctive belief in pain, ignominy and defeat as vital in expanding and developing the consciousness. The life of Christ ... was my original guide in this' (Natterstad 1974: 38). Stuart's profile here corresponds with Susan Gubar's description of Judas 'as a personification of spiritual recalcitrance' (2009: 246).

19 Barrington describes *Victors and Vanquished* as 'a fantasy of the war Stuart perhaps wished he had had' (2000: 50), and as 'embarrassingly inferior to *Black List*' (53).

20 It's ironic, of course, that Stuart found the exemplar of his 'outsider' in the figure of the Jew, when, as Brendan Barrington has shown, he had (like so many others of the period) trafficked in a kind of casual anti-Semitism throughout the earlier part of his writing career.

21 Besides de Man, Stuart's case warrants comparison with many of the high-profile cases of betrayal and collaboration emerging from World War Two, including those involving writers such as Ezra Pound, Knut Hamsun and Louis-Ferdinand Céline.

22 For the background to the controversy, as well as a chronology of de Man's life and a wide range of contributions to the debate, see Hamacher *et al.* (1989).

23 Natterstad speculates on the influence of his father as 'a symbol of the outcast and the afflicted, with whom Stuart himself was to identify' (1974: 14).

24 Colm Tóibín is the only critic I have encountered who, whilst acknowledging the self-consciousness, and indeed self-indulgence, of Stuart's attitude, regards it as the strategy of 'a damaged self, someone who was clearly weak' (2001: 3).

7 'Cangled both to treachery'

1 McCabe was born in Glasgow in 1930, but returned to the family farm near Clones in Co. Monaghan during the early years of the Second World War. He first came to literary prominence with his play *King of the Castle* (1964). Thereafter he managed to combine his farming activities with the production of a wide range of drama and short fiction.

2 The precise location of Clonoula, the farm on which the novel is set, is unclear. The actual townland of 'Clonoula' is to the east of the Upper Lough, in a Co. Monaghan enclave, near the Cavan Road (now the N54). Yet the description in *Farms, Families and Dwelling Houses of Fermanagh*, quoted on pp. 20–1 of the text, says that there's a view of Upper Lough Erne from the eastern side of the farm, which would place it to the west of the lake, and somewhere to the south of Enniskillen. The same source locates the farm three miles from Tully Castle, which would actually place it to the north-west of Enniskillen on the shores of the Lower Lough. See n. 7 below.

3 See McCabe (2004/5).

4 In the same interview, McCabe alludes to the cases of the legendary Queen Maeve and Charles Stewart Parnell, and goes on to make explicit links with post-Crash Ireland.

5 Thompson (2004: 287). The complex post-Plantation religious history of Fermanagh – in particular the frequently fraught relations between various Protestant denominations – is tracked in Hill (2004). See also the chapter entitled 'Modes of Minority: Protestants, 1886–1912' in Stewart (1977: 167–73).

6 'The medicals later concurred in their assessment to Mallon that the men had been killed with long and very sharp knives, of good temper. They may have been surgical knives, or boning knives made especially keen or they might also have been bowie knives' (Molony 2006: 48–9).

7 As with the geographical issues noted above, the text incorporates a number of temporal anomalies. A newspaper in Ward's house refers to the 'Execution of Joe Brady Last and Youngest of the Phoenix Park Murderers Day Appointed Thursday May 17th 1883': in fact Brady was neither the youngest nor the last to die, and his execution date was 14 May. On the same evening Liam Ward ponders the death of 'his uncle-in-law, James Carey, killed a few days ago at Port Elizabeth' (194); Carey was not killed until 29 July.

8 During his testimony, Carey had mentioned that he had joined the Fenian movement in 1861, when one of his comrades was Thomas Brennan, subsequently secretary to the Land League. He also implicated other prominent Land Leaguers, such as P.J. Sheridan and the British Branch secretary, Frank Egan (Molony 2006: 146ff.).

9 Confronting his servant Mercy Boyle with her unintentional betrayal, Billy resorts to archetypes: 'Who would you pick between, the Fenian-betrayer James Carey or the Christ-betrayer, Judas Iscariot?' (132).

10 A contemporary anonymous account in a volume entitled *The Mysteries of Ireland* lists the 'Rewards to Witnesses and Informers' involved with the Invincibles case; these include £1,000 for a fringe figure named Robert Farrell, 'in consideration of the fact that he came forward to inform the authorities before he was arrested' (Anon. 1883?: 302).

11 Quoted at www.advertiser.ie/galway/article/21496.

12 See Larkin (1975: 315) and Foster (1993: 248). These were the events that inspired James Joyce to write his essay 'L'Irlanda alla sbarra' (2000: 145–7, translating as 'Ireland at the Bar') for the *Piccolo della Sera* in Trieste on 16 September 1907.

13 The material relating to the Maamtrasna murders must have been written in the period between 18 August, when the story broke, and 3 November, when Trollope suffered a stroke. He died in London on 3 December.

14 In an article in his journal *Kavanagh's Weekly* in May 1952, Kavanagh wrote: 'Parochialism and provincialism are direct opposites ... The parochial mentality ... is never in any doubt about the social and

artistic validity of his parish. All great civilizations are based on parochialism – Greek, Israelite, English' (quoted in Smyth 1998: 108).

15 The three stories included in *Christ in the Fields* (1993) were written and are set in the 1970s. The novella *Victims* (93–198) is as close as McCabe gets to a traditional 'Troubles thriller', telling the story of an IRA unit which takes over a Fermanagh stately home in order to bargain for the freedom of some high-profile prisoners. Despite its unlikely premise, *Victims* anticipates *Death and Nightingales* in so far as it's a story in which betrayal features strongly at both thematic and structural levels. For changing critical responses to Ulster fiction see Wilson Foster (1974), Magee (2001) and Magennis (2010).

16 A ballad composed in 1879 on the legend of Noon's murder contains the verse: 'Within the mountain nature made, / A deep and dismal cave, / That suited well the murderers said, / To be a traitor's grave, / The flung the lifeless body below – / A groan they thought it gave' (quoted in Willis (n.d.) www.bbc.co.uk/northernireland/yourplaceandmine/fermanagh/A954182.shtml).

17 *By Thrasna River* features a central character, Jan, who, like Billy Winters, temporarily leaves his Protestant rural background to seek an education in the big city of Dublin; like Billy, Jan returns home to a religiously divided (although on the whole contented) Fermanagh with a healthy scepticism about the benefits of formal learning. For Bullock himself, Dublin was only a staging post on the way to London.

18 It might be argued that the same sense of ambivalence underpinned the largely Protestant-inspired 'Celtic Revival' of the 1890s; see Campbell (1991: 293), and Murphy (1997: 6).

19 In a chapter entitled 'Public Sphere and Domestic Circle: Gender and Political Economy in Nineteenth-Century Ireland', Timothy P. Foley describes a perception at large at that time: 'Women, by nature sensitive, altruistic, self-giving … virtually Christlike in their self-abnegation, were unfitted to the outdoor rigours of the public sphere and so needed the "protection" afforded by the enclosing domestic circle, though this fortress was increasingly seen by many women as a prison. Women were the keepers of tradition, the exemplars of morality as traditionally defined, the disinfecting element in a morally dissolute society' (1997: 21). Against the idea of religious determination see Lee (1978), who discusses the economic impact of the Famine on women's social standing, and McLoughlin, who suggests that 'sexual prudery in nineteenth-century Ireland had little to do with the Church and all to do with the economics of the emerging middle class' (1994: 272).

20 The 'Emily Brontë' title on Beth's bookshelf can only be *Wuthering Heights* (1847) – a novel in which a betrayed ghost (also named Catherine) plays havoc with the next generation.

21 See also Radcliffe's *The Italian* (1797), in which concealment and duplicity feature as central motifs.

22 Another of the stock gothic motifs – incest – is implicit in the narrative in so far as there's a possibility that Liam and Beth could be half-siblings. After making love he presses her about her 'untrue' father who, she muses, 'must be heartless, a betrayer or liar, or already married perhaps' (93).

23 In the same interview in which he highlights the theme of betrayal in the novel (see n. 10), McCabe acknowledges the importance of the date (1990) of its composition.

24 On the politics of 'trauma' as engaged in Irish cultural theory see Conor Carville's chapter '"Keeping the wound green": Luke Gibbons, Traumaculture and the Subject of Exclusion' (2011: 23–59). See also Chapter 8 of this volume.

25 Graham Dawson quotes a Catholic priest's description of how the aftermath of Enniskillen left his congregation with a 'sense of frustration, a sense of total hopelessness and ... fear' (2007: 291).

26 The 'game' motif is prevalent throughout the canon of 'Troubles' fiction; see Smyth (1998: 115).

27 The contemporary critical climate is encapsulated in books such as Luke Gibbons's *Transformations in Irish Culture* (1996), David Lloyd's *Anomalous States* (1993) and Edna Longley's *The Living Stream* (1994). For an astute overview of those debates see Colin Graham's *Deconstructing Ireland* (2001).

8 'A family – a whole fucking country – drowning in shame'

1 Inglis 1998: 15–17. Also important in this context is the concept of 'familism' described by Conrad M. Arensberg and Solon T. Kimball in *Family and Community in Ireland*, first published in 1940.

2 The extent to which the Catholic Church's rigid control of sexuality may have actually contributed to the prevalence of inappropriate sexual desire remains at issue; see Inglis (1998: *passim*).

3 Such attitudes were underpinned by accounts such as Chris Moore's *Betrayal of Trust: The Father Brendan Smyth Affair and the Catholic Church* (1995). See also *The Cloyne Report* (2009), *The Murphy Report* (2009) and *The Ryan Report* (2009). Debbie Ging argues that '[the] revelations of clerical abuse by the media, while they have played a crucial role in giving voice to those who have been silenced by an oppressive, autocratic and deeply patriarchal culture, have also served to skew the realities of child abuse in Ireland' (2009: 64).

4 In *Irish Child Care Services*, Gilligan describes 'sexual abuse' as 'the involvement of dependent, developmentally immature children and adolescents in sexual activities which they do not truly comprehend,

to which they are unable to give informed consent or that violate the social taboos of family roles' (1991: 62).

5 Of the Church's failure to act on its knowledge of known paedophiles within its ranks, O'Gorman writes: '[All] I see is the betrayal of the boy I was, of my family, my community and even my faith. The depth of that betrayal left me breathless' (2009: 176).

6 This is an unfortunate designation since, as Jeffrey Masson points out, 'it implies some form of participation by the child' (1984: 3). Richard Haslam (1999) suggests 'molestation theory' as a more accurate description of Freud's intentions.

7 The proposition that childhood abuse 'leads to huge developmental damage which has ongoing implications' (Walker 1992: 1) has become axiomatic in the field. Besides the more theoretical registers adopted by Masson and Miller, see Briere (1992), Gilligan (1991), Parton (1985) and Thompson (1992).

8 See Caruth (1995), Crews (1995) and Scott (1996) for analyses of the scope and tenor of the debates.

9 Parton (1985) traces the evolution of the British state's attempts to codify the treatment of children through a series of laws, including such key mechanisms as the Prevention of Cruelty to and Protection of Children Act of 1889 and the Children Act of 1908. Time and again, he points out, such laws encoded a stand-off between the rights of the private family and the responsibilities of a civilised society.

10 Although I can't pursue the point here, I would argue that O'Faolain's memoir should be regarded as the principal intertext for Enright's novel, both in terms of its style as well as its numerous thematic correspondences. These include a family of nine children, a temporary relocation to relatives in order to relieve the mother's stress, a sexual assault and an alcoholic brother, traumatised by domestic violence, found dead in England. As in *The Gathering*, this latter development necessitates a traumatic trip by the narrator to England to deal with the body. See also Fiona Doyle's high-profile *Too Many Tears* (2013) – an account of parental abuse whose details (even down to the suicide of a brother in England) also follow Enright's fictional treatment closely.

11 In Veronica's account, Liam evinces many of the symptoms of the abused child: '[disturbances] of mood (low self-esteem, feelings of guilt, depressive episodes), self-damaging behaviour (attempted suicide, self-mutilation, substance abuse, eating disorders), interpersonal problems (isolation, insecurity, discord, inadequacy), stress disorders giving rise to various psychological problems (e.g. panic or anxiety states or psychosomatic disorders) and sexual difficulties (problems of sexual dysfunction or orientation, subsequent experience of rape, involvement in prostitution or compulsive sexual behaviour)' (Gilligan 1991: 64).

12 Hansson argues that the post-national society described in *The Wig My Father Wore* (1995) and *What Are You Like?* (2000) 'is defined mainly in negative terms: fragmentary, not whole, confusing, not stable, transitory, not solid' (2009: 229). My suggestion in this chapter is that Enright found the embodiment of those troubled experiences in the figure of the abused child.

13 In 'The Aetiology of Hysteria', Freud alluded to the role of the witness in corroborating the abusive event: an unassailable proof might be provided, he writes, 'if the statements of someone who is being analysed were to be confirmed by someone else, whether under treatment or not' (1896: 274). The latter clause raises the possibility of Veronica's own ongoing traumatised response to her role as witness to her brother's abuse, as well as her betrayal of the responsibility to adopt that role.

14 A Catholic presence features in *The Gathering* in the form of the priest who, when the children light candles in a church without paying, 'marked Kitty's upper arm with a ring of bruises, giving us, as he held on to her, a lecture on wickedness that was dense with rage' (50).

References

(Place of publication is London unless otherwise indicated. The date in parentheses is the date cited in the text and notes; details of the edition used are given in the reference.)

Allen, K. (2009). *Ireland's Economic Crash: A Radical Agenda for Change*. Dublin, Liffey Press.

Anon. (1883?). *The Mysteries of Ireland: Giving a Graphic and Faithful Account of Irish Secret Societies and Their Plots from the Rebellion of 1798 to the Year 1883*. Milner & Co.

Arensberg, C.M. and S.T. Kimball (1940). *Family and Community in Ireland*. Cambridge, MA, Harvard University Press, 1968.

Armstrong, J. (1976). *The Novel of Adultery*. Macmillan.

Arnold, B. (2009). *The Irish Gulag: How the State Betrayed its Innocent Children*. Dublin, Gill & Macmillan.

Austin, J.L. (1962). *How to Do Things with Words*. Oxford University Press.

Barrington, B. (2000). *The Wartime Broadcasts of Francis Stuart 1942–1944*. Dublin, Lilliput Press.

Bell, S.H. (1951). *December Bride*. Belfast, Blackstaff Press, 2000.

Bellamy, J.G. (1970). *The Law of Treason in England in the Later Middle Ages*. Cambridge, Cambridge University Press.

—— (1979). *The Tudor Law of Treason: An Introduction*. Routledge & Kegan Paul.

Benda, J. (1927). *The Betrayal of the Intellectuals*. Trans. R. Aldington. Boston, Beacon Press, 1955.

Berresford Ellis, P. (1972). *A History of the Irish Working Class*. Pluto Press, 1996.

—— (1995). *Celtic Women: Women in Celtic Society and Literature*. Constable.

Bickley, F. (1912). 'Deirdre', *Irish Review* 2.17 (July), 252–55.

Blamires, H. (1966). *The Bloomsday Book: A Guide through 'Ulysses'*. Methuen.

Bloom, H. (1994). *The Western Canon: The Books and School of the Ages*. Harcourt Brace.

Borges, J.L. (1964). *Labyrinths*. Penguin, 2000.

Boucicault, D. (1860). *The Colleen Bawn; Or, The Brides of Garryowen: A Domestic Drama in Three Acts*. Samuel French, n.d.

Boveri, M. (1956). *Treason in the Twentieth Century*. Trans. J. Steinberg. Macdonald, 1961.

Bowen, E. (1929). *The Last September*. Harmondsworth, Middlesex, Penguin, 1983.

—— (1935). *The House in Paris*. Harmondsworth, Middlesex, Penguin, 1946.

—— (1938). *The Death of the Heart*. Harmondsworth, Middlesex, Penguin, 1962.

—— (1942). *Bowen's Court*. Cork, The Collins Press, 1998.

—— (1949). *The Heat of the Day*. Penguin, 1976.

—— (1950). *Collected Impressions*. Longman.

—— (1975). *Pictures and Conversations*. New York: Knopf.

—— (1986). *The Mulberry Tree: Writings of Elizabeth Bowen*. Ed. H. Lee. Virago.

—— (1999). *Collected Stories*. Vintage.

Breatnach, C. (1994). 'Oidheadh Chloinne Uisnigh', *Ériu* 45, 99–112.

Brewster, S. and M. Parker (eds) (2009). *Irish Literature since 1990: Diverse Voices*. Manchester, Manchester University Press.

Briere, J.N. (1992). *Child Abuse Trauma: Theory and Treatment of the Lasting Effects*. Sage.

Brown, R. (1985). *James Joyce and Sexuality*. Cambridge, Cambridge University Press.

Brown, T. (1985). *Ireland: A Social and Cultural History 1922–1985*. Fontana.

Budgen, F. (1934). *James Joyce and the Making of 'Ulysses' and Other Writings*. Oxford, Oxford University Press, 1972.

Bullock, S. (1895). *By Thrasna River*. Memphis, TN, General Books, 2012.

—— (1924). *The Loughsiders*. Turnpike Books, 2012.

Cahill, S. (2011). *Irish Literature in the Celtic Tiger Years 1990–2008: Gender, Bodies, Memory*. Continuum.

Campbell, F. (1991). *The Dissenting Voice: Protestant Democracy in Ulster from Plantation to Partition*. Belfast, Blackstaff Press.

Carleton, W. (1843–44). *Traits and Stories of the Irish Peasantry*. Gerrards Cross, Buckinghamshire, Colin Smythe, 1990.

Caruth, C. (1995). *Unclaimed Experience: Trauma, Narrative, History*. Baltimore, MD, Johns Hopkins University Press.

Carville, C. (2012). *The Ends of Ireland: Criticism, History, Subjectivity*. Manchester, Manchester University Press.

Caterson, S. (1996). 'Francis Stuart, Hitler and the Lure of Fascism', *Irish Studies Review* 16 (autumn), 18–22.

—— (1997). 'Joyce, the *Künstlerroman* and Minor Literature: Francis Stuart's *Black List, Section H*', *Irish University Review: A Journal of Irish Studies* 27.1 (spring/summer), 87–97.

Cave, R. (2004). 'Representations of Women in the Tragedies of Gregory and Yeats', *Irish University Review: A Journal of Irish Studies* 34.1, Special Issue: Lady Gregory (spring/summer), 122–32.

Cleary, J. (2007). *Outrageous Fortune: Capital and Culture in Modern Ireland*. Dublin, Field Day Publications.

Collins, A. (2001). *A History of Sex and Morals in Ireland*. Cork, Mercier Press.

Corcoran, N. (2004). *Elizabeth Bowen: The Enforced Return*. Oxford, Clarendon Press.

Costello, P. (1996). *Liam O'Flaherty's Ireland*. Dublin, Wolfhound Press.

Craig, W.J. (ed.) (1965). *Shakespeare: Complete Works*. Oxford University Press.

Crawford, E.M. (2004). 'Food, Famine and Fever', in Murphy and Roulston (eds), 267–85.

Crews, F. (1995). *The Memory Wars: Freud's Legacy in Dispute*. New York, New York Review of Books.

Cronin, A. (1997). 'Stuart: An Innocent Abroad', *Sunday Independent* (30 November), 12.

Cronin, M. (2000). *Across the Lines: Travel, Language, Translation*. Cork, Cork University Press.

Cullingford, E. (1981). *Yeats, Ireland and Fascism*. Macmillan.

D'Arbois de Jubainville, H. (ed.) (1892). *Cours de littérature celtique*, vol. V, *L'épopée celtique en Irlande*. Paris, Ernest Thorin.

Daruwala, M.H. (2001). 'Yeats and the Mask of Deirdre: "That love is all we need"', *Colby Quarterly* 37.3, 247–66.

Dawson, G. (2007). *Making Peace with the Past? Memory, Trauma and the Irish Troubles*. Manchester, Manchester University Press.

Deane, S. (1985). *Celtic Revivals: Essays in Modern Irish Literature*. Faber & Faber.

Del Collo, S. (1999). 'Yeats, Fergus(on), O'Grady, and Deirdre', *South Carolina Review* 32.1, 158–67.

De Man, P. (1983). *Blindness and Insight: Essays in the Rhetoric of Contemporary Criticism*. Methuen.

Derrida, J. (1986). 'Declarations of Independence', *New Political Science* 15, 7–15.

—— (1988). 'Like the Sound of the Sea Deep within a Shell: Paul de Man's War' (trans. P. Kamuf), *Critical Inquiry* 14 (spring), 590–652.

—— (1991a). *The Gift of Death*. Trans. D. Wills. Chicago, University of Chicago Press, 1995.

—— (1991b). 'Speech and Phenomena'. Trans. D.B. Allison, in Kamuf (ed.), 6–30.

De Vere, A. (1884). 'The Sons of Usnach', in *The Poetical Works of Aubrey de Vere*, vol. II. Kegan Paul, Trench & Co.

Dickson, A. (ed.) (1990). *The Penguin Freud Library*, vol. XIV, *Art and Literature*. Penguin.

Donoghue, E. (1997). '"How could I fear and hold thee by the hand?" The Poetry of Eva Gore Booth', in Walshe (ed.), 16–42.

Dottin, G. (1892). 'Exil des fils d'Usnech, autrement dit: Meurtre des fils d'Usnech et de Derdriu', in d'Arbois de Jubainville (ed.), 217–319.

Doyle, F. (2013). *Too Many Tears*, Dublin, Penguin.

Doyle, P. (1988). *The God Squad*. Corgi, 1989.

Duggan, J.P. (1985). *Neutral Ireland and the Third Reich*. Dublin, Gill & Macmillan.

Dunbar, R. (2012). *The Science of Love and Betrayal*. Faber & Faber.

Eagleton, T. (1998). *Crazy John and the Bishop and Other Essays on Irish Culture*. Cork, Cork University Press.

Ehrman, B.D. (2006). *The Lost Gospels of Judas Iscariot: A New Look at Betrayer and Betrayed*. Oxford, Oxford University Press.

Elborn, G. (1990). *Francis Stuart: A Life*. Dublin, Raven Arts Press.

Ellis-Fermor, U. (1939). *The Irish Dramatic Movement*. Methuen, 1967.

Ellmann, M. (2004). *Elizabeth Bowen: The Shadow across the Page*. Edinburgh, Edinburgh University Press.

Ellmann, R. (1949). *Yeats: The Man and the Masks*. Faber & Faber, 1960.

—— (1959). *James Joyce*. New York, Oxford University Press, 1983.

—— (ed.) (1966). *Letters of James Joyce*, vol. II. Faber & Faber.

—— (ed.) (1969). *The Artist as Critic: Critical Writings of Oscar Wilde*. New York, Vintage Books.

—— (ed.) (1975). *Selected Letters of James Joyce*. Faber & Faber.

English, R. (1994). *Radicals and the Republic: Socialist Republicanism in the Irish Free State*. Oxford, Clarendon Press.

Enright, A. (1991). *The Portable Virgin*. Vintage, 2002.

—— (1995). *The Wig My Father Wore*. Minerva, 1996.

—— (2000). *What Are You Like?* Vintage, 2001.

—— (2002). *The Pleasure of Eliza Lynch*. Vintage.

—— (2004). *Making Babies: Stumbling into Motherhood*. Jonathan Cape.

—— (2007). *The Gathering*. Vintage, 2008.

—— (2008). *Taking Pictures*. Jonathan Cape.

—— (2011). *The Forgotten Waltz*. Jonathan Cape.

Fanon, F. (1961). *The Wretched of the Earth*. Harmondsworth, Middlesex, Penguin, 1967.

Ferguson, S. (1864). 'Deirdre', in *Lays of the Red Branch*. Dublin, T.F. Unwin, 1897, 35–86.

Fisk, R. (1983). *In Time of War: Ireland, Ulster, and the Price of Neutrality 1939–1945*. Deutsch.

Foley, T.P. (1997). 'Public Sphere and Domestic Circle: Gender and Political Economy in Nineteenth-Century Ireland', in Kelleher and Murphy (eds), 21–35.

Forster, E.M. (1951). *Two Cheers for Democracy*. Edward Arnold.

Foster, R. (1976). *Charles Stewart Parnell: The Man and His Family*. Hassocks, Sussex, Harvester Press.

—— (1993). *Paddy and Mr Punch: Connections in Irish and English History*. Allen Lane.

—— (1997). *W.B. Yeats: A Life. I – The Apprentice Mage, 1865–1914*. Oxford, Oxford University Press.

—— (2003). *W.B. Yeats: A Life. II – The Arch-Poet 1915–1939*. Oxford, Oxford University Press.

—— (2007). *Luck and the Irish: A Short History of Change 1970–2000*. Allen Lane.

Foucault, M. (1976). *The History of Sexuality*, vol. I, *The Will to Knowledge*. Trans R. Hurley. New York, Vintage, 1980.

Freud, S. (1896). 'The Aetiology of Hysteria', in Masson (1984), 259–90.

—— (1900). *The Interpretation of Dreams*. Trans. and ed. J. Strachey. Allen & Unwin, 1961.

—— (1905a). *On Sexuality: Three Essays on the Theory of Sexuality and Other Works*. Trans. J. Strachey. Penguin, 1981.

—— (1905b). 'Fragment of an Analysis of a Case of Hysteria ("Dora")'. Trans. A. and J. Strachey, in Richards (ed.) (1983), 31–164.

—— (1909). 'Family Romances', in Freud (1905a), 217–25.

—— (1912). 'On the Universal Tendency to Debasement in the Sphere of Love', in Freud (1905a), 243–60.

—— (1919). 'The Uncanny', in Dickson (ed.) (1990), 335–76.

—— (1930). *Civilization and its Discontents*. Trans. J. Strachey. New York, Norton, 1989.

Freyd, J.J. (1996). *Betrayal Trauma: The Logic of Forgetting Childhood Abuse*. Cambridge, MA: Harvard University Press.

Fuller Torrey, E. (1984). *The Roots of Treason: Ezra Pound and the Secrets of St. Elizabeths*. Sidgwick & Jackson.

Gerald of Wales (1982). *The History and Topography of Ireland*. Trans. J. O'Meara. Penguin.

Gibbons, L. (1996). *Transformations in Irish Culture*. Cork, Cork University Press / Field Day Publications.

Giddens, A. (1992). *The Transformation of Intimacy: Sexuality, Lover and Eroticism in Modern Societies*. Cambridge, Polity Press.

Gilligan, R. (1991). *Irish Child Care Services: Policy, Practice and Provision*. Dublin, Institute of Public Administration.

Ging, D. (2009). 'All-Consuming Images: New Gender Formations in post-Celtic-Tiger Ireland', in Ging *et al.* (eds), 52–70.

Ging, D., M. Cronin and P. Kirby (eds) (2009). *Transforming Ireland: Challenges, Critiques, Resources*. Manchester, Manchester University Press.

Girvin, B. and G. Roberts (eds) (2000). *Ireland and the Second World War: Politics, Society and Remembrance*. Dublin, Four Courts Press.

Glendenning, V. and J. Robertson (eds) (2008). *Love's Civil War: Elizabeth Bowen and Charles Ritchie*. Pocket Books.

Gore-Booth, E. (1905). *The Three Resurrections and The Triumph of Maeve*. Longmans, Green & Co.

—— (c. 1908). *The Buried Life of Deirdre*. New York, Longman, 1930.

—— (1923). *A Psychological and Poetic Approach to the Study of Christ in the Fourth Gospel*. Longmans, Green & Co.

Graham, C. (2001). *Deconstructing Ireland: Identity, Theory, Culture*. Edinburgh, Edinburgh University Press.

Gregory, A. (1902). 'Fate of the Sons of Usnach' from *Cuchulainn of Muirthemne*, in *Selected Writings*. Penguin, 1995, 167–97.

—— (1904). *Gods and Fighting Men: The Story of the Tuatha de Danann and of the Fianna of Ireland*. John Murray.

—— (1962). *Selected Plays*. Gerrards Cross, Buckinghamshire, Colin Smythe, 1975.

Griffin, G. (1829). *The Collegians*. Belfast, Appletree Press, 1992.

Griffin, R. (2010). *Modernism and Fascism: The Sense of a Beginning under Mussolini and Hitler*. Palgrave Macmillan.

Gubar, S. (2009). *Judas: A Biography*. New York, Norton.

Hamacher, W., N. Hertz and T. Keenan (eds) (1989). *Responses: On Paul de Man's Wartime Journalism*. Lincoln, University of Nebraska Press.

Hand, D. (2011). *A History of the Irish Novel*. Cambridge, Cambridge University Press.

Hanley, B. (2002). *The IRA, 1926–1936*. Dublin, Four Courts Press.

Hansen, J. (2009). *Terror and Irish Modernism: The Gothic Tradition from Burke to Becket*. Albany, NY, SUNY Press.

Hansson, H. (2009). 'Anne Enright and Postnationalism in the Contemporary Irish Novel', in Brewster and Parker (eds), 216–31.

Hardy, T. (1874). *Far from the Madding Crowd*. Oxford: Oxford World's Classics, 1998.

Hart, P. (2003). *The I.R.A. at War 1916–1923*. Oxford, Oxford University Press.

Hederman, M.P. (1985). 'The "Mind" of Joyce: From Paternalism to Paternity', in Kearney (ed.), 244–66.

Hederman, M.P. and R. Kearney (eds) (1981). *The Crane Bag Book of Irish Studies*. Dublin, Blackwater.

Hedva, B. (2001). *Betrayal, Trust and Forgiveness: A Guide to Emotional Healing and Self-Renewal*. Berkeley, CA, Celestial Arts.

Hepburn, A. (ed.) (2008). *People, Places, Things: Essays by Elizabeth Bowen*. Edinburgh, Edinburgh University Press.

—— (ed.) (2010). *Listening In: Broadcasts, Speeches, and Interviews by Elizabeth Bowen*. Edinburgh, Edinburgh University Press.

Hill, M. (2004). 'Protestantism in County Fermanagh, c. 1750–1912', in Murphy and Roulston (eds), 387–408.

Hillis Miller, J. (1989). 'An Open Letter to Professor Jon Wiener', in Hamacher *et al.* (eds), 334–42.

Hull, E. (1898). *The Cuchulain Saga in Irish Literature*. David Nutt.

Hyde, D. (1899). *A Literary History of Ireland from Earliest Times to the Present Day*. Ernest Benn Ltd., 1967.

Ingersoll, E.G. (1993). 'Who Is Bartell D'Arcy and Why Does He Sing in Both "The Dead" and *Ulysses*?', *Irish University Review: A Journal of Irish Studies* 23.2 (autumn/winter), 250–57.

Inglis, T. (1998). *Lessons in Irish Sexuality*. Dublin, UCD Press.

James, S. (2005). *Exploring the World of the Celts*. Thames & Hudson.

Jones, E. (1951). *Essays in Applied Psycho-Analysis*, vol. I, *Miscellaneous Essays*. Hogarth Press.

Joyce, James (1914). *Dubliners*. Oxford, Oxford World's Classics, 2000.

—— (1916). *A Portrait of the Artist as a Young Man*. Oxford, Oxford World's Classics, 2000.

—— (1918). *Exiles*. Nick Hern Books, 2006.

—— (1922). *Ulysses*. Oxford, Oxford World's Classics, 1993.

—— (1944). *Stephen Hero*. Jonathan Cape, 1969.

—— (2000). *Occasional, Critical and Political Writings*. Ed. K. Barry. Oxford, Oxford World's Classics.

Joyce, P.W. (1879). 'The Fate of the Sons of Usna', in *Old Celtic Romances*. Dublin, Roberts Wholesale Books, 1907.

Joyce, R.D. (1876). *Deirdre*. Dublin, M.H. Gill & Son.

Joyce, S. (1958). *My Brother's Keeper: James Joyce's Early Years*. Cambridge, MA: Da Capo Press, 2003.

Kamuf, P. (ed.) (1991). *A Derrida Reader: Between the Blinds*. New York, Columbia University Press.

Kearney, R. (ed.) (1985). *The Irish Mind: Exploring Intellectual Traditions*. Dublin, Wolfhound Press.

Keating, G. (*c.* 1634). *The History of Ireland*, vol. II. Ed. P. Dinneen. Irish Texts Society, 1908.

Kelleher, M. and J.H. Murphy (eds) (1997). *Gender Perspectives in Nineteenth-Century Ireland: Public and Private Spheres*. Dublin, Irish Academic Press.

Kelly, A.A. (ed.) (1996). *The Letters of Liam O'Flaherty*. Dublin, Wolfhound Press.

Kennelly, B. (2002). *The Little Book of Judas*. Hexham, Northumberland, Bloodaxe Books.

Keogh, D. and M.H. Haltzel (eds) (1993). *Northern Ireland and the Politics of Reconciliation*. Cambridge, Cambridge University Press.

Kiberd, D. (1979). *Synge and the Irish Language*. 2nd edn. Dublin, Gill & Macmillan, 1993.

Kickham, C. (1879). *Knocknagow, or the Homes of Tipperary*. Otley, Woodstock Books, 2002.

Kiely, K. (2007). *Francis Stuart: Artist and Outcast*. Dublin, Liffey Press.

Kirby, P. (2002). *The Celtic Tiger in Distress: Growth with Inequality in Ireland*. Basingstoke, Palgrave.

—— (2010). *Celtic Tiger in Collapse: Explaining the Weaknesses of the Irish Mode*. Basingstoke, Palgrave.

Kirschner, S.R. (1996). *The Religious and Romantic Origins of Psychoanalysis: Individuation and Integration in Post-Freudian Theory*. Cambridge, Cambridge University Press.

Kostick, C. (1996). *Revolution in Ireland: Popular Militancy 1917–1923*. Pluto Press.

Lacan, J. (2006). *Écrits: The First Complete Edition in English*. Trans. Bruce Fink. New York: Norton.

Lane, J. and B. Clifford. (2009). *Elizabeth Bowen: 'Notes on Eire'*. 3rd edn. Millstreet, Co. Cork, Aubane Historical Society.

Larkin, E. (1975). *The Roman Catholic Church and the Creation of the Modern Irish State, 1878–1886*. Dublin, Gill & Macmillan.

Lawson, A. (1988). *Adultery: An Analysis of Love and Betrayal*. Oxford, Blackwell.

Leckie, B. (2003). 'The Simple Case of Adultery', *James Joyce Quarterly* 40.4 (summer), 729–52.

Lee, H. (1981). *Elizabeth Bowen: An Estimation*. Vision.

Lee, J.J. (1978). 'Women and the Church since the Famine', in MacCurtain and Ó Corrain (eds), 37–45.

Leerssen, J. (1996). *Remembrance and Imagination: Patterns in the Historical and Literary Representation of Ireland in the Nineteenth Century*. Cork, Field Day Publications.

Le Fanu, J.S. (1864). *Uncle Silas: A Tale of Bartram-Haugh*. Penguin, 2000.

Lemon, R. (2006). *Treason by Words: Literature, Law, and Rebellion in Shakespeare's England*. Ithaca, NY and London, Cornell University Press.

Lever, C. (1872). *Lord Kilgobbin*. Smith, Elder & Co.

Lewis, G. (1988). *Eva Gore-Booth and Esther Roper: A Biography*. Pandora.

Lloyd, D. (1987). *Nationalism and Minor Literature: James Clarence Mangan and the Emergence of Irish Cultural Nationalism*. Berkeley, University of California Press.

—— (1993). *Anomalous States: Irish Writing and the Post-Colonial Moment*. Dublin, Lilliput Press.

Longley, E. (1994). *The Living Stream: Literature and Revisionism in Ireland*. Newcastle upon Tyne, Bloodaxe Books.

Lukács, G. (1950). *Studies in European Realism: A Sociological Survey of the Writings of Balzac, Stendhal, Zola, Tolstoy, Gorki and Others*. Trans. E. Bone. Hillway.

—— (1971). *Writer and Critic and Other Essays*. Trans. A. Kahn. Merlin Press.

McCabe, E. (1964). *King of the Castle*. Loughcrew, Co. Meath, Gallery Press, 1997.

—— (1992). *Death and Nightingales*. Minerva, 1993.

—— (1993). *Christ in the Fields: A Fermanagh Trilogy*. Minerva.

—— (1999). *Tales from the Poorhouse*. Loughcrew, Co. Meath, Gallery Press.

McCartney, A. (2000). *Francis Stuart Face to Face: A Critical Study*. Belfast, Institute of Irish Studies.

McCormack, W.J. (1993). *Dissolute Characters: Irish Literary History through Balzac, Le Fanu, Yeats and Bowen*. Manchester, Manchester University Press.

—— (1994). *From Burke to Beckett: Ascendancy Tradition and Betrayal in Literary History*. Cork, Cork University Press.

McCourt, F. (1996). *Angela's Ashes*. HarperCollins.

McCourt, J. (2000). *James Joyce: A Passionate Exile*. Orion.

MacCurtain, M. and D. Ó Corrain (eds) (1978). *Women in Irish Society: The Historical Dimension*. Dublin, Arlen House.

Macdonell, A.C. (1913). 'Deirdre: The Highest Type of Celtic Womanhood', *Celtic Review* 8.32 (May), 347–56.

McLoughlin, D. (1994). 'Women and Sexuality in Nineteenth-Century Ireland', *Irish Journal of Psychology* 15.2–3, 266–75.

McWilliams, D. (2008). *The Pope's Children: The Irish Economic Triumph and the Rise of Ireland's New Elite*. Hoboken, NJ, Wiley.

Maddox, B. (1988). *Nora: A Biography of Nora Joyce*. Hamish Hamilton.

Magee, P. (2001). *Gangsters or Guerrillas? Representations of Irish Republicans in 'Troubles Fiction'*. Belfast, Beyond the Pale.

Magennis, C. (2010). *Sons of Ulster: Masculinities in the Contemporary Northern Irish Novel*. Peter Lang.

Magennis, P. (1874). *The Ribbon Informer: A Tale of Lough Erne*. F. Bell & Co.

—— (1877). *Tully Castle: A Tale of the Irish Rebellion*. Dublin, M.H. Gill & Son.

Maguire, M.J. (2009). *Precarious Childhood in Post-Independence Ireland*. Manchester, Manchester University Press.

Marlowe, L. (2012). 'Righteous Anger at Betrayal of Trust, says President', *Irish Times* (1 May), 5.

Martin, A. (1965). 'Stephens' *Deirdre*', *Irish University Review: A Journal of Irish Studies* 3.7 (spring), 25–38.

—— (1977). *James Stephens: A Critical Study*. Dublin, Gill & Macmillan.

—— (ed.) (1990). *James Joyce: The Artist and the Labyrinth*. Ryan.

Martland, P. (2003). *Lord Haw Haw: The English Voice of Nazi Germany*. The National Archives.

Masson, J.M. (1984). *The Assault on Truth: Freud's Suppression of the Seduction Theory*. Harmondsworth, Middlesex, Penguin, 1985.

Maume, P. (2004). 'Shan Bullock's Perspectives on Nineteenth-Century Fermanagh', in Murphy and Roulston (eds), 459–77.

Miller, A. (1981). *Thou Shalt Not Be Aware: Society's Betrayal of the Child*. Trans. H. and H. Hannum. Pluto Press, 1985.

Milton, J. (1667). *Paradise Lost*. Oxford, Oxford World's Classics, 2004.

Molony, S. (2006). *The Phoenix Park Murders: Conspiracy, Betrayal and Retribution*. Cork, Mercier Press.

Moore, C. (1995). *Betrayal of Trust: The Father Brendan Smyth Affair and the Catholic Church*. Dublin, Marino.

Moore, T. (1910). *The Poetical Works of Thomas Moore*. Ed. A.D. Godley. Oxford University Press.

Murphy, E.M. and W.J. Roulston (eds) (2004). *Fermanagh: History and Society*. Dublin, Geography Publications.

Murphy, J.H. (1997). *Catholic Fiction and Social Reality in Ireland, 1873–1922*. Greenwood Press.

Murphy, R.T. (2004). 'A Minority of One: Francis Stuart's *Black List, Section H* and the End of the Irish Bildungsroman', *Irish University Review: A Journal of Irish Studies* 34.2 (autumn/winter), 261–76.

Murray, C. (1997). *Twentieth-Century Irish Drama: Mirror Up to Nation*. Manchester, Manchester University Press.

Natterstad, J.H. (1974). *Francis Stuart*. Lewisburg, PA, Bucknell University Press.

Nietzsche, F. (1872). *The Birth of Tragedy and The Genealogy of Morals*. New York, Doubleday, 1956.

Ní Siúdlaig, M. (1904). 'Deirdre', *The Gael* (March), 85–6.

Norris, C. (1987). *Derrida*. Fontana.

Ó Broin, L. (1976). *Revolutionary Underground: The Story of the Irish Republican Brotherhood 1858–1924*. Dublin, Gill & Macmillan.

O'Connor, E. (2004). *Reds and the Green: Ireland, Russia and the Communist Internationals 1919–1943*. Dublin, UCD Press.

O'Connor, S. and C.C. Shepard (eds) (2008). *Women, Social and Cultural Change in Twentieth-Century Ireland: Dissenting Voices?* Newcastle upon Tyne, Cambridge Scholars Press.

O'Connor, U. (1990). 'Joyce and Gogarty – Royal and Ancient, Two Hangers-On', in Martin (ed.), 333–54.

O'Curry, E. (1862). 'The "Tri Thruaighe na Scéalaigheachta" (i.e. the "Three Most Sorrowful Tales") of Erinn: "The Exile of the Children of Uisneach"', *Atlantis* 3.6, 377–422.

O'Day, A. and J. Stevenson (eds) (1992). *Irish Historical Documents since 1800*. Dublin, Gill & Macmillan.

O'Donoghue, D. (1998). *Hitler's Irish Voices: The Story of German Radio's Wartime Irish Service*. Belfast, Beyond the Pale.

Ó Drisceoil, D. (2000). 'Censorship as Propaganda: The Neutralisation of Irish Public Opinion during the Second World War', in Girvin and Roberts (eds), 151–64.

O'Faolain, N. (1996). *Are You Somebody?* Dublin, New Island Books.

O'Flaherty, Liam (1923). *Thy Neighbour's Wife*. Dublin, Wolfhound Press, 1992.

—— (1924). *The Black Soul*. Dublin, Wolfhound Press, 1981.

—— (1925). *The Informer*. New English Library, 1971.

—— (1928). *The Assassin*. Jonathan Cape.

—— (1930). *Two Years*. Jonathan Cape.

—— (1931). *I Went to Russia*. Jonathan Cape.

—— (1934). *Shame the Devil*. Grayson & Grayson.

O'Flanagan, T. (1808). 'Deirdri, or, The Lamentable Fate of the Sons of Usnach', *Transactions of the Gaelic Society of Dublin* 1, 1–135.

O'Gorman, C. (2009). *Beyond Belief*. Hodder & Stoughton.

O'Grady, S.J. (1878). *History of Ireland: The Heroic Period*. Sampson, Low, Searle, Marston & Rivington.

O'Malley, E. (1978). *The Singing Flame*. Dublin, Anvil Books.

O'Sullivan, N. (ed.) (1983). *Revolutionary Theory and Political Reality*. Brighton, Wheatsheaf Press.

O'Toole, F. (2010). *Enough Is Enough: How to Build a New Republic*. Faber & Faber.

Parton, N. (1985). *The Politics of Child Abuse*. Basingstoke, Macmillan.

Patten, E. (2012). *Imperial Refugee: Olivia Manning's Fictions of War*. Cork, Cork University Press.

Pelaschiar, L. (1998). *Writing the North: The Contemporary Novel in Northern Ireland*. Trieste, Edizioni Parnaso.

Petriglieri, G. (2005). 'In Praise of Loving "Betrayal": Reflections on the Steiner–Novellino Letters and the Life of Behavioral Science Organisations', *Transactional Analysis Journal* 35.3 (July), 285–90.

Peyre, H. (1963). *Literature and Sincerity*. New Haven, CT and London, Yale University Press.

Piette, A. (1995). *Imagination at War: British Fiction and Poetry 1939–1945*. Macmillan.

Pinter, H. (1978). *Betrayal*. Eyre Methuen.

Radcliffe, A. (1794). *The Mysteries of Udolpho*. Oxford, Oxford World's Classics, 2008.

—— (1797). *The Italian*. Oxford, Oxford World's Classics, 1998.

Regan, J.M. (1999). *The Irish Counter-Revolution 1921–1936: Treatyite Politics and Settlement in Independent Ireland*. Dublin, Gill & Macmillan.

Richards, A. (ed.) (1983). *The Pelican Freud Library*, vol. VIII, *Case Histories I: 'Dora' and 'Little Hans'*. Harmondsworth, Middlesex, Penguin.

Scott, A. (1996). *Real Events Revisited: Fantasy, Memory and Psychoanalysis*. Virago.

Sealy Lynch, R. (1993). '"Soft Talk" and "An Alien Grip": Gallagher's Rhetoric of Control in O'Flaherty's *The Informer*', *Irish University Review: A Journal of Irish Studies* 23.2 (autumn/winter), 260–68.

Sheehan, R. (1981). 'Novelists on the Novel: An Interview with Francis Stuart and John Banville', in Hederman and Kearney (eds), 408–15.

Sheeran, P.F. (1976). *The Novels of Liam O'Flaherty: A Study in Romantic Realism*. Atlantic Highlands, NJ, Humanities Press.

Shelley, M. (1818). *Frankenstein, or, 'The Modern Prometheus'*. Oxford, Oxford World's Classics, 2008.

Sharp, W. (Fiona Macleod) (1900). *The House of Usna*. Thomas B. Mosher, 1903.

Sigerson, G. (1897). *Bards of the Gael and the Gall: Examples of the Poetic Literature of Erinn*. T. Fisher Unwin.

Smyth, G. (1998). *Decolonisation and Criticism: The Construction of Irish Literature*. Pluto Press.

—— (2008). *Music in Contemporary British Fiction: Listening to the Novel*. Basingstoke, Palgrave.

—— (2009). *Music in Irish Cultural History*. Dublin, Irish Academic Press.

Squire, C. (1905). *Mythology of the British Islands*. Blackie & Sons.

Stephens, J. (1912a). *The Charwoman's Daughter*. Macmillan.

—— (1912b). *The Crock of Gold*. Macmillan.

—— (1914). *The Demi-Gods*. Macmillan.

—— (1918). 'Hunger: A Dublin Story' (as James Esse). Dublin, The Candle Press.

—— (1923). *Deirdre*. Macmillan.

Stewart, A.T.Q. (1977). *The Narrow Ground: The Roots of Conflict in Ulster*. Faber & Faber.

Stoker, Bram. (1897). *Dracula*. Penguin, 2012.

Stokes, W. (1887). *The Death of the Sons of Uisneach*, in *Irische Texte mit Übersetzungen und Wörterbuch*, vol. II.ii. Ed. W. Stokes and E. Windisch. Leipzig, Hirzel, 109–84.

Stringer, C. (2011). *The Origin of Our Species*. Allen Lane.

Stuart, F. (1948). *The Pillar of Cloud*. Dublin, New Island Books, 1994.

—— (1949). *Redemption*. Dublin, New Island Books, 1994.

—— (1959). *Victors and Vanquished*. Cleveland, OH, Pennington Press.

—— (1971). *Black List, Section H*. Harmondsworth, Middlesex, Penguin, 1982.

—— (1984). *States of Mind: Selected Short Prose 1936–1983*. Dublin, Raven Arts Press.

Synge, J.M. (1910). *Deirdre of the Sorrows: A Play*. Dublin, Maunsel & Company, 1911.

Tanner, T. (1979). *Adultery in the Novel: Contract and Transgression*. Baltimore, MD, Johns Hopkins University Press.

Thompson, F. (2004). 'The Land War in Country Fermanagh', in Murphy and Roulston (eds), 287–306.

Thompson, Helen (ed.) (2006). *The Current Debate about the Irish Literary Canon: Reassessing 'The Field Day Anthology of Irish Writing'*. Lampeter, Edwin Mellen Press.

Thompson, N. (1992). *Child Abuse: The Existential Dimension*. Norwich, Social Work Monographs.

Tiernan, S. (2008). '"No measures of 'emancipation' or 'equality' will suffice": Eva Gore-Booth's Revolutionary Feminism in the Journal *Urania*', in O'Connor and Shepard (eds), 166–82.

Tobin, F. (1984). *The Best of Decades: Ireland in the 1960s*. Dublin, Gill & Macmillan.

Todhunter, J. (1896). 'The Fate of the Sons of Usna', in *Three Bardic Tales*. J.M. Dent & Co., 47–143.

Tóibín, C. (1997). 'Stuart's raison d'être is to be Outside the Pale', *Sunday Independent* (7 December), 3.

—— (2001). 'Issues of Truth and Invention', *London Review of Books* 23.1 (4 January), 3–11.

—— (2012). 'Dreamers and Chancers', *The Guardian* (16 June), 2–4.

Toolis, K. (1995). *Rebel Hearts: Journeys within the IRA's Soul*. Picador.

Trench, H. (1901). *Deirdre Wedded*, in *Collected Works*, vol. I. Jonathan Cape, 1924, 5–48.

Trollope, A. (1883). *The Landleaguers*. Oxford, Oxford University Press, 1993.

Turnaturi, G. (2007). *Betrayals: The Unpredictability of Human Relations*. Chicago and London, University of Chicago Press.

Waldron, J. (1992). *Maamtrasna: The Murders and the Mystery*. Dublin, Deburca, 2004.

Walker, M. (1992). *Surviving Secrets: The Experience of Abuse for the Child, the Adult and the Helper*. Buckingham, Open University Press.

Walpole, H. (1765). *The Castle of Otranto: A Gothic Story*. Oxford, Oxford World's Classics, 2008.

Walshe, É. (ed.) (1997). *Sex, Nation and Dissent in Irish Writing*. Cork, Cork University Press.

—— (2006). '"A Lout's Game": Espionage, Irishness and Sexuality in *The Untouchable*', *Irish University Review: A Journal of Irish Studies* 36.1 (spring/summer), 102–15.

—— (ed.) (2011). *Elizabeth Bowen's Selected Irish Writings*. Cork, Cork University Press.

Welch, R. (1993). *Transformations in Modern Irish Writing*. Routledge.

West, R. (1964). *The New Meaning of Treason*. New York, Viking Press.

Wiener, J. (1989). 'The Responsibilities of Friendship: Jacques Derrida on Paul de Man's Collaboration', *Critical Inquiry* 15 (summer), 797–803.

Wills, C. (2007). *That Neutral Island: A Cultural History of Ireland during the Second World War*. Faber & Faber.

Wilson Foster, J. (1974). *Forces and Themes in Ulster Fiction*. Dublin, Gill & Macmillan.

—— (2008). *Irish Novels, 1890–1940: New Bearings in Culture and Fiction*. Oxford, Oxford University Press.

Windisch, E. (1880). *Longes mac nUisnig*, 'Die Verbannung der Söhne Usnechs', in *Irische Texte mit Übersetzungen und Wörterbuch*, vol. I. Ed. E. Windisch. Leipzig, Hirzel. Text reprinted in *Gaelic Journal* 1 (1883), 378–91.

Wood, K. and P. O'Shea (1997). *Divorce in Ireland: The Options, the Issues, the Law*. Dublin, The O'Brien Press.

Woodrow, J. (1769). *Carthon, the Death of Cuchulain, and Darthula*. Edinburgh, J. Dickson.

Yeats, W.B. (1907). *Deirdre*, in *Selected Plays*. Ed. A.N. Jeffares. Macmillan, 1964, 49–78.

—— (1933). *Collected Poems*. Macmillan, 1981.

Other sources

Bunting, Madeleine (2009). 'An Abuse Too Far by the Catholic Church', *The Guardian* (21 May), www.theguardian.com/commentisfree/belief/2009/may/21/catholic-abuse-ireland-ryan.

The Cloyne Report (2009). Report of Investigation into Catholic Diocese of Cloyne, www.justice.ie/en/JELR/Pages/Cloyne_Rpt.

Gore-Booth, E. (1904). *Unseen Kings*. Longmans, Green, & Co., www.archive.org/stream/unseenkings00gorerich#page/n7/mode/2up.

Haslam, R. (1999). 'A Race Bashed in the Face: Imagining Ireland as a Damaged Child', *Jouvert: A Journal of Postcolonial Studies* 4.1, http://english.chass.ncsu.edu/jouvert/v4i1/hasla.htm.

Hayes O'Grady, S. (1894). *The Coming of Cuculain*. Dublin, The Talbot Press, http://www.gutenberg.org/files/5092/5092-h/5092-h.htm.

Hyde, D. (1887). 'Deirdre', in *The Three Sorrows of Storytelling and Ballads of Saint Columcille*. T. Fisher Unwin, 1–39, www.archive.org/stream/threesorrowssto01hydegoog#page/n8/mode/2up.

Leahy, A.H. (1905). 'The Exile of the Sons of Usnach', in *Heroic Romances of Ireland*, vol. I, David Nutt, www.sacred-texts.com/neu/hroi/hroiv1.htm.

McCabe, E. (2004/5). Interview, *Teaching English* (winter), http://www.pdst.ie/sites/default/files/Winter%20Magazine%202004(1).pdf.

MacPherson, J. (1760). 'Dar-Thula', www.exclassics.com/ossian/oss24.htm.

The Murphy Report (2009). Commission of Investigation Report into Catholic Archdiocese of Dublin, www.justice.ie/en/JELR/Pages/PB09000504.

Rolleston, T.W. (1911). *Myths and Legends of the Celtic Race*, George G. Harrap, https://archive.org/details/mythslegendsofc00roll.

RTÉ News (2009). 'Reopening of redress agreement not ruled out' (21 May), www.rte.ie/news/2009/0521/117609-abuse/.

Russell, G. (1901). *Deirdre: A Legend in Three Acts*, in *Imaginations and Reveries*. Dublin, Maunsel, 1915, www.gutenberg.org/files/8105/8105-h/8105-h.htm#2H_4_0030.

The Ryan Report (2009). Residential Institution Redress Board, www.childabusecommission.ie/rpt/.

Simpson, J.A. and E.S.C. Weiner (eds) (1989). *The Oxford English Dictionary*. 2nd edn. Oxford, Clarendon Press.

Willis, B. (n.d.). 'Noon's Hole/Arch Cave', www.bbc.co.uk/northernireland/yourplaceandmine/fermanagh/A954182.shtml.

Index